Praise for LIFE AFTER DEATH

"Deepak Chopra has written a masterpiece that is long overdue in our spiritual culture. *Life After Death: The Book of Answers* is a bold and comforting guide into the afterlife. Eternity is the true home of the soul, yet we fear to explore experience of death and our place beyond now. Deepak has brilliantly accomplished this journey on our behalf."

—CAROLINE MYSS, author of *Anatomy of the Spirit* and *Sacred Contracts*

"Here is the paradox: life's greatest mystery—death—seems to be its opposite and its very denial. However, anyone who reads Deepak Chopra's penetrating and insightful investigation into this great mystery with an open mind will come to realize that the opposite of death is birth, not life. Life, which in essence is consciousness, is eternal and has no opposite. There is no death, only the metamorphosis of life-forms, consciousness appearing as this or that. This is the liberating truth the book continuously points to."

—ECKHART TOLLE, author of *The Power of Now*

"Wide-ranging and thought-provoking, this book puts the question of life after death in a vast perspective. It is an excellent antidote to any self-imposed limitations we may have on our thinking about the nature of life, death and consciousness."

—RUPERT SHELDRAKE, Ph.D., biologist and author of *The Presence of the Past*

"Who is not curious about what happens after death? And even when there are many answers available, both ancient and modern, even some based on new science, the question 'What does Deepak Chopra have to say about this?' is an important one for our age. Well, finally, Deepak's answer is here, and it is very affirming on meaningful questions. I like that. Need I say more? This is a great book for your easy reading."

—AMIT GOSWAMI, Ph.D., author of *The Self-Aware Universe, Physics of the Soul,* and *The Quantum Doctor*

"This fascinating, provocative and profound book is written with exquisite ease and with a very personal warmth that makes its invitations to expansion of consciousness all the more delicious and powerful."

—ANDREW H

"What if life and death are like two locked boxes, each containing the key to the other? In this book Dr. Chopra looks at life after death from this intriguing perspective and proposes that death may not constitute the extinction of life, as usually imagined, but rather its extension by other means. He draws upon a dazzling array of sources, from ancient myths to the findings of modern science, to produce a work of compelling novelty on an eternal mystery."

—ARVIND SHARMA, Birks Professor of Comparative Religion, McGill University

"Deepak Chopra has been my friend and mentor for nearly twenty years. Now, when we baby-boomers are finally admitting our own mortality, he has tackled the ultimate subject which fascinates us all: life after death. Drawing from many cultures, and emphasizing the idea of Karma from his own, Deepak interweaves mythical lore with first-hand spellbinding anecdotes to somehow make the subject of death very useful and relevant to making the most time on the Earth here and now. A must-read for everyone who will die."

—CANDACE B. PERT, PH.D., author of *Everything You Need to Know to Feel Good*

"In this remarkable book, Deepak Chopra turns to the anomalies in science that modern physicists are trying to explain, and considers how the rishis, the ancient sages of Vedanta, dealt with the very same questions. According to the 'observer effect' in physics, for example, the very act of looking at an electron forces it to leave the quantum soup of pure potential and take specific form. Vedic rishis believed that seeing is the ultimate act of creation—that through consciousness each of us shapes the universe we experience. By marrying science and wisdom in *Life After Death*, Chopra builds his case for an afterlife in which our most essential self, the seer that observes our experiences in this temporary home that we call the self, uses the end of this lifetime to pass over into the next. This is an intellectual and spiritual tour de force."

—PROFESSOR ROBERT THURMAN, Columbia University, author of *Infinite Life* and *The Tibetan Book of the Dead*

"In this book, Deepak brilliantly creates a remarkable tapestry for opening our hearts, minds and consciousness to explore for ourselves the mysteries of life, death and the mind. He cleverly interlaces mystical stories, childhood memories, thoughts on creation, scientific data about many areas, and questions that will allow the reader to reexamine and to question old beliefs about our own identity. With an open-minded approach, this book stretches our mind and our imagination to explore a reality of truth that is far beyond our physical reality."

—GERALD G. JAMPOLSKY, M.D., author of *Love Is Letting Go of Fear* and founder of the International Center for Attitudinal Healing (Sausalito, California)

"If I had any doubts about the afterlife, I don't have them anymore. Deepak Chopra has cast his inimitable light on the darkened corners of death. I think this is his greatest contribution yet."

—MARIANNE WILLIAMSON, author of *The Gift of Chang*

"As I shuttled between East and West cultures, the greatest difference that I have found has been attitudes toward death and life-after-death. Deepak Chopra has combined East and West in his Being. He is familiar with Vedanta, the laws of Karma, and Hindu myths for he grew up in a Hindu family in India. But then he went to a Catholic school, where he learned the fathers' take on death and afterlife. He is familiar with Western science so we have quantum physics and consciousness theories in the mix, and then he is a Western physician, which makes him familiar with Near-Death Experiences (NDEs). In this book he incorporates these parts of his Being to provide us with a masterful treatment of life-after-death."

—RAM DASS

"Chopra illuminates, brilliantly, a wonderful variety of extraordinary experiences documented by scientists and engineers, and weaves them into a tapestry embracing different religious traditions, by grouping, comparing and analyzing them. This radical empiricism in the William James tradition succeeds beautifully, as did James, in putting the 'burden of proof' squarely on the reductionist materialists who have, for several decades now, while claiming to speak for science, been allowed to ignore the bedrock of science: facts.

Chopra then compares these data/experiences with some of the metaphors with which we, in the world of science, amuse ourselves, and impress the masses. Deepak has thrown down the gauntlet demanding the burden of proof from the reductionist materialists. I can confidently predict that the best they will do is to try to ignore it."

—RUSTUM ROY, professorships at Pennsylvania State University, Arizona State, and University of Arizona; elected to the National Academies of Science or Engineering of The United States, Sweden, Japan, Russia, and India

"As we enter the twenty-first century it is clear that we have crossed into an unprecedented global age in which widely diverse worldviews intersect, meet, and often compete or collide in the marketplace of our cultures. Deepak Chopra has established himself as a unique global voice for our time who lives and speaks from the global perspective and through a global lens that brings our diverse worlds together. In his global story it is clear that the collective wisdom of the ages, including the wisdom of frontier science, concurs that Reality must be an infinite unified field of interconnectivity that calls for a radical revision in how most of us see and understand ourselves and approach our life and death.

In his powerfully accessible narrative Chopra helps all readers cross into this ancient, yet newly revealed, global perspective that clarifies a new common sense that overcomes chronic ignorance, fear and denial of our passage through death. This lucid book shifts the burden of proof about life after death onto the older dysfunctional egocentric cultures and myopic perspectives whose time have now passed. This book is another clear historic marker of our transition into our new global story and self-image in which humans may flourish together across all our old artificial borders."

—ASHOK GANGADEAN, Professor and Chair of Philosophy, Haverford College; founder-director of the Global Dialogue Institute; co-convenor of the World Commission on Global Consciousness; host of the TV show Global Lens; author of *The Awakening of the Global Mind* (www.awakeningmind.org)

"*Life After Death: The Book of Answers* opens the doorway to an ever-evolving future Now. With mastery and compassion, Chopra combines the wisdom of the Vedic tradition with quantum physics, and his experience as a doctor, to reveal that we are not and never have been limited creatures trapped in physical bodies, but are already multidimensional beings, creating our future beyond this life through every thought, word and deed. His view of the nature of reality is precious, illuminating, life-giving. I love the book."

—BARBARA MARX HUBBARD, President, Foundation for Conscious Evolution

"A unique initiative to understand Life After Death and dispel one of our greatest fears of the unknown: death. Weaving between religious scriptures, science, and our common cultural/societal understanding, Deepak has very articulately reasoned the myth of death and simply made it just another aspect of life. Surely this book serves to expand our understanding to go beyond and deeper into the unknown, cherish life, and embrace death with love."

—BAWA JAIN, Secretary General, World Council of Religious Leaders

"Three cheers for Deepak's courage to express his beliefs and wisdom about a subject many fear and avoid. This book will help us to open a door to a subject few seemed prepared to explore because they cannot explain it. I know from personal experience that near-death and past- life experiences are not a matter of the imagination. I can believe because I have had the experience. Consciousness exists when our bodies do not. From my own life and my work with patients I know that we are aware of the future and the past at an unconscious level, which when made conscious helps us to understand and survive. Life is a mystery, so read on and help us to enter the darkness and light a candle."

—BERNIE SIEGEL, M.D., author of *365 Prescriptions for the Soul* and *101 Exercises for the Soul*

"I, perhaps like many others, most often think of and look to Deepak Chopra as a physician, pioneer, and major influence in the huge positive change in Western attitudes toward holistic medicine. In this book he is much more than that. He addresses the ultimate mystery—death—as a physician, a philosopher, and a teacher. His presentation of concepts such as the 'journey of the soul,' or the 'music of the spheres,' reminded me of the readings of my grandfather, Edgar Cayce, who many years ago also provided the world with a more hopeful view of the transition we are all destined to make. I recommend this book for all of us who are concerned about our own eventual death, and the death of those closest to us."

—CHARLES THOMAS CAYCE, Executive Director, Association for Research and Enlightenment, Inc.; President, Edgar Cayce Foundation, Inc.

"Deepak Chopra masterfully navigates a bewildering but profoundly important landscape in *Life After Death: The Book of Answers*. Gracefully weaving parables, poignant experiences, religious lore and scientific evidence, Chopra's survey of the afterlife is at once contemplative, heartening and satisfying."

—DEAN RADIN, Ph.D., senior scientist, Institute of Noetic Sciences.

"This is not an 'easy' but thoroughly fascinating book that could well become one of the important reads of your lifetime."

—DORIS WILSDORF, Professor Emeritus, University of Virginia, and inventor

"A fabulous read! While western science continues to watch the world with its nose pressed to precise lenses with limited focus, Deepak takes you by the hand and leads you on a wonderful journey right through those looking glasses to the very inside of eternally creative consciousness as revealed by the Vedic rishis and reflected in other great world cultures. Then he shows you why this inside view better explains the data of western science than its own worldview! In short, this is a highly effective preview of the integral global science of the future that will dramatically change the way we see and act in our world. As you take this fascinating journey with Deepak, the immortality promise of its title is easily fulfilled along the way."

—ELISABET SAHTOURIS, PH.D., evolution biologist and futurist; professor; author of *EarthDance: Living Systems in Evolution*

"In his captivating book *Life After Death*, the immensely talented Deepak Chopra invites us to join him in an exhilarating and irresistible eternal dance whereby death equals love and freedom. Chopra, with his distinctive wisdom and ingenuity, takes us deeper into a timeless consciousness that encompasses all of life. *Life After Death* is a scintillating amalgamation of science and spirit as it lyrically intertwines ancient tales, modern literature, and Chopra's own intriguing encounters. *Life After Death* is a stunning work, a magnificent achievement, and an inspiring antidote to mankind's anxiety and despair!"

—T. BYRAM KARASU, M.D., Silverman Professor and University Chairman of the Department of Psychiatry and Behavioral Sciences at Albert Einstein College of Medicine; author of the best-selling *The Spirit of Happiness*

"Deepak Chopra presents a compelling portrait of the afterlife, one he bases on the wisdom of religious teachings and supports with the findings of scientific research. The result provides readers much food for thought as well as the opportunity to approach death in a new, more hopeful way."

—JIM B. TUCKER, M.D., researcher at the University of Virginia Division of Perceptual Studies, and author of *Life Before Life: A Scientific Investigation of Children's Memories of Previous Lives*

"'The shortest distance between the human heart and truth is a story,' according to one wisdom saying. The story Deepak Chopra tells of Savitri in his insightful and wonderful book *Life After Death: The Book of Answers* not only makes the human heart and truth kiss, but also penetrates to the heart of this extraordinary insight into life after death. Reading this book as a Catholic priest and spiritual teacher, I am amazed at the way Dr. Chopra is able to make sense to a Christian of the profound truth of life and death from his own culture and deep learning. I encourage everyone—be he or she Christian, Buddhist, Hindu, or atheist—to read this extraordinary work. Your mind and your soul will be uplifted and enlightened."

—REV. J. FRANCIS STROUD, S.J. DeMello Spirituality Center, Fordham University

"East meets West in *Life After Death*. This treasure of a book is graceful and thoughtful, inspiring and enlightening, practical and mystical, an adventure of the mind and heart. If Deepak Chopra is correct—and contemporary afterlife research supports his belief—we should not fear death, but 'respect it as a miracle' and celebrate our inherent ability to conceive and experience the eternity of life. Prepare to be awakened."

—GARY E. SCHWARTZ, PH.D., professor and director, Laboratory for Advances in Consciousness and Health, University of Arizona, and author of *The Afterlife Experiments* and *The G.O.D. Experiments*

"Deepak Chopra continues to be a significant figure in the emerging dialogue of world cultures and faiths. Here he deepens the conversation by tackling the 'Big One,' the eternal issue of death and the possibility of life on another plane. Instead of focusing on beliefs, he turns to the medium through which most people receive the ancient wisdom of a tradition: stories. Thus he expands the whole idiom in which such questions are understood by recalling the ancient Indian insight that we exist at the intersection of multiple realities and that the line between life and death is not a wall, as we often imagine, but one permeable crossing point among many, many others. Also by drawing on the most recent science, he makes this book thought-provoking for people of any faith or none at all."

—HARVEY COX, Harvard University, author of *When Jesus Came to Harvard*

"Deepak Chopra, M.D., has become a physician to our time. His latest medicine is *Life After Death: The Book of Answers*. With care and humility he uses story, the teachings of the masters of wisdom in the East, new science, and cosmology to hospice the fatally constricting reductionism of the materialist worldview and open our minds and souls to a universe permeated with consciousness, spirit and Life. Be prepared for a truly masterful exposition on the nature of karma that brings together Eastern philosophy and modern neuroscience. Chopra reminds us that both ancient wisdom and frontier science point us toward a Reality that will persist long after the sound bites of contemporary culture have bitten the dust. I loved the book."

—JAMES O'DEA, President, Institute of Noetic Sciences

"Harvesting the wisdom of East and West, of science and spirituality, Deepak Chopra carries the reader on a profound exploration of the greatest of mysteries. It is a revelation to waking consciousness of the source of our existence, the passion of our unending journey, and the Field of Being that calls us into Union."

—JEAN HOUSTON, PH.D., author of *A Passion for the Possible*

"Mind-expanding! Acting as a trusty guide whose words spring not from this-is-so or believe-this but from what-if? and why-not?, Deepak Chopra takes us on a fascinating exploration of a vast continent of beliefs, stories, myths, testimonies and brain research, demystifying a hitherto foggy domain while facilitating our self-examination. Like the rishis of old, Chopra invites us to participate in an endless experiment. The journey includes surprises (our reality here may determine our afterlife) as well as comforts (death is a creative leap). One cannot read *Life After Death* with any degree of openness without being delighted, empowered, and changed."

—JIM BALLARD, author of *Mind Like Water*

"Some books are divinely inspired transmissions with the power to change the way we think, act and live. This is one of them, written by a scientist and physician who is also one of the most luminous spiritual teachers of our time. If you've ever wondered about the meaning of life and longed to awaken to your full potential, this book is sacred treasure."

—JOAN BORYSENKO, PH.D., author of *Minding the Body, Mending the Mind* and *Seven Paths to God*

"Belief in life after death is a universal constant. This book will help many find certainty and comfort in this possibility by exploring many lines of evidence pointing to the infinite, eternal nature of human consciousness."

—LARRY DOSSEY, M.D., author of *The Extraordinary Healing Power of Ordinary Things*

"Deepak Chopra has written what will be considered his most brilliant book yet: Life After Death: The Book of Answers. He skillfully draws the reader into his inquiring and limitless mind on a topic relevant and fascinating to all of us, Death itself, and he does that in a way that we are profoundly touched, expanded, and inspired.

In his writings and talks, Deepak always gives us the gift of freeing us from the limitations of our mistaken confining identity. Readers of Deepak's also know we can always count on him to liberate us from the prison of our greatest and most petty fears. In this breathtaking book, he does all of that again and more. Through exquisite prose, mystical poetry, and riveting storytelling, the reader is given a whole new way of seeing death and therefore life itself.

As a scholar and teacher, physician and healer, master communicator and twenty-first century sage, Deepak Chopra has written a masterpiece that draws on many disciplines, communicates on multiple dimensions, and delivers a sweeping transformation on every level. I was hooked from the moment I started reading and found myself buzzing with excitement, moved to tears, filled with awe, and profoundly altered by this book. My unexamined and unconscious beliefs and assumptions about death have been unearthed and overturned.

I absolutely loved this book and am transformed by its message in ways I am just beginning to understand. I urge everyone to read it. It will change your life and your death."

—LYNN TWIST, President, Soul of Money Institute

"In *Life After Death*, Deepak Chopra opens the door to our true potential: the afterlife. He shows us that death can be a profound confrontation with the radiance of our soul. And he guides us in a hundred irresistible ways into this journey which begins now. This book is a must-read for those who want to find out how 'passing on' can be the most meaningful adventure of your life."

—MARGOT ANAND, author of *The Art of Everyday Ecstasy*

"With profound wisdom and clarity, Deepak Chopra reveals an awesome kaleidoscopic view of infinite possibilities in the akashic field. Crystallized in story form, one can easily identify with personal experience in the cycle of everyday life. Every culture, religion and individual can access the spiritual path of their choice in this remarkable work where 'love, truth, compassion, birth and death are equal' and eternity is NOW."

—SISTER JUDIAN BREITENBACH, R.N., Catholic Order of the Poor Handmaids of Jesus Christ, Namaste Center for Holistic Education, La Porte, Indianapolis

"In *Life After Death*, Deepak Chopra takes his readers to the gateway that is death and encourages them to keep their eyes open for what lies beyond. Exploring different traditions, he shows death not as a threat, but an opportunity. Chopra deftly combines ancient mythology with cutting-edge science and psychology. He is a master storyteller who makes Eastern wisdom accessible for the Western reader."

—VICTOR CHAN, Founding Director, Dalai Lama Center for Peace and Education; coauthor, with HH the Dalai Lama of *Wisdom of Forgiveness: Intimate Conversations and Journeys*

"In *Life After Death*, Deepak Chopra proves himself to be a spiritual alchemist. Using the power of language, he takes diverse elements such as Vedic philosophy, particle physics, psychology, and neuroscience and transforms them into literary gold. His insights into what happens after we die will transform the way you see what lies ahead. An inspiring and profoundly reassuring book."

—ARIANNA HUFFINGTON, editor, huffingtonpost

LIFE AFTER
DEATH

ALSO BY DEEPAK CHOPRA

Creating Health

Return of the Rishi

Quantum Healing

Perfect Health

Unconditional Life

Ageless Body, Timeless Mind

Journey into Healing

Creating Affluence

Perfect Weight

Restful Sleep

The Seven Spiritual Laws of Success

The Return of Merlin

Boundless Energy

Perfect Digestion

The Way of the Wizard

Overcoming Addictions

Raid on the Inarticulate

The Path to Love

The Seven Spiritual Laws for Parents

The Love Poems of Rumi
(edited by Deepak Chopra; translated
by Deepak Chopra and Fereydoun Kia)

Healing the Heart

Everyday Immortality

The Lords of the Light

On the Shores of Eternity

How to Know God

The Soul in Love

The Chopra Center Herbal Handbook
(with coauthor David Simon)

Grow Younger, Live Longer
(with coauthor David Simon)

The Deeper Wound

The Chopra Center Cookbook
(coauthored by David Simon and
Leanne Backer)

The Angel Is Near

The Daughters of Joy

Golf for Enlightenment

Soulmate

SynchroDestiny

The Book of Secrets

Fire in the Heart

The Seven Spiritual Laws of Yoga
(with coauthor David Simon)

Magical Beginnings, Enchanted Lives
(coauthored by David Simon and
Vicki Abrams)

Deepak Chopra

Life After Death

THE
BOOK
OF
ANSWERS

RIDER

LONDON • SYDNEY • AUCKLAND • JOHANNESBURG

13

Published in 2008 by Rider, an imprint of Ebury Publishing
First published in the USA by Harmony Books, an imprint of
Crown Publishing Group, in 2006

Ebury Publishing is a Random House Group company

The Random House Group Limited Reg. No. 954009

Addresses for companies within the Random House Group can be found at
www.randomhouse.co.uk

A CIP catalogue record for this book is available from the British Library

Design by Lauren Dong

ISBN 9781846041006

Copies are available at special rates for bulk orders.
Contact the sales development team on 020 7840 8487 or visit
www.booksforpromotions.co.uk for more information.

To buy books by your favourite authors and register for offers,
visit www.randomhouse.co.uk

Penguin Random House is committed to a sustainable future for
our business, our readers and our planet. This book is made from
Forest Stewardship Council® certified paper.

Printed and bound in Great Britain by Clays Ltd, St Ives plc

To my beloved parents

CONTENTS

ACKNOWLEDGMENTS

My longtime editor, Peter Guzzardi, encouraged me to write a book on death and dying, which evolved into this book. As always, his instincts were astute, and he has been an invaluable guide every step of the way.

To David, Carolyn, Felicia, and the entire staff at the Chopra Center, I am reminded every day of your dedication and kindness to me. Thank you.

To my family, who gives me more loving devotion than I could ever return in a lifetime.

MEMOIR: THE LIFE BEYOND

WHILE WRITING THIS book on the afterlife, I kept being drawn back to stories that I'd heard in India as a child. Parables are a powerful way to teach children, and many of the ones told to me have lasted all my life. So I decided to weave the book around tales of the kind I heard at home, around the temples, and at school, hoping that the reader would be enticed by a world where heroes battle darkness in order to emerge into the light.

In this case the hero is a woman, Savitri, and the enemy she must defeat is Yama, the Lord of Death. Yama shows up in her front yard one day, waiting to take away her husband the moment he returns from his work as a woodcutter. Savitri is terrified. What strategy could possibly turn Death away from his inexorable mission?

I had no trouble imagining these characters. I was frightened for Savitri and anxious to find out how her battle of wits with Death turned out. Their world flowed easily into my own, because the India of my childhood was not that far removed from ancient India. I want to take a moment to convey what death and the world beyond meant back then. It may seem like a very esoteric place. If so, you can come back to it after reading the main body of the book. However mysterious and exotic, here is where I began.

What was most magical in my childhood was transformation. Death itself was seen as a brief stopping point on an endless soul journey that could turn a peasant into a king and vice versa. With the possibility of infinite lifetimes extending forward and backward, a soul could experience hundreds of heavens and hells. Death ended nothing; it opened up limitless adventures. But at a deeper level, it's typically Indian not to crave permanence. A drop of water becomes vapor, which is invisible, yet vapor materializes into billowing clouds, and from clouds rain falls back to earth, forming river torrents and eventually merging into the sea. Has the drop of water died along the way? No, it undergoes a new expression at each stage. Likewise, the idea that I have a fixed body locked in space and time is a mirage. Any drop of water inside my body could have been ocean, cloud, river, or spring the day before. I remind myself of this fact when the bonds of daily life squeeze too tight.

In the West the hereafter has been viewed as a place akin to the material world. Heaven, hell, and purgatory lie in some distant region beyond the sky or under the earth. In the India of my childhood the hereafter wasn't a place at all, but a state of awareness.

The cosmos that you and I are experiencing right now, with trees, plants, people, houses, cars, stars, and galaxies, is just consciousness expressing itself at one particular frequency. Elsewhere in spacetime, different planes exist simultaneously. If I had asked my grandmother where heaven was, she would have pointed to the house we lived in, not only because it was full of love, but because it made sense to her that many worlds could comfortably inhabit the same place. By analogy, if you are listening to a concert orchestra, there are a hundred instruments playing, each occupying the same place in space and time. You can listen to the symphony as a whole or, if you wish, put your attention on a specific instrument. You can even separate out the individual notes played by that instrument. The presence of one frequency does not displace any of the others.

I didn't know it as a child, but when I walked around the crowded Delhi market where more humanity was packed into one bazaar than was possible to imagine, the world I couldn't see was even more crowded. The air that I breathed contained voices, car noises, bird songs, radio waves, X-rays, cosmic rays, and an almost infinite array of subatomic particles. Endless realities lay all around me.

Every frequency in nature exists simultaneously, and yet we experience only what we see. It's natural to fear what we can't see, and since death snatches a person out of sight, we react to it with fear. I certainly wasn't immune to this. The death of a pet made me anxious and sad; the death of my grandfather, which happened suddenly in the middle of the night, was devastating. My younger brother kept running around the house crying, "Where is he? Where is he?" It would be years before I realized that the correct answer was "Here and everywhere."

Different planes of existence represent different frequencies of consciousness. The world of physical matter is just one expression of a particular frequency. (Decades later, I was fascinated to read that according to physicists, there is a background hum to the universe that is so specific as to sound like the note B-flat, although it vibrates millions of times lower than human hearing.) In India a child would never hear such a complicated quasi-scientific idea, but I did hear about the five elements, or *Mahabhutas*: earth, water, fire, air, and space. These elements combined to form everything in existence, which sounds crude to someone versed in Western science, but it contained a valuable truth: All transformations come down to a few simple elements.

In the twentieth century Western science came to understand that all solid objects are actually made of invisible vibrations. In my childhood, solid things were seen to have a large portion of the earth element. To put it another way, solid things had dense vibrations, or vibrations on a lower plane. Vaporous things had a fine vibration, on a higher plane.

Just as there are different planes of material things, there are also different spiritual planes, a shocking notion to the pious Catholic brothers, mostly Irish, who were my teachers at school. To them the only spirit was the Holy Ghost that lived in heaven. We children were politic enough not to disagree, yet in our cosmos it only made sense that if the Earth was a dense spiritual world, there must be higher spiritual planes, known to us as *Lokas,* which in Western mystical circles became known as "astral planes." There are an almost infinite number of astral planes, divided into a higher and lower astral world, and even the lowest ones vibrate at a higher frequency than the material world.

Long ago the West gave up trying to hear the music of the spheres, but in India it is believed that a person with finely tuned consciousness can go inward and actually hear the vibration of various higher planes. In the astral plane you can see your own body, for instance, yet it might change in age from moment to moment.

In the lower astral planes we find clairvoyance, telepathy, and other refinements of the five senses, as well as ghosts, disembodied souls, and spirits that for one reason or another are "stuck." As a child I was certain that when a cat or dog paused to assess the air, it saw something I couldn't. So it came as no surprise to later read, in various texts both Eastern and Western, that lower astral planes sometimes sensed by humans in higher states of awareness are often sensed by animals. Nor was I surprised to meet a psychiatry resident who told me that if the hospital room was dimly lit enough, he could see—on the very edge of visibility—when the soul left a dying person. Every Indian child devours comic books about the exploits of various heroes who fought their battles in faraway Lokas. Slipping in and out of material existence was our version of traveling to outer space. Our comic book heroes would come across thought forms and thought clouds, astral bodies traveling during sleep, astral colors and auras. All these are vibrations in the lower astral plane.

In the Indian tradition every physical body is assigned an accompanying astral body. Your astral body is a complete mirror of your physical body; it has a heart, liver, arms, legs, a face, etc., but since it operates at a higher frequency, most people are unaware of it. During life, the physical body provides a garment for the soul; it gives it the appearance of being localized in the material world. In death, as the physical body begins to disintegrate, the departing soul enters an astral plane that corresponds to its existence on the material plane, the frequency that corresponds most closely to its former life.

The general notion that you go where you belong rested easily in my mind back then. I imagined dogs going to dog heaven, and people who loved dogs joining them. I imagined bad people no longer hurting anyone except themselves because they were isolated in a kind of karmic jail. This was consoling, an assurance that the good people who loved me but were now gone lived in a place of goodness. But my view had limitations. I was never sure whether my wise grandfather met his wise grandfather in the hereafter, who showed him how to proceed, or if that job was carried out by angels, or enlightened spirits. Much later when I began to research karma I found that after we die, we remain self-motivated. A soul moves according to its desire from one astral plane to another, projecting as in a dream whatever sights and people, guides and astral entities it needs for its own advancement.

All these planes ultimately were imagined by Spirit, just as it imagined the material world. The Indian word for Spirit is *Brahman,* which is Everything, the one consciousness that fills every plane of existence. But Indians are relaxed about terminology, as befits a very old culture. We said God. Rama. Shiva. Maheshwara. The important thing wasn't the name but the concept of a single consciousness that creates everything and continues to do so in infinite dimensions at infinite speed. On the astral planes Spirit continues to play roles.

There, one can actually see images of gods and goddesses, angels and demons. These are ultimately illusions, however, for each astral plane provides the experience of Spirit. Here, on our plane, we experience Spirit as matter, solidity. On the astral planes we experience subtle beings and the landscapes they inhabit—what we might call dreams.

The cosmos is nonlocal; that is, it can't be mapped as a location. After death we gradually stop being local. We see ourselves as we really are from the soul's perspective: everywhere at once. This adjustment is probably the biggest obstacle any of us will encounter in the astral planes. Right now you are at the center of the universe because infinity extends in all directions, yet someone on the other side of the world is also at the center of the universe, because infinity extends on all sides of him, too. If both of you are centers of the universe, you must both be at the same location. The fact that you appear to be in different places is a sensory artifact. It's based on sights and sounds, which are local events. You are not a local event.

Similarly, each moment is the center of time, because eternity stretches around each moment in all directions. Therefore every moment is the same as every other. The cosmos, being nonlocal, has no up or down, north or south, east or west. These are only points of reference for our convenience at our particular frequency (i.e., inside a body). The transformational process after death is not a movement to some other place or time; it is just a change in the quality of our attention. You can only see what you vibrate to.

I had an uncle who loved to travel and visit the various saints and sages who so densely populate India. Sometimes, to my fascination, he brought me along. I saw renunciates who sat in one posture for years at a time; others who barely breathed. I know now that my eyes were deceiving me. I only saw a chrysalis, inside of which marvelous transformations were taking place. Silently, these figures were tuning in to different frequencies beyond the outside world. Through a shift in attention they could speak to Rama (or Buddha or Christ, though that was less likely in India). Deep meditation wasn't an inert state; it was a launching pad for consciousness. In the ER when someone dies of a heart attack, only to be resuscitated with reports of a near-death experience, he or she uses a different launching pad. In both cases there was a shift in the quality of attention.

The big difference is that when a cardiac patient goes into the light, the journey is involuntary. Those silent yogis from my past were exercising an intention. By having a desire at a deep enough level of awareness, they went through a process that parallels death. The senses fade one by one. (The last one to leave when a person dies is sound, which was the first to come in at birth. This fits the Indian notion that the five elements come and go in a specific order; since sound is the equivalent of vibration, which holds the body together, it makes sense that it would be the last to go.)

As the gross senses become duller, the subtle senses sharpen. We still see and hear after we die, but now the objects aren't physical. They consist of anything we want to see on the astral plane: celestial sights and sounds, heavenly beings, and brilliant lights. In near-death experiences the most typical manifestations are faces, voices, or an emotional presence. In other cultures people might expect to encounter ghosts or animals. Often a dying person feels something subtle around him—a certain warmth, a faint form or sound before leaving the body. Somehow these can be accessed on the dying person's vibrational frequency. Anyone who has spent time with the dying knows that they may say that they've been joined in the room by a departed spouse or other long-dead loved one. Some kind of astral contact is being made in the transition zone from physical to subtle.

At death the astral counterpart of the physical body separates from it. According to Vedic teachings, the departed soul then sleeps for a time in the astral region, which I translate as its incubation period.

New ideas percolate in the mind before they lead to action, and something similar happens with the soul. Normally the soul sleeps peacefully, but if a person dies suddenly or prematurely, or has many unfulfilled desires, this sleep may be restless and disturbed. The horrors of a violent death would continue to reverberate, and so would more mundane torments like unrequited love or grief. Suicides experience the same inner pain that led them to take their lives.

Unfulfilled desires don't have to be negative. A longing for pleasure also represents an inability to let go. My uncle the spiritual devotee heard many detailed accounts of souls stuck in lower astral planes. Days, months, and years aren't the yardsticks of the soul's perspective. When people die suddenly or unnaturally, they haven't had time to work out their personal karma; until they fully process their attachments and obligations, they will remain drawn to this denser plane.

Saints and sages have the advantage of being able to travel freely through astral planes, unrestrained by desires. Disturbed souls remain caught between two worlds, and if loved ones left behind keep calling to the soul through prayers, grief, unfulfilled love, or attempts to contact the dead, the soul will continue to be perturbed. The soul is meant to sleep in the astral body as it did in the womb, and peaceful death makes this possible.

Then there is the matter of seeing your life flash before your eyes. Since this is experienced by people on the brink of dying, such as drowning victims, it must be part of a transition, not actually connected to death per se. I was never told about this as a child, although I did meet a doctor later on who told me that he had nearly drowned off the Great Barrier Reef in Australia. He described it as a peaceful experience accompanied by a rapid sequence of images spanning his whole life—more like a slide show than a movie, he said. (I wonder if he would have become a restless soul had the lifeguards not reached him in time.)

Swamis talk extensively about the afterlife, and according to a number of them, seeing your life flash before your eyes is a specific karmic process. Karma is wound around the soul like thread around a spindle. Whenever a person is exposed to the possibility of sudden death, the thread unwinds rapidly, and one sees images of the events that have already occurred. In this sequence only significant karmic moments become visible.

In cases where someone is dying over a period of weeks and months, karma unwinds slowly. The person may become intensely absorbed in the past, reflecting upon it. At the moment of dying, entering into the astral plane is accompanied by a quick karmic review, with images unwinding like a film unspooling off its reel.

However, purists in India might see this image too as pure illusion. The phenomenon of seeing your life flash before you in a split second, they say, is a demonstration that every second contains the whole of eternity. During the deep sleep of the soul between births, all the memories of past events in the physical body get impressed onto the soul, forming the karmic software that will give rise to its future life.

One spiritual practice that I still perform is to lie in bed before falling asleep and review the events of the day. I do this in backward order, for the same reason karma unspools in this way: to understand and come to peace with what has happened to me. My own feeling is that a dying person must be given the same opportunity.

The period of the soul's slumber varies according to how evolved the soul is at the time of death. The main reason for the sleep of the soul is to shed its attachments. The strength of its attachments will determine how long it takes to shed them. When the soul awakens it can only enter a plane of existence that is familiar. If you were to enter a plane higher than your level of evolution, you would become confused and uncomfortable. Likewise, you cannot go backward in your evolution: you can only progress.

A kind of cocoon surrounds the sleeping soul. When it wakes up it sheds this shell, which eventually fades away. During the astral journey souls meet other souls vibrating at a similar level of evolution. You may meet some souls that you encountered in the physical world if they are on your frequency. Most people deeply desire to join their loved ones in the afterlife. Their souls aren't drifting through the astral atmosphere but are directed by love itself. Love is a vibration, older than humanity itself. But the principle of directedness is very human: we go where our deepest desires take us.

When Spirit moves in the world of physical objects, its vibration is very slow and dense, almost stilled by the physical casing of the body. When it operates at a very high vibration, Spirit is also still because it experiences only pure awareness—in other words, itself. In between those two extremes lies the whole range of creation. In the astral world, the soul can visit planes of vibration lower than itself at will, but can only visit higher planes through evolution, much the way when you pass particles through finer and finer sieves, any particle can always pass back to a grosser level but can only advance when it has reached the correct level of refinement.

The Christian brothers who taught me loved to talk about what life would be like in heaven, and for them God's home was as real and solid as any building in Delhi. The swamis and yogis agreed with that, but only because they believed that Spirit permeates every plane of existence. Depending on your level of awareness, you project your own heavens, hells, and purgatories, to work through on the physical plane as well as astral planes. In the physical world, if you want to build a house, you need to collect the bricks, put them on top of one another, and so on. In the astral world you could just imagine the house the way you want it, and it will appear seemingly as real and solid as the one in the physical world.

In the astral plane suffering and enjoyment occur in the imagination, even though they appear to be real. Ironically, someone who has been a skeptic in this world will likely be a skeptic in the astral planes; he won't realize that he's in the very place he doesn't believe exists. The body you inhabit in the astral world is the one you've most identified with in the previous physical life. Since this is an imaginary body, you can keep it or change it during your astral life. Evolution on both the physical or astral planes is gradual—it takes time.

My Christian schoolteachers relished the idea that every desire would come true in heaven, and once again the swamis agree in their way. Desire is still crucial after death. Evolution is really the process of fulfillment of desire. In the astral world you fulfill and refine desires left over from your last physical life. You also refine your knowledge and experiences from the material world. The astral is like a graduate school for your previous physical incarnation. Here the soul also stores up energy for its higher, more evolved desires so that they might be fulfilled on its next visit to the physical plane when it inhabits a new body.

I wasn't sure why people died in the Christian scheme. Some who died were loaded down with sin, it seemed, like criminals who have come to the end of their bad actions, while others died to meet God, eager that their time had come. In India someone dies after reaching the maximum evolution allotted to that lifetime; they have come to the end of what their karma can teach them. The same holds true in the mirror of the astral world. The cycle closes on itself to produce a rebirth, which seemed totally natural to me as a child. So natural, in fact, that it didn't occur to me how mysterious the process must be. Somehow the soul finds a set of suitable parents so it may be reborn to continue its evolution. Thanks to what has taken place on the astral plane, reincarnation occurs at a higher level than where one left off. The specific calculations are made by the universe itself or, as some scriptures claim, by the lords of karma.

As a child I imagined a scene rather like a courtroom in which wise judges sit and consider every case—so wise, in fact, that they know every lifetime a soul has ever had. With complete impartiality they mete out the events that will arise in the next lifetime. Their aim isn't to reward or punish, but to lay out opportunities to evolve. Later on in life, it occurred to me that there is no need for lords of karma, since the universe is already correlating not just every lifetime but every event in nature. The courtroom scene stands as a symbol for our own clarity of judgment. Between lifetimes we are perfectly capable of making our own evolutionary choices for the future. For the great sages and saints none of this happened unconsciously. They recalled their own past-life experiences as clearly as you or I might evoke yesterday's events. But for those of us without their liberated awareness, only a faint memory remains of what has gone before.

Being born means arriving at a new level of insight and creativity. The process repeats itself over and over, each time progressing to a slightly higher plane. When your karma has been sufficiently worked out, you reach the maximum limit for that plane, your soul slips back into slumber, and the cycle continues.

The soul's trajectory is always upward. Any suffering on the astral plane, even the most tormenting hell, is only a temporary detour. By working itself out, your karma sees to it that your actions will always be better next time. I know this contradicts the popular belief that reincarnation can demote a person to the level of an animal or even an insect if one's actions merit it. India is a very old, complex culture, and when I grew up I was astonished to discover how contradictory its spiritual teachings could be—beliefs changed from town to town like the food. Indians are omnivorous. At one time or another they have believed everything. My Catholic schoolteachers were just the latest item on a centuries-old menu. Eventually I concluded that the only way to learn anything about spiritual matters was to experience and read as much as I could.

According to the India of my childhood, we don't choose our next incarnation voluntarily, but an element of choice does come into play.

The degree of choice you have depends on how clearly you can view yourself in the astral plane. This faculty, called witnessing, is comparable to what we experience here and now. Those who have the least freedom of choice are driven by obsessions, compulsions, addictions, and unconscious impulses. To the extent that you become free of these, you have more choice. The same is true of a soul contemplating its next physical incarnation.

Saints and sages are clear witnesses in this lifetime. The Buddha was said to be able to close his eyes and in an instant see thousands of his past incarnations in complete detail. By contrast, most people are so preoccupied with desire that when they try to see themselves truly as they are, they see only fog or blankness.

By developing your ability to witness, to be aware of your situation, you will be able to influence the lives you incarnate into. You will also be able to speed up the process of working through your karma. In the same way, you can also develop skills and talents on the astral plane. (This explains, among other things, how great artists and musicians can exhibit their abilities at uncanny ages, often before they turn three; being born with a talent is no accident.) When you are born, you bring along the talents you have developed from all your previous existences.

Soul bonds occur on the astral plane just as they occur in the physical world. Relationships in the astral plane mean that you are vibrating in concert with someone else's soul and therefore feel a heightened sense of love, unity, and bliss. It is not a relationship in spatial or physical terms, because the astral world is populated only by thought forms. When the disembodied soul tunes in to the frequency of a loved one back on the physical plane, that person may feel the presence of the departed; two souls can commune even though one is vibrating in the material plane and the other in the astral plane.

The soul's motivation to keep coming back to the material plane is twofold: to fulfill desires and to rejoin with familiar souls. We relate now to those people whose souls we related to in the past; we end relationships with people whose souls no longer vibrate with ours.

When I was a boy the only thing that really troubled me about this scheme was how the story ended. In the West it has been a long time since people longed for the next life more than they did this one. Since the Middle Ages we have become firmly entrenched in the desirability of being here. India has always been more ambivalent. There's enough pain in life that the prospect of repeating it forever creates anxiety. How does one get off the wheel of karma?

In one version of Indian belief, once a soul has completely worked out all its karma, it loses all earthly desires. It has transcended material objects and attachments to become enlightened. And once it is free of karma, there is no need to be reborn on either the physical or astral planes. Such a soul continues to spiral upward in its evolution, but on planes we cannot imagine. In Eastern philosophy these are known as causal planes; here, consciousness takes on such a subtle form that it offers no visual image for us to cling to. We will know the causal world only when we are ready to experience it, and that time is different for each person. We may glimpse it in an epiphany, but we will dwell there only when the soul's vibration is high enough to sustain it.

In another Indian variation, karma is infinite and is constantly being renewed. Trying to get to the end of your karma would be like emptying water out of a boat with one hand and pouring it back in with the other, so evolution works somewhat differently in this scheme. When you achieve self-realization, you no longer identify with your body, mind, ego, or desires. You become a pure witness, and in that state you can choose to transcend karma. The end of karma isn't the end of life, however. It's like getting out of debt and being left with the freedom to spend money without constraint.

The impulse to be liberated has waxed and waned in me, as it does in everyone. In the Indian tradition, we are reborn, after all, for a positive reason, to express and exhaust the force of desire. Even as a boy I knew that the Christian brothers didn't agree, since the only good reason to be born into their world of sin was to find a path to Jesus. The ideal Christian would be in such a rush to be redeemed that he would renounce this world altogether, as many Christian saints did—and many Indian ones, too.

India has imbibed from ancient cultures that long preceded the rise of Hinduism, and even under the influence of Islam and Christian conquerors has kept its eye on eternity. In the Indian mind there is no end to the celestial realms that belong to higher frequencies of existence, but as we've seen, at a certain high level of evolution, some souls may choose to complete their path. Once a soul has reached these levels it would not normally want to take another human birth except to provide a particular service, but these souls are exceptions. Buddhism calls these souls *bodhisattvas*, those who don't return to Earth driven by the force of evolution, but choose to come instead to serve the cause of enlightenment. When I asked a Tibetan lama what a bodhisattva was, he said, "Imagine that you are no longer dreaming, and although you enjoy being awake, you also enjoy helping others who are still asleep."

Of course most people are unaware of all this, and for them the karmic cycle continues spontaneously. Right here and now we are surrounded by an infinity of planes. If you could shift your awareness into a higher frequency, you could be with the angels this very minute, if you so desired. In the field of infinite possibilities you exist on all these levels at the same time, but at the level of experience you exist on only one. According to some Indian teachings, we all yearn for these other planes so much that we travel to them at night in our sleep. Then the astral body actually leaves the physical body, remaining attached by a filament that brings it back again. If the filament gets severed, the way back is lost. It is also dangerous to flirt with the lower astral planes if you don't understand them. However, once you truly realize that the whole scheme of worlds is imagined by Spirit, from the lowest to the highest, from demons to angels, there can be nothing dangerous about creation.

In this overview I have tried to immerse you in the world I found myself in sixty years ago. This was the Vedic perspective as I understood it. It was a vast spiritual ocean, and in typically Indian fashion you were invited to dip your cup in and take as little or as much as you wanted. It's nearly impossible for a society to embrace infinity, and India is no exception. People remain as troubled there about death and dying as do people here, and there are those who have completely turned their backs on the ocean of knowledge that laps at their feet. In the West we have our own version of this phenomenon. We deny that anyone could know what lies beyond death, which conveniently closes the door on our anxiety for a time. Or we say that spiritual knowledge is relative; all that matters is faith, not the thing you have faith in.

It is these limitations that this book strives to overcome. Ultimately the question of "What happens after we die?" comes down to "What happens after I die?" The issue becomes personal, emotional, and inescapable. If a devout Muslim landed in a Christian heaven (or vice versa), he'd be very unhappy: eternity wouldn't meet with his expectations. I was fortunate as a boy, because the simple scheme I was presented with—and which I've elaborated on in this overview—allows for every soul to find the home to which it belongs.

What has also remained with me are certain themes that will figure prominently in this book:

The afterlife is a place of newfound clarity.
The afterlife isn't static. We continue to evolve and grow after
we die.

Choice doesn't end with death; it expands.

Earthly images carry us into the afterlife (we see what our culture has conditioned us to see), but then the soul makes creative leaps that open new worlds.

I set out to see how credible these premises are, since they go far beyond the Christian story of heaven and hell that most children learn in the West. An old culture makes room for love and death together, not as enemies but as entwined aspects of one life. The great Bengali poet Rabindranath Tagore wrote,

> *The night kissed the fading day*
> *With a whisper.*
> *"I am death, your mother,*
> *From me you will get new birth."*

The afterlife I grew up with is open-ended, like life itself. The old spiritual wisdom has stuck with me for decades, modified by experience and reflection. The only conception of death that makes sense to me allows us to experience everything. Now I hope to give readers a chance for that same freedom, here and in every world to come.

Part One

LIFE AFTER

DEATH

DEATH AT THE DOOR

LONG AGO, IN the dense forests that once encircled the holy city of Benares, there was ample work for woodcutters. One of these was the handsome Satyavan, who was all the more handsome because he had so much love for his wife, Savitri. Many mornings Satyavan found it hard to leave his hut to work in the woods.

One day Savitri lay dreamily in bed contemplating her happiness, which seemed complete. Suddenly she noticed a figure sitting cross-legged in the dusty clearing that served for a front yard. A wandering monk, she thought. She put rice and vegetables in a bowl and rushed out to offer them to the holy man, since hospitality was a sacred duty.

"I need no food," the stranger said, pushing away the bowl that Savitri had placed on the shade-dappled ground. "I will wait here."

Savitri drew back in horror, because suddenly she knew who her guest was. Not a wandering monk but Death himself, who is known in India as Lord Yama.

"Who are you waiting for?" she asked, her voice trembling.

"For one named Satyavan." The Lord of Death spoke politely. He was used to having absolute authority over mortals, and he approached them simply, with just a touch of imperiousness.

"Satyavan!" Savitri cried out. She could hardly keep from fainting when she heard her husband's name. "But he's strong and healthy, and we love each other dearly. Why should he die?"

Yama shrugged. "Everything will be as it will be," he said indifferently.

"But if you care so little," Savitri said, her wits coming back to her, "then why not take someone else? There are sick and wretched people begging for the release of death. Visit them and leave my house in peace."

"I will wait here," Yama repeated, unmoved by her plea and by the tears welling in Savitri's eyes. In Yama's face she saw a world where everything is nameless and without pity.

The young wife rushed back inside. She paced the floor, frantic in the knowledge that her husband would come home to meet his doom. Tigers feared the swing of brave Satyavan's axe, but here was an enemy no blade could touch. Then Savitri had an idea born of desperation. Throwing a cloak around her shoulders, she ran out the back door into the woods.

Savitri had heard that there was a sacred place on the mountain, a space in the earth as large as a cave formed by the roots of a huge banyan tree. A reputed holy man lived there. Savitri would beg for his help. But she didn't know her way and soon found herself following deer paths and washed-out gullies. Fear drove her as hard as breath and strength would allow, and so Savitri wandered, higher and higher, until she was totally exhausted. She collapsed on the ground and slept for a time; she couldn't tell how long.

When a shaft of sunlight opened her eyes, Savitri found herself at the foot of a huge banyan tree. She spied the cavernous hole among the roots and peered into it anxiously. Before she could summon the courage to enter, a voice from inside said, "Go away!" It was so loud and sudden that she jumped.

"I can't go away," Savitri replied, her voice trembling. She explained her desperate plight, but the voice from the darkness said, "How are you different from everyone else? Death is two steps behind us, from cradle to grave."

Tears welled up in Savitri's eyes. "If you are wiser than ordinary people, you must have something more for me."

The voice said, "You wish to bargain with Death? All who have tried that have failed."

Savitri got to her feet with dignity. "Then let Yama take me in my husband's place. What everyone says is true. Death is absolute. My only hope is that he will kill me and spare someone who doesn't deserve to die."

The voice was more gentle this time. "Be calm," it said. "There is a way." Savitri heard a stirring in the darkness, and then the holy man emerged from his cave. He was an ascetic, his thin body clad in a loin-cloth with a monk's silk shawl thrown over his shoulders. He looked surprisingly young, however, and he told Savtiri that his name was Ramana.

"You know a way to defeat Death? Tell me," Savitri implored.

The monk Ramana squinted in the sunlight, ignoring her for the moment. He had a gaze that she couldn't read, then he stooped down to pick up a worn old reed flute lying on the ground.

"Come," he said. "Perhaps you will be able to learn. I make no promises, but certainly you are desperate enough."

As if forgetting her, Ramana began to play on his flute and wandered down a nearby deer path. Savitri stood for a moment, dismayed and confused, but as the notes of the flute faded into the forest, she had no choice but to run after them.

THE MIRACLE OF DEATH

Every life is framed by two mysteries. Only one of them, birth, is considered a miracle. If you are a religious person, birth brings a new soul into the world from its home with God. If you are not, the miracle is that a single fertilized cell in a mother's womb can divide and subdivide again a mere fifty times to produce a complete new person. A blob of protein and water somehow knows how to shape itself into eyes, hands, skin, and a brain.

This nine-month transformation keeps accelerating, so that by the end a million new brain cells are appearing every minute. At the moment the newborn emerges, like a space shuttle undocking from the mother ship, every system that needs to function independently—heart, lungs, brain, and digestive tract—suddenly realizes that the moment is now and not a moment later. Organs detach from total dependence on the mother, and with astonishing precision they begin to act as if they had always been on their own. In a split second life chooses to live.

The other mystery that occurs, usually decades later, death, is very different. It brings to an end all the things birth struggled so hard to achieve. A thready heartbeat crosses an invisible line and becomes still. The bellows of the lungs, which have pumped some 700 million times, refuse to pump even once more. A hundred billion neurons cease to fire; a trillion billion cells throughout the body receive the news that their mission is over. Yet this abrupt finale is as much a mystery as birth, for at the moment life ends, 99% of our cells are typically still functional, and all 3 billion codons, the individual letters in the book of human DNA, remain intact.

Death comes without the miraculous coordination of birth. Some cells don't even get the news for some time. If the dead person is revived within ten minutes or so, before the brain gets permanently damaged by hypoxia, the body's machinery will go back to work as if nothing had happened. Indeed, death is such a blurry event that eyelids can continue to blink ten or twelve times after a head is severed from a body (a grisly fact discovered at the foot of the guillotine during the French Revolution).

Religion doesn't consider death a miracle. In Christianity death is linked to sin and Satan—the Western equivalent of the Lord of Death. Death is the enemy, and God saves us from its clutches. But with God's help dying is the doorway to a far more important event—the beginning of the afterlife. To the religious mind death brings the presence of God near, and witnesses throughout history have claimed to actually see the soul depart. (Not all of these witnesses are religious. I know of a prominent psychiatrist whose atheism was deeply shaken in medical school when he entered a cancer patient's room at the exact moment of death and saw a ghostly, luminous form emerge from the body and disappear.) There is a persistent legend that 21 grams of mass disappear when we die, which must be the weight of the soul. In fact, no such change occurs.

Whatever it is that occurs at death, I believe it deserves to be called a miracle. The miracle, ironically, is that we don't die. The cessation of the body is an illusion, and like a magician sweeping aside a curtain, the soul reveals what lies beyond. Mystics have long understood the joyousness of this moment. As the great Persian poet Rumi puts it, "Death is our wedding with eternity." But not only mystics have seen through death's illusion. The eminent twentieth-century philosopher Ludwig Wittgenstein wrote, "For life in the present there is no death. Death is not an event in life. It is not a fact in the world."

I believe that death accomplishes the following miraculous things:

It replaces time with timelessness.
It stretches the boundaries of space to infinity.

It reveals the source of life.

It brings a new way of knowing that lies beyond the reach of the five senses.

It reveals the underlying intelligence that organizes and sustains creation (for the moment we won't use the word "God," for in many cultures a single creator is not part of dying or the afterlife).

In other words, death is a fulfillment of our purpose here on earth. Every culture offers a deep faith that this is true, but ours demands a higher standard of proof. I think that proof exists, but it cannot be physical, since by definition death brings physical life to an end. To see this proof, we must expand the boundaries of consciousness so that we know ourselves better. If you know yourself as someone beyond time and space, your identity will have expanded to include death. The reason that human beings keep seeking fulfillment beyond the stars is that we sense that our own mystery lies there, not here in the realm of physical limitation.

Eternity Now

Being an invisible miracle, death is extremely elusive. But we get tantalizing clues that what lies on "the other side" is actually very close to us right now. People don't comprehend how important this is in terms of the afterlife. The very word "after" implies that time hasn't changed at the moment of death, that it still moves in a straight line, carrying a person from earthly time to heavenly time. This is wrong on two counts. First, eternity is not a function of time. In Christianity, sinners consigned eternally to hell wouldn't be punished for a long time. They would be punished *outside* time. Good people who find salvation also live in that same region where clocks never tick. So our ordinary sense of time has no relevance to what comes "after."

Secondly, our everyday sense of time is itself based on eternity. The universe exploded into existence 14 billion years ago, and started the cosmic clock going. Our bodies experience time because of atomic vibrations at the level of hydrogen, oxygen, nitrogen, and carbon, the building blocks of organic chemicals. We measure outside events using the inner clock of the brain, which is nothing but these organic chemicals. A snail's brain clicks so slowly that it takes five seconds before one event passes and a new one appears. In that five seconds you could pick up a snail and move it ten feet, and to the snail it would appear that he had teleported through space. The human brain ticks fast enough that we can sense events lasting only a few thousandths of a second (the darting of a mosquito, the blur of hummingbird wings), but it is too slow to observe the flight of a bullet or the million neutrinos that pierce our bodies every minute.

Before the Big Bang time wasn't ticking away; a second was equal to eternity. We surmise this because quantum physics has pierced the illusion of time, detaching from the atomic clock to go deeper into the fabric of Nature. At the deepest level vibrations cease. The universe flatlines like a dead brain. Yet the appearance of death is illusory, for the frontier where all activity ends marks the beginning of a new region, known as virtual reality, where matter and energy exist as pure potential. The basis for virtual reality is complex, but in simplest terms, a nonphysical region must exist to give birth to the physical universe. This region is a void, but it's far from empty. Just as when you are dozing on the couch your mind is empty but can awaken instantly to an infinite choice of thoughts, so the virtual realm awakens to an infinite realm of new events. Creation leaps from the void to complete fullness, just as eternity leaps from timelessness into the fullness of time.

If eternity is with us now, underlying all physical existence, it must underlie you and me. The illusion of time tells us that you and I are shooting in a straight line from birth to death, when in fact we are inside a frothy bubble let loose by eternity.

Actually, the event of death has never been all that far away, and the fixed boundary between life and death isn't impenetrable. A woman I know named May is a fifty-year-old divorcée from New Mexico. As a teenager she suffered the shock of having her adored older brother die suddenly in a car accident. "I was fifteen, he was nineteen, and he was the only person I've ever truly worshipped. When he died, poof, just like that, I couldn't even wrap my mind around it," May says. She was in a state of intense grief that dragged on for several years.

"I retreated completely. I stopped seeing anyone. I kept asking, *Why? I want an answer. Tell me.* Day after day no answer came." May had given birth to a child, so she decided to return to society for her baby's sake. "I knew it wasn't good for him to grow up as a recluse, so I decided to start seeing a few people at a time."

At the first social gathering she went to, May felt a sudden strange sensation. "I was talking to someone with a glass of wine in my hand when I realized that my feet had gone numb. The numbness quickly moved up both legs, and I had a flash. *This is it.* Immediately the room disappeared, and I was flying through space faster than I could imagine. It was like everything was incredibly compressed and expanded at the same time. I had no idea how long I was gone. The party was at a farm out in the country, so it took fifty minutes before the ambulance arrived. By then I had come to again; my friends told me they had felt a weak pulse the whole time. Nobody knew if I'd fainted or had a stroke."

I asked her how she interpreted her experience. "It's still here," she said, holding her palm about a foot from her chest. "About that far."

"What's still here?" I asked.

"Eternity. I'm sure that's what I experienced, and the feeling has never left me. It reassures me that I exist outside my body. In my thirties I had a tough time with breast cancer, but I wasn't afraid of dying, not for a minute. How could I be? I've seen eternity."

I want to put a human face on immortality before we get to the science that supports it. Facts are useless if we can't relate to them personally, and nothing is more personal than dying. In ancient India the idea that eternity could be experienced was widely accepted, so let's venture there to see how that was possible. Thousands of years ago there were people who searched the depths of spirit for answers without offending God or trespassing on his domain. They were the *rishis,* or sages of Vedic India, who rose into prominence when Hinduism was in its earliest flowering, perhaps as far back as four thousand years ago or as recently as a thousand. The names by which the rishis are known, such as Vyassa, Brighu, and Vasistha, may or may not be historical, but the body of work they left behind numbers in the thousands of pages. Many writings lack a proven author, much like the Old Testament, but the teaching of the rishis, known as Vedanta, isn't a religion.

The spiritual landscape of India was replete with gods and goddesses; there were innumerable Lokas, or nonphysical worlds. There were also hierarchies of angels and demons to rival anything in Dante. In the face of such bewildering diversity, the rishis didn't offer one God. They offered one reality that encompassed every possible experience, both in this life and beyond. They posited that every level of existence was actually a state of awareness. Other worlds—all worlds, in fact—were formed in consciousness. Therefore, as creators of these worlds, we could experience them and influence them at will. That's the essence of Vedanta. What the rishis were proposing was more than a philosophy; it was an invitation to participate in an endless experiment. The purpose of the experiment was to test the truth of reality by exploring it within yourself.

The invitation is still open. When you or I accept it, we are linked to the Vedic rishis by what Aldous Huxley called "the perennial philosophy," which returns in every age to suit the demands of a new generation. It would be pointless to haul an ancient tradition into the present if it didn't apply to us, but Vedanta does. For one thing, doubt has replaced dogma in many people's lives. The present spiritual confusion may not be as exotic as the profusion of temples and gods in ancient India, but listen to the voices that circulate around us:

> *I was in the Alzheimer's unit when my grandfather died. He was a totally different person by the end—out of his mind, doped up on morphine to the max. It was like watching a vegetable die. It was like nothing changed when his breathing stopped.*
> *My ex-husband is such a bastard. I told him when he dies he's got a ticket straight to hell. First class.*
> *I'm a Buddhist. When I drop the body I will become pure consciousness.*
> *I'm Hindu. I am pure consciousness already.*
> *Who are they kidding? When you're gone, you're gone. Period.*

That last voice is the voice of materialism, which regards death as final because it sees life only in the physical body. We may claim that denying the afterlife is scientific, but in fact it merely indicates a belief in materialism. The rishis believed that knowledge wasn't external to the knower but woven inside consciousness. Thus they had no need for an external God to solve the riddle of life and death. The rishis had themselves instead, which is very fortunate, because so do we. Each person is conscious. Each person has a self. Each person is certain of existence, that is, of being alive. With these raw ingredients, Vedanta declares, anyone can come up with firsthand knowledge of anything, no matter how deep the mystery appears.

Then why haven't we? Perhaps it's because we don't contact the deepest part of ourselves, which the rishis called *Atman.* The closest equivalent word in English is "soul." Soul and Atman are a spark of the divine, the invisible component that brings God's presence into flesh and blood. The biggest difference between them is that in Vedanta the soul isn't separate from God. Unlike the Christian soul, Atman cannot come from God or return to him. There is unity between the human and the divine; awareness of this unity is the necessary step that makes reality dawn.

To say "I am God" comes naturally with Atman. It's much less natural for us. Years ago I had a friend who was capable of intense spiritual experiences like leaving his body and seeing white light in his heart—or so he said. I told him that personally I didn't have such experiences. "Neither do I," he replied. "I have them impersonally."

He gave me insight at that moment, because something eternal, boundless, and unchanging *cannot be personal*. Out of habit we say "my" soul, but that's misleading. The soul doesn't belong to me the way my house does, as a possession, or as my children do, as an extension of my flesh and blood. It doesn't belong to me like my personality, or my memories, because senility and mental disorder can disable the brain and take away both.

Death isn't about what I possess but about what I can become. Today I see myself as a child of time, but I may become a child of eternity. I see my place here on earth, but I may be on a journey to the universe. Human beings have a deep intuition that our destiny is infinite, but we fear death because it tests our wishes and dreams. We fear to be tested because if we turn out to be wrong, then all our aspirations feel empty. In my medical career I've seen how afraid people can be at the last. Dying isn't more real than any other moment, but it is more definitive. No matter how rich and gifted you are, death is the great equalizer. (I remember when a renowned guru was giving a talk about how being absorbed into the light was the ultimate spiritual reward. The woman sitting next to me was fidgeting; she leaned over and whispered in my ear, "Sounds a lot like death to me.")

For the afterlife to have meaning, it has to be fully as satisfying as this life. Bringing money, power, sex, family, achievement, and physical pleasure to an end is not a trivial thing. Much that we love and depend on will be extinguished when this life comes to an end. And yet we can bring something to that moment. Many years ago when I was an inexperienced medical resident in Boston, an older couple was admitted to the hospital together. The husband was at the end of a long struggle with colon cancer. The wife, although she had a history of cardiac disease, was in much better shape. The two shared a room, and over the few days that I visited them, I could see how attached they were to each other.

The husband lingered for days, passing in and out of consciousness, in considerable pain. His wife sat beside him holding his hand, hour after hour. Then one morning I came in to find her bed empty—she had died suddenly of cardiac arrest during the night. The husband was having a lucid period, so I told him the news, reluctantly, since I was afraid of the shock it would give. But he seemed very calm.

"I think I'll go now," he said. "I've been waiting."

"For what?" I asked him.

"A gentleman always allows the lady to go first," he said. He lapsed back into unconsciousness and passed away that afternoon.

He reminds me of what we can choose to bring to dying. Grace, calm, a patient acceptance of what's to come: These are all qualities that can be cultivated, and when they are, death is a test we will not fail. Our fault is not that we fear death but that we don't respect it as a miracle. The most profound subjects—love, truth, compassion, birth and death—are equal. They belong to our destiny but also to our present life. Ultimately the goal of this book is to bring death into the present and thereby make it equal to love.

To that end, I will continue the story of Savitri, a woman who sought to use love to outwit death, as an interlude in our discussion of the afterlife. In the fullness of love there is a secret that she learned and we must relearn. Tagore hints at it quite beautifully in the following poem.

WHAT WILL YOU GIVE?

What will you give
When death knocks at your door?

The fullness of my life—
The sweet wine of autumn days and summer nights,
My little hoard gleaned through the years,
And hours rich with living.

These will be my gift.
When death knocks at my door.

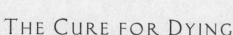

THE CURE FOR DYING

AS THEY WANDERED farther up the mountain, Savitri became more and more anxious, but Ramana paid no attention to her. He left the deer path, following a cut among some huge boulders, and was lost from sight. Scrambling after him, Savitri spied a stream, and beside it sat the monk. He pulled out his reed flute, which was tucked into his saffron robe, and began to play.

"My music doesn't make you smile?" he asked, noticing the anxious look in Savitri's eyes. All she could think about was the Lord of Death awaiting her at home.

"We have so little time," she implored. "Teach me what you would teach."

"What if I could teach you the cure for dying?" asked Ramana.

Savitri was startled. "I'm sure everyone dies."

"Then you believe in rumors. What if I told you that you've never been happy? Would you believe me?"

"Of course not. I was happy this morning, before all this trouble began," said Savitri.

Ramana nodded. "We all remember being happy, and no one can talk us out of that knowledge. So let me ask you another question. Can you remember *not* being alive?"

"No," Savitri said hesitantly.

"Try harder. Cast your mind back to when you were very, very small. Try as hard as you can to remember *not* being alive. This is important, Savitri."

"All right." Savitri tried her best, but she had no memory of never being alive.

"Perhaps you can't remember not being alive because you always have been," said Ramana. He pointed to a locust clutching to a twig over her head. "If you see a locust emerging from the ground after seven years' sleep, does that mean it was dead before that?"

Savitri shook her head.

"Yet the only reason you believe that you were born is that your parents saw you emerge from the womb. They thought they witnessed the moment when you began to exist, so they spread the rumor that you had been born." Savitri was astonished at this line of reasoning.

Ramana became insistent. "Look at this stream. All you see is a short stretch of it, yet would you say you know where the stream begins or where it ends? Heed me, Savitri. You accept death because you accept birth. The two must go together. Forget these rumors that you were ever born. That is the only cure for dying."

Ramana stood up and tucked his flute back in his robe; he was ready to walk on. "Do you believe me?"

"I want to believe you, but I am still afraid," Savitri admitted.

"Then we will keep going." Ramana began to walk away and Savitri followed, pondering what he had said. It seemed irrefutable that if she'd never been born, she could never die. Was it really true?

Ramana caught her thoughts. "We can't base reality on what we don't remember, only on what we do. Everyone remembers being; nobody remembers nonbeing."

After a moment she gently touched his arm. "Play a little more for me, please. I wish to remember being happy."

Vedanta's assertion that the soul is always near brings us face to face with the fascinating phenomenon of near-death experiences, which have become a fixed part of popular belief. (In a 1991 Gallup poll, 13 million Americans, roughly 5% of the population, reported that they had had such an experience.) Near-death is a momentary brush with another reality, or so it seems to those who report the experience. A person is lying in the emergency room or intensive care unit. His heart stops, and for all intents and purposes death ensues. Yet some of these patients, typically those who suffered cardiac arrest, can be resuscitated. When they are, nearly 20% report at least one of the familiar symptoms of NDE (as near-death experience is abbreviated in the medical literature)—leaving their bodies, looking down and seeing themselves on the operating table, watching medical procedures being performed as doctors tried to restart their hearts, finding themselves in a tunnel, going toward a bright light, feeling the presence of a higher power, hearing or seeing loved ones beckoning them on.

Dr. Pim van Lommel, the cardiologist who conducted a major Dutch study on this subject, was astonished by the finding that patients were having a full-blown NDE after their brains had ceased any activity—they were flatline until revived. Suddenly death becomes robed in the trappings of a miracle. How can a person experience any event after the brain's clock has stopped? Other cultures, however, have ventured even further into the timeless, and they assure us that time may end, but consciousness continues.

A woman named Dawa Drolma sits quietly inside a black felt tent at the base of a Himalayan peak. This is her home, but there's little privacy here as visitors stream in and out all day to ask questions and to get her blessing. Dawa Drolma has been famous throughout eastern Tibet ever since she came back from the dead. Her death occurred from a sudden illness when she was sixteen, and for five full days her corpse lay untouched by family or priests. After that time Dawa re-entered her body with a full memory of what had happened in the *Bardo,* the subtle world of Tibetan Buddhist afterlife.

In those five days Dawa spent time in many heavens and hells. (These are Christian terms, but they correspond to places described in Buddhism where the righteous are rewarded and evildoers punished.) The goddess of wisdom took personal charge of showing Dawa each place, pointing out who was there and why. She felt the rapture of those souls who were prayed for by their still-living families. She heard the agonized screams and pleas for mercy of evildoers who had committed sins on earth. Dawa met the god of death, who gave her messages to impart to the living. He knew, and so did she, that Dawa would return to life. In fact, her dying wasn't a chance event; she consciously undertook her journey, first considering all the risks and dangers. The local lamas warned her not to do it, but Dawa had a conviction that her life was going to be entirely about her death.

Year after year she repeated her story; it took a long time to convince people. Tibetan culture wasn't prepared to give spiritual prominence to a woman, except under extraordinary conditions. But the direct knowledge Dawa brought back from the Bardo—and from the "Clear Light" that lies beyond—was unimpeachable. She showed people where to find buried gold. She knew secrets about their private lives and details about departed relatives that no one could possibly guess at. She debated learned lamas and equaled or outdid them in Buddhist theology.

Dawa Drolma isn't unique in Tibet. People who come back to life are called *delogs* (or *deloks*), and one, the famed Lingza Chokyi, left a vivid account in the sixteenth century. "I was still in the room, but instead of being sick in bed I left my body and floated up to the ceiling. I saw my body like a dead pig dressed in my clothes. My children wept over me, and this caused me such intense pain. I tried to talk to my family, but no one could hear me. When they ate, I cried and got angry that they didn't feed me. When they said prayers over me, I suddenly felt much better."

Stages of Awakening

One amazing thing about delogs is their consistency; the experience of Dawa Drolma in the twentieth century mirrors that of Lingza Chokyi four hundred years previously. They see the same six levels of the Bardo, are guided by the White Tara, the goddess of wisdom, and receive messages to bring back to the living. These messages tend to center on being a good Tibetan Buddhist (just as apparitions of the Virgin Mary in every century tend to center on being a good practicing Catholic).

Experts in near-death experiences find much common ground between NDEs and delogs. They both describe leaving the physical body, looking down on themselves and the surroundings, being unable to talk to the people they see, and then traveling elsewhere using the power of thought. When delogs report that in the other world they had "a body from the golden age"—which is to say, young and perfect—we're reminded that some NDEs remember that once they died they seemed to be back in the prime of physical life, somewhere in their twenties or early thirties. Deceased relatives appear on the other side, a region the Tibetans call "the Bardo of becoming." When the newly dead person tries to join them, he is pushed back into the physical world with a sense that it isn't the right time or that somehow a mistake has been made. In both cases there can be a profound sense of coming into contact with God or the supreme Light, after which the fear of death holds no more power.

There are significant parallels, then, between the experience of NDE and the delogs of Tibet. Since delogs provide more detailed and extended accounts, it seems fair to assume that an NDE is just the beginning of the awakening taking place that moves the dying person through all the stages needed for the soul to reveal itself. If we shed the specific geography of Christian heaven, the Buddhist Bardo, and the many Lokas, or divine realms, of Hinduism, the first stage of the afterlife emerges with certain consistent events.

"CROSSING OVER"
How the afterlife dawns

1. The physical body stops functioning. The dying person may not be aware of this but eventually knows that it has occurred.

2. The physical world vanishes. This can happen by degrees; there can be a sense of floating upward or of looking down on familiar places as they recede.

3. The dying person feels lighter, suddenly freed of limitation.

4. The mind and sometimes the senses continue to operate. Gradually, however, what is perceived becomes nonphysical.

5. A presence grows that is felt to be divine. This presence can be clothed in a light or in the body of angels or gods. It can communicate to the dying person.

6. Personality and memory begin to fade, but the sense of "I" remains.

7. This "I" has an overwhelming sense of moving on to another phase of existence.

This sevenfold awakening isn't the same as going to heaven. Researchers often call this the "inter-life" phase, a transition between the mental state of being alive and the mental state of realizing that one has passed on. There are many specifics that change from person to person. Not all NDEs "go into the light." Some patients report traveling to various planets in space or to other worlds according to their religious beliefs. Some experience a judgment scene that can be quite harsh, or even hellish; it can also be full of satisfaction, however.

The nature of the person plays a large part. A child can come back from heaven and report that it was full of baby animals at play, a cardiac patient can report sitting on God's lap and being told by the Almighty that he must return to Earth, and a delog can see every detail of Tibetan theology. These images clearly depend on the culture they reflect. Huston Smith, an expert on world religions, declares, "Everything we experience in the Bardos is a reflection of our own mental machinations." One can substitute "afterlife" for Bardos, since Christians see Christian images, not Buddhist ones, and Muslims see Islamic images.

Crossing over is only a transition, however. The full reality of the soul hasn't yet revealed itself. For delogs, still ahead lies the experience of "the mind's pure nature," as Buddhists would call it. Delogs are quite clear that they haven't actually gone anywhere, that every level of the journey exists in consciousness. What is actually real isn't heaven and hell but the "Clear Light" that lies beyond them. Dawa visited that brilliant white light before descending back through the intermediate worlds in her return to physical existence.

As her son writes, "Despite the fact that the realms of cyclic existence are in the absolute sense empty in nature, mere projections of [the] mind's delusions, on a relative level the suffering of beings trapped there is undeniable." Westerners argue over whether the afterlife could be as real as the physical world; Easterners declare that both are mental projections. Westerners limit the human life cycle to a short span between birth and death; Easterners see an eternal cycle of birth, death, and rebirth.

Thus there is huge room for variation even in the same journey: "As if in a dream or hallucination, beings float in and out of Dawa Drolma's perception like flakes of snow. In one instant she encounters an acquaintance enduring the most hideous torments of hell; in the next she meets a virtuous person on the way to a pure realm.

Occasionally, she sees entire processions of Bardo beings leaving for the pure realms shepherded by a great lama . . . who by the power of his or her altruistic aspirations, has come to save [them]."

A Wealth of Expectations

If different cultures see such different things after death, we must face the possibility that we create our own afterlife. Perhaps the vivid images that appear to dying people are projections, the soul's way of helping us adjust to leaving behind the five senses. I accept that the afterlife is created in consciousness. But as a noted biologist told me with a sigh recently, "The minute you begin to use that word 'consciousness,' you are immediately shut out of science." I can pick up a recent *Time* magazine to read the following from Professor Eric Cornell, a Nobel Prize winner in physics: "Science isn't about knowing the mind of God; it's about understanding nature and the reasons for things. The thrill is that our ignorance exceeds our knowledge."

I'm sure that many people would agree, without realizing that "understanding nature" has limited value when you don't understand human nature. Why are we leaving ourselves out of the experiment?

WHEN CONSCIOUSNESS ISN'T a viable possibility, explanations can only come from materialism. Drugs (for example, marijuana, hashish, LSD, ketamine, mescaline) can induce the brain to experience both a white light and a tunnel effect. So can putting someone in a centrifuge and spinning them at high enough rates to press blood out of the frontal lobes—astronauts and test pilots have such experiences when trained in centrifuges. Extreme stress can bring on hallucinations; patients hospitalized in intensive care during the aftermath of a heart attack are especially prone to them.

Is it possible that medicine has all the answers after all? Dr. van Lommel, who conducted the Dutch study of near-death experiences, doesn't think so. He screened 344 patients whose heart had defibrillated (gone into chaotic twitching instead of a normal regular heartbeat) in the hospital. Talking to them within days of being revived, van Lommel discovered that anesthesia or medications didn't affect their experience. What he marvels most at, however, are those reports of consciousness in the absence of brain activity. Years afterward this paradox still fills him with awe: "At that moment these people are not only conscious; their consciousness is even more expansive than ever. They can think extremely clearly, have memories going back to their earliest childhood and experience an intense connection with everything and everyone around them. And yet the brain shows no activity at all!"

These observations undercut the dying-brain theory of materialism, since the brain has stopped functioning before the NDE begins, in that 4- to 10-minute limbo when resuscitation is possible without permanent brain damage. Van Lommel also points out that any physiological explanation, if true, should apply to everyone. He found that 82% of resuscitated patients couldn't remember any near-death experience; why did their dying brains deprive them of one when the brains of 18% of patients had experiences?

Maybe consciousness isn't in the brain. That's a startling possibility but one consistent with the world's most ancient spiritual traditions. What if an NDE is a step into the afterlife that is still governed by memories and expectations?

There is no doubt that heaven is the expectation of many people in Western society, and therefore we will have to examine its promises next, to consider if Paradise is the choice we really want to make.

3

DEATH GRANTS THREE WISHES

AFTER TWO HOURS of walking through the woods, Savitri and Ramana came to a fork in the path.

"If we went that way we would arrive at Yama's castle. Did you know that Death lives so close by?" he said.

Savitri shuddered. "I'm happy not to know."

"Really?" Ramana seemed genuinely surprised. "I ran across the castle when I was out wandering one day. I was very curious to meet Death face to face."

Savitri felt frightened simply to be reminded of something she so dreaded. Ramana reached out and took her hand. "Come, I can tell you about it as we walk." He had a strong grip, and Savitri felt calmer, as if his strength was seeping into her.

"I immediately knew that I had stumbled on to Yama's home," Ramana continued, "because skulls were stuck on pikes surrounding the gate. So I sat down and waited for my host to appear. I waited all that day and the next. The next day Yama returned home. When he saw me he became distressed. 'I've made you wait outside my gate for three whole days,' he said. 'Not even Death can break the sacred vow of hospitality. Therefore I grant you three wishes, one for each day.'

"'That pleases me well,' I replied, 'for I have long wanted to gain knowledge of you, the wisest of all beings in creation.' Yama bowed regally. 'My first wish,' I said, 'is to know the way back home. I'm not a fool, and I have no desire to remain with you forever.'

"Yama smiled and pointed to the east. 'You will find your way back to the living if you go that way, where the sun rises.'

"'My second wish,' I said, 'is to know if you have ever felt love.'

"Yama didn't look so pleased now, but reluctantly he answered. 'The role of love is to create; my role is to destroy. Therefore, I have no need of love.' Hearing that, I pitied Yama, but he glared proudly, scorning any attempt at compassion. He said, 'Now be quick and name your third wish.'

"I said, 'The great sages declare that the soul survives beyond death. Is this true?' A black cloud came over Yama's countenance. He sputtered with rage, but there was nothing for it but to answer me. 'I will tell you the truth,' he said. 'There are two paths in life, the path of wisdom and the path of ignorance. The path of wisdom is to pursue the Self. The path of ignorance is to pursue pleasure. Pleasure, being born of the senses, is temporary, and whatever is temporary falls under the sway of death. Thus the ignorant fall into my clutches. But the Self is the light of immortality. It shines forever. Few are wise enough to see this light, even though it is inside them and nowhere else. The Self is but the light of your soul. Now go. It will please Yama never to behold your face again.' And off he stalked to nurse his rage."

Savitri found this tale fascinating, but she was puzzled. "How can we miss finding the soul if its light shines inside us?"

Ramana stopped and looked around. He spied a rain puddle along the path and drew Savitri toward it. "Do you see the sun reflected in that puddle?"

Savitri nodded. "I do."

"Then watch."

Ramana stepped into the water, stirring up the mud and roiling the water's smooth surface. "Can you still see the sun's reflection?" Savitri admitted that she couldn't. "This is why people cannot find the soul," said Ramana. "It is muddied by the mind's constant activity and confusion. When I destroyed the sun's reflection I didn't kill the sun. It is eternal, and nothing I do can extinguish it. Now you know the secret of the soul, which even Death cannot extinguish."

Savitri grew grave and thoughtful. "This is something I want to believe."

"You are still afraid," Ramana said gently, "but learn this one thing: Do not trust reflections, not if you want to see reality."

Savitri looked thoughtful as they continued to walk, her hand softly placed in the monk's.

A QUESTION OF BELIEF

The worst afterlife I can imagine is hell.
The second worst may be heaven.

I scribbled these sentences on the page of a notebook in the summer of 2005. The words "heaven" and "hell" immediately strike a Christian note, but I was thinking generally. Heaven is where you go if you are good enough for God; hell is where you go if you aren't. Aren't they both synonyms for "the end"?

Vedanta holds that every afterlife is created to give us what we expect. If that's true of heaven and hell, what kind of expectations do they stand for? Why should bad deeds doom you to a prison where your wrongdoing is punished without mercy or hope of reprieve?

That's an easy question compared to the opposite. Why should being good lead to a fantasy land above the clouds where virtue is rewarded with endless indolence, also without reprieve?

In the summer of 2005 these issues were close at hand for me. Death was something I had to think about constantly because my mother had lapsed into a coma. *Hurry,* an urgent voice said on the phone from India. I was on a jet immediately. From moment to moment it was uncertain whether I would reach her bedside in time to say good-bye.

It's hard to imagine someone you love dying. My mother was nearly eighty and had been gradually fading for the past five years. Her body was a husk of what it had been even six months before. Everyone in the family agreed that it would be a blessing for her suffering to end.

I found myself thinking about just a single cell in my mother's heart. As a doctor I could imagine that cell as clearly as if it were under a microscope. Any heart cell has exchanged all its atoms many times over during one lifetime. My mother's weak heart, so full of a lifetime's experience, was not a static object. It was a firestorm of change. Because every cell is like that, my mother has been passing in and out of life since the day she was born.

Old heart cells can't go to heaven, yet they survive physical death in their own way. Your whole body does the same, putting itself into the grave and rising from the dead thousands of times a minute as old matter is exchanged for new.

Since molecules can always be replenished, only the death of knowledge matters. Knowledge is a cell's essence, which no one will ever see or touch. When millions of oxygen atoms fly away on an exhaled breath, floating out into the world, what remains is far more important: how to build a cell, how a cell behaves, how it relates to other cells.

How can a string of simple molecules along a strand of DNA know all this? When we die we go in pursuit of the answer, because then we confront our essence behind the mask of matter. "Essence" means a distillation, boiling down something crude into something refined, extracting the pure from the impure. There's no need to get tangled up in terminology here. Essence, soul, Atman, or holy spirit all suffice. After the initial stage of "crossing over," the rest of the afterlife is beyond images; it concerns the soul.

My mother passed away, still in a coma, a few hours after I arrived at her bedside. It was a modern death, undramatic and swaddled in the caring cocoon of a hospice. The time to grieve had come, but knowing that Mother was now free to discover who she really was sustained me. Millions of people do not think in this way, relying on the time-honored idea of heaven, but that's changing.

The erosion of traditional faith has not left Paradise untouched. After the *Columbia* space shuttle disaster in 2003, in which the craft exploded in the atmosphere over central Texas and killed all seven people aboard, President Bush said he was sure that the dead astronauts "are now in heaven." Yet in Tennessee, pollsters asked people if they agreed, and although 74% said they believed in the afterlife, only about half of them (37% of the total) thought the astronauts were in heaven, with another third saying they didn't know.

One only has to look at a leading indicator like church attendance. While 44% of Americans say they attend church regularly, reliable statistics show that perhaps half that number is more realistic. Every major denomination is declining—as is also true in fifteen out of eighteen developed countries. (One exception is Christian fundamentalism, which claims growth in the United States and worldwide.)

To get some idea of where you fall in the spectrum of religious belief, ask some basic questions of yourself, as follows:

Read the following statements and then rate each one:

A *Agree—This is true to my beliefs.*
D *Disagree—This is opposed to my beliefs.*
N *No Opinion—I am uncertain, or don't think about this.*

A D N   I believe in God.

A D N   I think God is in heaven.

A D N   I expect to go to heaven when I die.

A D N   Going to heaven depends on being a good person.

A D N   Going to heaven means believing in what the Bible says (substitute Koran or other scriptures).

A D N   If you believe in God you have a better chance of going to heaven than if you don't.

A D N   God is merciful, but he still created Hell.

A D N   Hell is for the punishment of sin.

A D N   Both heaven and hell are eternal.

A D N   Whether I am punished or achieve salvation, the outcome will be just.

A D N   It comforts me to think that I won't disappear when I die.

A D N   Scientific proof of heaven will never come.

A D N   What happens after we die is known by faith.

A D N   Near-death experiences are real.

A D N   When people "go into the light" and then come back, this is a foretaste of the afterlife.

A D N   The near-death experiences I've read about increase my belief in heaven.

A D N   The loved ones I've lost will meet me in heaven.

A D N   I expect to join my mother and father after I die.

A D N Communicating with the dead is real.
A D N Reincarnation is real.

Total A _____
Total D _____
Total N _____

Compare the number of times you agreed, disagreed, or had no opinion and find one category that's dominant.

High A (14–20 points) You are a *believer.* Believers fall into two categories, those who closely hold the tenets of an organized religion and those who pursue spirituality even though they have dropped out of church. As a believer you feel secure about the afterlife and take comfort from that certainty. You feel you have come to terms with fear of dying. Your God is benign—a higher being who will look after your soul when you die. What you know about near-death experiences totally confirms your belief.

High D (14–20 points) You are a *skeptic.* As a skeptic your approach to life is likely to be logical and materialistic. Although not necessarily a scientist, you trust the scientific model over models of faith, to the point that for you the two cannot coexist. You disbelieve in life after death and have made peace with that. You suspect that near-death experiences must be a strange kind of brain dysfunction. Your mind could be changed by more convincing evidence, but so far you've seen none; you suspect that every proof of the afterlife is either a fantasy or wish fulfillment. Since no one returns from the dead, you feel pretty certain we will never have reliable information about it.

High N (14–20 points) You are either *agnostic* or *noncommittal.* Despite the difference between these two groups, both agree that the afterlife may or may not exist. You may be someone who doesn't think about dying, preferring to wait until there is no other choice but to face it. Or you may feel that the afterlife, like God, will never be explained. Accounts of near-death experiences mildly interest you.

If you don't score 14 to 20 points in any category, consider yourself *open-minded*. Such people find credence in spiritual notions but also in materialistic or scientific ones. You are intrigued by near-death experiences but not totally convinced. You may experience a certain anxiety about having no fixed beliefs; you may consider yourself confused. Most likely you are comfortable with having no certainties because there is no certainty, in your opinion, to be had when it comes to the afterlife. (At the prospect of going to heaven, you sigh and think it would be nice. But you're not counting on it.)

IT SHOULD COME as no surprise to discover that you are a believer, skeptic, or agnostic. Yet when you look at where other people fall, which could be very far outside your belief system, it may be disturbing to consider that *you might all be right.*

Believers may go to the heaven (or hell) that matches their religious background. In the afterlife they will meet their most cherished version of God—or gods. They will find themselves surrounded by angels or bodhisattvas. The emotional tone of that afterlife could be one of total bliss, if that is the tone they anticipate, or it could feel more ambiguous, even sad. Catholic theology allows for a weeping Jesus and his mother, Mary, sorrowing over the fate of sinners.

The experience could even feel like nothing. Skeptics may find that the afterlife is a blank, devoid of conscious sensation. For them, dying could lead to a long sleep without any perception of the self. The question is how long this state will last or what it might become.

For agnostics the afterlife is problematic. They may perceive that they remain themselves, occupying a kind of limbo where good and bad deeds form a hazy cloud that never resolves decisively. In this kind of afterlife the same worries and ambiguities that reside at the center of the agnostic worldview may persist. For Christians purgatory fits this description.

And the undecided or open-minded people? They may be in for the biggest surprise, because someone who is truly open-minded dies without any expectations. If your approach to life is to take it one day at a time, the very last day won't be any different. In short, the ability of consciousness to shape our lives is the most permanent thing about us, the one aspect of the mind we can expect to continue.

Somewhere in the Gap

As long as the physical and the metaphysical remain confused, we are trapped in the gap between them. Since belief isn't a given in our society, why should we all expect the same afterlife? Choice and conditioning must play a huge part in the outcome. Consider the following two people whose lives diverge in many ways:

Marion was born into a large Catholic family. She took Communion and was a believer until her mother died of ovarian cancer before she was forty. Watching her mother's suffering killed something in Marion. She stopped believing in God's mercy, although she hardly acknowledged this, even to herself. When she married a man who had long ago dropped his faith, she turned to career and family, and together they achieved success. Decades went by without any undue calamities. After her last child left home for college, Marion began to feel lonely, and within a few years she had vague, somewhat guilty impulses that made her reconsider joining the Church again. At fifty-two, she again feels the need for the faith she grew up in.

Aaron comes from a small family of nonpracticing Jews. As the only son his needs were nurtured as a child, perhaps to a fault, and when he developed a talent for mathematics, his father encouraged him to become an accountant (for the financial security). Aaron pursued the law instead, and by age thirty was established in a prominent Manhattan law firm. Since then he has never looked back. He married late to a woman who is also a lawyer, and together they own an apartment in the city and a summer cottage at the beach. They have no children, and when he found out that his wife was cheating on him, Aaron got over his shock rapidly. He arranged a divorce settlement that benefited him as much as possible. At fifty he hasn't decided whether to remarry, and his career gives him little time to consider the prospects. So far as he is aware, he hasn't had a spiritual thought in years.

It's obvious that these two people have led very different lives. One is a placid follower, the other a fierce competitor. One put her energies into raising a family, the other into making a career. Key words for Marion include stability, intimacy, caring, togetherness, cooperation, listening, and patience. The key words for Aaron include independence, self-reliance, competition, power, ambition, and success. When two lives are different in so many core values, why should they anticipate the same afterlife?

Everyone's basic choices, which have shaped their lives, begin at the level of consciousness. At this level choices aren't simple. They depend on memory and conditioning, on culture and expectation. All these ingredients factor into what happens in the afterlife. Only some of the beliefs that make a difference center on religion. Looming much larger are the infinite other choices we make every day, for they create our personal reality.

What you choose today will ripple throughout a thousand tomorrows.

4

❧

ESCAPING THE NOOSE

FROM THE MOMENT she ran away from home, Savitri had been counting the minutes until Satyavan would return from his woodcutting. But now her mind grew quieter. This wasn't just the influence of Ramana's wisdom or the silence of the woods. Fate had a scheme in mind for Savitri. Fate was leading her in circles until it was satisfied that she could face Yama on her own.

Before, all she could see in her mind's eye was her beloved husband coming home to his doom, but now she saw nothing. Perhaps this was a good sign, because Ramana began to speak.

"I'm not promising you that we can save Satyavan, but others have escaped death."

Savitri's heart rose. "Tell me."

"I remember a boy who was born under a terrible curse. His father was a great rishi, the most revered sage for many miles. This rishi had longed for a son, yet his wife was barren. Finally the rishi decided that he would demand a son from God. Only the wisest know the secret that God was created to do our bidding, not we to do His.

"The rishi called upon God, but at first He refused to appear. The rishi had great patience, however, and he kept telling God to grant him a son, year after year. Finally God appeared to him and said, 'I will give you offspring, but you must choose. Do you want a hundred sons who will live long but be fools, or do you want one son who will be intelligent but die young?'

"The rishi didn't hesitate to choose the intelligent son, who God decreed would die on his sixteenth birthday. To the boundless joy of the rishi and his wife, she became pregnant and gave birth to a boy. He grew up to be extremely intelligent, and his parents cherished him all the more knowing the curse he was born under. They intended to tell the boy his fate in time. Somehow the years passed, and they kept putting it off.

"Finally the boy's sixteenth birthday arrived, and still he knew nothing. When he knelt before his father to get his blessing, the rishi said, 'I want you to stay beside me and not leave the house today.' His son was puzzled, especially when he saw the tears in his father's eyes. Obediently he stayed beside him the whole day, but the rishi was called away for a moment, and his son seized the opportunity to run out the back door. He owed an offering to God on his birthday, which a father cannot forbid.

"When the boy got to the temple he stood in front of the altar, not noticing that Yama had followed him there, carrying the noose that he uses to snare his victims. He threw it over the boy's head to drag him away.

"But at that very moment the boy bowed before the altar in gratitude for the gift of life. Yama's noose missed and caught the sacred images on the altar instead, which crashed to the floor. When they broke, God leaped up, enraged at this insult. He kicked Yama out of the temple and granted the boy a reprieve from death. Some say that he kicked Yama so hard that he killed him, but then God gave him life again when he realized that people were so used to dying that they couldn't do without it."

Savitri listened to this tale intently. Her intuition told her that the boy was none other than Ramana, but she decided to keep that to herself. "What did the boy learn from this?" she asked instead.

Ramana replied, "He learned that when Death comes to grab you, let him grab God instead. If God is in you, Yama's noose will always miss. That is the secret for escaping his clutches."

As it happened, they were passing a meadow that gleamed with flowers in a clearing. Savitri said, "Let's lie down here for a while. I've been so anxious that I forgot to be grateful that I am alive."

"A good idea, Savitri."

They sat down in the afternoon light that turned every flower into radiant gold, and Savitri meditated on her soul.

A RISHI'S HEAVEN

The notion of heaven keeps things human, and that's one reason it has survived so long. The image of returning home after we die, resting from our labors, and receiving our just reward offers powerful reassurance. (It's difficult not to come to tears listening to the old gospel hymn with its gentle, rocking refrain: "Softly and tenderly Jesus is calling, *Come home . . . Come home.*") In an age of doubt, however, the shakiest assumptions about heaven are the two it can't do without:

1. We go somewhere when we die.
2. The place we go to is the same heaven or hell for everyone.

When we talked about the transition stage known as "crossing over," we saw that step-by-step the dying person comes to terms with losing a physical body and the many attachments of a personality. But this is just the first stage of what transpires. A destination lies ahead, which for most religious people implies a real place, not simply a state of mind.

Of all possible destinations, heaven is the easiest. It offers reassurance that we will remain physically the same, with our personality intact. (People get even more specific. I was talking with a breast cancer patient who had undergone a radical mastectomy. We both knew there was a chance she might not survive, but being a devout Christian she was easy about going to heaven. "What do you expect to see when you get there?" I asked. "My boobs," she shot back immediately.)

Heaven flies in the face of Vedanta, which holds that our destination is a meeting with the unknown. After the familiar images of "crossing over" disappear, the unexpected unfolds. Consciousness can take a creative leap. The conventional heaven we were all told about as children was just such a creative leap that has become a cliché. We can remain in its well-worn groove, but in a culture of doubt, I don't think this is fixed. Doubt has the advantage of opening new possibilities.

One of these is the possibility that death can be as creative as living. A painter knows that he's using the raw material of pigment, but the vast majority of people do not realize that they are using the raw material of consciousness. If they think about consciousness at all, what comes to mind are its contents. Like a room full of furniture, your consciousness is filled with thoughts and memories, wishes and fears, desires and dreams. Some of this content gets changed, but some of it is permanent—the fixed furniture of the mind. It isn't creative to keep using those same contents over and over, yet that's essentially what heaven amounts to: reused furniture.

Take a piece of paper and mark one column "heaven" and one column "hell." As quickly as you can, list the words and images that come to mind for each word. Most people, whether they consider themselves believers or skeptics, come up with a list along the following lines:

58

HEAVEN

harps
fluffy white clouds
angels
home of God
everlasting peace
bliss eternal
the soul's true home
Paradise—lost and then regained
reward for the righteous
great white father on his throne
nice but boring
one big family again
opiate of the masses
I want to go there

HELL

devil, pitchfork, sulfur
torments of the damned
fire
Dante's Inferno—circle after circle
unending pain
scary beyond belief
cloven hooves
fear keeps people in line
glamour of evil
Satan the ultimate rock star, seductive bad boy
I don't want to go there

These were the entries I came up with, writing as fast as I could. I immediately notice two things: my images are entirely secondhand, inherited from the culture I live in. There is no ambiguity. Heaven is one thing, hell is the opposite. Without room for ambiguity, the afterlife can't be creative. But our minds prefer things to be clear-cut. Every fairy tale opposes absolute good with absolute evil. We don't tell our children that after Cinderella came home from the ball she was so happy to see her stepsisters there that they became better friends. Or that once the glass slipper fit her foot she decided to go on a trial date with the prince. Despite centuries of theology about Satan and his relationship to God, our minds simplify their roles into villain and hero.

According to Catholic belief we see God imperfectly while we are alive here on earth. His reflection is cast in a mirror like our own face and body (Saint Paul's "seeing in a glass darkly"). We imagine that he is human. But on arriving in heaven we will see God directly as he is. And that, according to the Church, raises a contradiction, because we will see both the "obscure and vague" image we had in mind and the real God "after the manner of His own Being." In other words, he will be real and unreal at the same time. This contradiction can't be settled; it's a mystery. On this Vedanta would agree. How, then, can we find mystery in Heaven?

The War in Heaven

The popular British writer H. G. Wells wrote, "This doctrine of the Kingdom of Heaven . . . is certainly one of the most revolutionary doctrines that ever stirred and changed human thought." What made heaven so revolutionary was a shift from this world to the next for which Jesus is almost single-handedly responsible. In fact, heaven is one of his most unique contributions.

In the Old Testament God promises the prophets and patriarchs a kingdom in the literal sense: They will rule the earth in His name. Thus God makes a covenant, a binding legal contract, with David that He will "never lack a man to sit upon His throne, forever." Since David was already a king, this promise was taken to mean that David's throne in Jerusalem would be God's for all eternity. Jesus himself seems to second this notion when he promises that the Kingdom of God is at hand, yet his teaching extends much further.

In Christ's conception heaven is **present**: It's an inward experience that can be felt by the righteous. Heaven is also **future**: It's returning home to be with God that the righteous await on Judgment Day. Heaven is **personal**: It is to be found "within you." At the same time, heaven is **universal**: It is an eternal abode beyond birth and death, a place outside Creation.

This teaching was revolutionary because Jesus built a bridge to the soul, exhorting every person to find his (or her) way across. Before, being righteous in the eyes of Jehovah was a matter of ritual, obeying the priests, and not breaking divine commandments. Whether the Old Testament even holds out any afterlife is a matter of debate. (Needless to say, Jews do not consider the New Testament an advance over the Old. As Judaism has evolved it came to include its own elaborate metaphysics. But for millions of Reform Jews, there is no afterlife. This puts pressure on every believer to live the most moral and righteous life possible here and now.)

After Jesus, people could go on a spiritual journey, and the urgency of the journey was something quite new. Heaven was a prize one had to win through one's own efforts. The urgency to win heaven has fueled Christianity to this day, and the most fervent believers declare that it must never be forgotten. But do they remember that the entire process happens inside?

In today's culture Christianity has become stuck in literal images—such as heaven that is literally a place. There's no hint of an inward journey and no room for creative exploration of the soul. People wind up arguing fiercely over an imaginary landscape far removed from Jesus' actual teaching. The ramifications of this war reach everywhere. In 2005 a forty-one-year-old brain-dead woman in Florida named Terri Schiavo became the focus for a war between faith and science. The heartache of Ms. Schiavo's condition, known as a persistent vegetative state (PVS), is that the brain-dead person may have brief periods of what looks like intermittent wakefulness as facial expressions change, the eyes blink, and the head possibly moves. These are all unconscious reflexes. If viewed through desperate eyes, slim signs of wakefulness can seem like "minimal consciousness," a medical term that implies a faint degree of hope. Terri Schiavo's parents had seen her eyes move after she emerged from her original coma, and this they interpreted as a sign of recognition from someone they loved. (Right-wing politicians blew these faint signs of awareness out of all proportion, claiming that Ms. Schiavo laughed and cried, knew her surroundings, and recognized her family.)

The idea that Schiavo was no longer alive—and hadn't been for fifteen years, ever since the day in 1990 when she collapsed from heart failure—was attacked vehemently by the religious right. President Bush flew overnight from his Texas ranch to Washington, D.C., so that an emergency bill in Congress could "save" the life of one endangered person, a move that was denounced in some circles as a cynical political stunt. Accusations of hypocrisy flew freely. Isn't the religious right also an eager supporter of capital punishment, a form of death that has taken scores of innocent lives? In the end, Terri Schiavo's feeding tube was removed by court order, despite the emergency congressional bill. She died two weeks later, in March 2005. The right to end the life of the brain-dead has been well established all the way up to the Supreme Court, and it was upheld again in this case.

In this story religion traps the mind in a welter of firmly held contradictory positions. Those people who so vociferously believe in heaven, weren't they also denying Terri Schiavo her chance to go there by trying to keep her alive? If heaven is the supreme reward, is euthanasia a crime or a gift? Medical science doesn't care when the soul enters the body or when it leaves. If a woman in PVS can't see, feel, or think, then taking her off life support isn't much of a change. She will go from dead to dead, experiencing merely a more complete definition of what "dead" means. Finally, there is a peculiarly Christian dilemma here: Was Terri Schiavo going to heaven now or on Judgment Day, in which case how much can it matter if she is allowed to die sooner or later? According to fundamentalists, her body will still have to wait until the End Time to rise from the grave and meet God face to face.

The schism between science and religion is more than faith versus materialism. Science absents itself from metaphysical questions, but most people assume that science disproves metaphysics, indeed, disproves all invisible things associated with God, the soul, heaven, hell, and so on. This assumption is skepticism, not science. Science in the age of quantum physics does not deny the existence of invisible worlds. Quite the contrary. And we can't claim that Jesus is only about metaphysics—he gives plenty of advice about living in this world. Which brings us to a puzzle. When Jesus tells his disciples that they should be in the world but not of it, his teaching seems unlivable. If I'm eating breakfast, how can I do that without being of the world? My physical body anchors me here every moment. But the soul manages to be in this world while remaining firmly outside time and space. Jesus is giving us a clue about the kingdom of heaven within.

Where the Rishis Go

Many times Jesus sounds like a rishi in the tradition of Vedanta. Certainly that's true about being in the world but not of it. In simple terms, he is telling his closest followers to stop thinking of themselves as physical creatures. Jesus becomes more explicit if we look outside the four Gospels to the fragmentary Gospel of Thomas, which was written very early, perhaps within a century after the Crucifixion, but was later excluded from the official canon.

Jesus said: "If those who lead you say to you: See, the kingdom is in heaven, then the birds of the sky will go before you; if they say to you: It is in the sea, then the fish will go before you. But the kingdom is within you, and it is outside of you. When you know yourselves, then you will be known, and you will know that you are the sons of the living Father." This passage shows how profound the roots of religion are, and how compatible the great traditions of wisdom would be if dogma didn't stand in the way. What Jesus says here supports the view that heaven is everywhere, but it goes further by saying that heaven is an inward experience—an experience in consciousness. Jesus sees the soul everywhere and thus he can see that the essence of people lies outside time and space. Like the rishis, Jesus was comfortable living with eternity. Why, then, aren't we?

Eternity can't be grasped by the mind in our ordinary waking state. Our waking state is dominated by time while eternity is not. There must be a link. Vedanta says that there is a continuum, in fact. *Every quality in yourself is actually a soul quality.* Think about the following sequence of words:

Contented
Happy
Thrilled
Overjoyed
Ecstatic
Blissful

This is the kind of continuum the rishis had in mind. A person can feel contented without knowing that there is any connection to the soul. When contentment intensifies, one is aware of being happy, and if happiness is intense enough, it feels thrilling. At rare moments we can rise to a higher level and say that we are overjoyed, or ecstatic. We are moving along a continuum, which may be invisible but is just as real as tasting increasingly sweet desserts.

Ecstasy represents the limit of happiness that can be felt personally, and even here the Latin root of the word "ecstasy" means "to stand outside." In common usage people will say, "I was so happy it felt unreal, like it was happening to someone else," or "I loved her so much it was like an out-of-body experience." In Vedanta there is one final step on the continuum: bliss. In Sanskrit the word is *ananda*. Bliss is a quality of the soul. From the perspective of everyday life, it cannot be imagined. The mind is as baffled by infinite happiness as the tongue would be if it tasted something sweeter than sweet.

Even though it is inside everyone, heaven isn't reached in a single leap of faith. As with bliss, there is a continuum with every quality of the soul. We all know this instinctively. Take kindness. The urge to perform a small act of kindness, such as giving spare change to a homeless person on the street, is expandable to giving welfare to the needy. Kindness crosses over into a religious act when faith-based groups engage in AIDS relief work in Africa. We see the essence of this impulse in Buddha, the Compassionate One, whose very nature is kindness.

We need this reminder that our best qualities can reach universality. Christianity may claim that Jesus was unique, as Buddhism claims that Gautama was unique, yet the continuum says otherwise. The following qualities become more intense as we get closer to the soul:

Compassion
Strength
Truth

Bliss
Beauty
Love
Wisdom
Power

Every act of kindness adds another brushstroke to the picture; every insight draws you nearer to your essence. You and I differ from each other in a thousand ways, depending on how we relate to our souls. On a given day I may be struck by a beautiful sunset, a loving smile from a child, a sudden truth about who I am. You may be struck by how much the poor deserve compassion, how wise a poem by Keats is, how beautiful it is to give of yourself. What keeps life fascinating is the constant creativity of the soul. After all is said and done, I believe in heaven, and when I die I expect to be there, not in a celestial garden but in a space described by T. S. Eliot's famous lines:

> We shall not cease from exploration
> And the end of all our exploring
> Will be to arrive where we started
> And know the place for the first time.

Truth, wisdom, beauty, and all the other qualities of the soul don't need physical settings. Pure love exists even in the absence of a person to love. Spiritual truth needs no crusade to follow. The soul in its full intensity takes center stage after we die but is foreshadowed long before.

"I've never married, and I've never been a mother, because I'm a man," a middle-aged writer told me once. He had been a spiritual seeker for a long time. "For some years I lived in an ashram in western Massachusetts where the orientation was Hindu and a lot was said about the Divine Mother. I'm not Christian enough to be attracted to the Virgin Mary. I guess you'd say I was always more male oriented. But I realize that the feminine is important.

"I have women friends who have joined Goddess groups. They perform rituals and dance under the full moon. I followed a more conventional path, basically meditating hours a day. No dancing, no singing, not even any prayers. I did this for five years. Then one day something very strange occurred.

"I was sitting in meditation when a gentle feeling came over me. It began as warmth in my heart, then it took on an emotional tone. Tenderness, sweetness, love. I sat there enjoying this when the intensity increased. I seemed to melt away. Within ten seconds I became pure. Nothing but love. *I was the Divine Mother.*

"How can I tell you what that's like? Imagine that you're watching a great movie actress. She embraces and kisses her children, and for a moment you forget that you're sitting in the dark watching the play of light on a screen. You are her. That's what this felt like, only a thousand times more intense. I was nothing but the Mother."

At unexpected moments we go beyond our usual place on the spiritual continuum. We don't feel mere affection, infatuation, romantic love, or deep devotion. We become absorbed into universal love itself. This man told me that he now looks at women very differently. "They exist as ordinary people but at the same time a totally impersonal force—the Mother—shines through them. I can be honking at a woman driver to move faster through a light, but if she turns her face toward me, I see *it*. *It* is doing everything, and when I realize that, honking my horn seems absurd. Can you honk your horn at God?"

In physical form there's only so much purity we can absorb, but sometimes that threshold is transcended. I'm thinking of Saint Teresa of Ávila, the sixteenth-century Spanish saint who experienced divine love as a golden arrow being pushed through her heart by an angel. Teresa described this as excruciatingly painful and blissful at the same time (hence her status as the patron saint of sufferers).

This brings us back to the paradox of heaven, that God is visible and invisible at the same time. So is the soul. We encounter it visibly through events that inspire us to feel love, truth, and beauty. The vessel that contains them—a loving spouse, a beautiful painting, a wise saying—will fade and disappear. But its essence remains, and it is this essence that allows us to look forward to feeling more love tomorrow. This is the path to heaven.

For someone who has died, the path is complete. Then what? Having arrived in the soul's domain, does experience stop? In physical terms, yes. The objects of love are gone. Only essence is real now. But as we will see, activity hasn't come to an end—far from it. The soul finds itself much freer to choose "on the other side," and the possibilities—so the rishis declare—are more interesting than ever.

THE PATH TO HELL

"I WONDER IF Yama fools himself?" Ramana mused. "He certainly fools everyone else."

"You talk as if he's pulling some kind of trick," Savitri said. It was wearing on her to be in the forest this long. She knew that time was running out.

"Yama *is* pulling a trick," Ramana agreed. "You wouldn't have run away from him if you'd known it." Ramana stopped, as if he had pronounced something obvious.

"Show me how the trick works," Savitri said.

"All right. I'll tell you the story of a monkey who was shut inside a small room in a castle tower. Nothing was happening in the room, and the monkey was restless.

"The monkey could only divert himself by going to the window and looking out at the world. This distracted him for a while, but then he started to think about his situation. How did he end up in this tower? Why had he been captured and put there? The monkey's mood began to darken. There was nothing to do, no one to talk to. His thoughts made him more and more depressed. The room seemed to close in; the monkey started to sweat anxiously. *No,* he suddenly realized, *I'm not in a room, I'm in hell.* Quickly his depression grew into anguish and anguish into torment. The monkey saw demons all around inflicting every imaginable pain.

"*This is it,* the monkey thought. *I am in eternal hell.* And so the torment continued, getting worse and worse. The monkey saw no way out. But gradually the monkey got used to his torment. How much time had elapsed? The monkey couldn't remember. But he began to feel better about his surroundings. It wasn't such a bad room, not really. In fact, it was rather pleasant to be by oneself looking out the window at all the fascinating things going on outside.

"Bit by bit the demons stopped torturing the monkey and withdrew. He began to feel better, and soon the day came when he was feeling optimistic. The monkey grew more cheerful, and then . . ." Ramana broke off. "No doubt you know where this story is headed."

Savitri nodded. "The monkey is going to heaven."

"Exactly. He starts to feel better and better, until he imagines himself in Paradise, and instead of being punished by demons he is being soothed by angels. *Ah,* the monkey thinks, *I am in eternal bliss.*"

"Until he gets bored again," Savitri remarked.

Ramana nodded. "The monkey is the mind, sitting alone in the tower of the head. As the mind expands with pleasure and contracts with pain, it creates every possible world, constantly falling for its own creations. The monkey will believe in heaven for a while, but then boredom will set in, and being the seed of discontent, boredom will pull him out of heaven and back down to hell."

Savitri felt despondent. "So we're all trapped."

"Only if you agree to be trapped. I didn't say the tower was locked," said Ramana. "There is an infinite domain outside the castle walls. You can take your mind beyond walls. There is freedom outside, and having achieved it, you will never have to go to heaven or hell again."

KARMA AND THE WAGES OF SIN

So far, I've offered a view of the afterlife that is open, creative, and full of choices. Step-by-step we fulfill our expectations and behold images that fit those expectations. But this view leaves out one aspect that looms large for many people: sin. In Christian belief sin cannot be overlooked, since God is constantly adding up our good and bad deeds. He must; otherwise everyone would go to heaven, and its mixture of good and bad people would too closely resemble earthly life.

I saw a Catholic bishop being interviewed on television recently, and he was asked a question that could have been posed to a bishop in the Middle Ages: "Do Christians really believe that this life only exists to prepare us for the life to come?" The bishop's immediate reply was yes—exactly what a Catholic bishop would have said in the Dark Ages. A thousand years hasn't changed a basic Christian belief that the material world is a vale of tears, that sin created death, and that the only escape is to reach heaven. "I'll be at peace when I get there. I'll be able to relax," the bishop said. In other words, what we suffer here and now plays a huge part in our image of what's to come.

Hell is payback for sin, but it's also an extension of earthly suffering. When escape is the ultimate reward, staying behind is the ultimate punishment. Christian theology basically says, "Be good or God will give you more of this life, only worse." The Vedic rishis looked at suffering not as a matter of sin but as a matter of lost freedom. According to Vedanta, whatever limits our freedom now will continue to operate after we die. In both cases, you are subject to the power of Karma.

Originally the Sanskrit word *Karma* meant "action," but it quickly expanded and now implies the eternal struggle between good and evil. (I will use capital "K" to refer to the cosmic aspect of Karma, small "k" to refer to its personal effects.) At the most superficial level you build good karma by being good and bad karma by being bad. This matches the Christian concept of choosing between good and evil actions, and being rewarded or punished accordingly. Millions of people, East and West, live by that belief. But Karma never ends; it's part of the soul's continuous journey, not just a single lifetime that leads once and for all to heaven or hell.

The catch is that no amount of good karma can win a person's freedom. The Vedic version of hell is never finding a way out of bondage, which makes it strangely congruent to Christian hell. Perfect goodness isn't achievable, and bit by bit the effect of karma will turn the saint's life into the sinner's, and vice versa. That's why "glue" might be a better translation of Karma than "action."

You can compare Karma to a cosmic clock with every gear perfectly meshed. You can compare it to a super-computer keeping track of every action in creation. You can compare it to an eternal judge weighing the good and bad results of every thought and deed. In truth the whole system—universe, brain, lower self, higher self, Atman, God—is bound together by Karma's invisible force. The law of Karma, which underlies every Eastern belief system, holds that none of us can escape paying our debts, and since we accumulate debts every day, we have no choice but to keep paying them off lifetime after lifetime.

Being Saved from Sin

According to the rishis, punishment in the afterlife is the result of unpaid karmic debts. If I commit a crime and don't pay for it here on earth, I will pay by suffering later. What is a karmic debt? Basically any cause that hasn't yet found its effect. There's a saying in India, "Karma waits on the doorstep," meaning that a person may try to walk away from past actions, but like a dog sleeping by the door until

72

its master returns, Karma can be endlessly patient. Eventually the universe will insist on redressing the balance of wrong with right.

Hell is the condition of karmic suffering. The vast majority of near-death experiences turn out to be positive, but some are not. Instead of moving toward a benign and welcoming light, a few people experience the features of hell. They see demons or even Satan himself; they hear sinners crying out in torment; a heavy blackness looms over everything. NDE investigators have even found a category of people whom they call "earthbound souls," haunted by evil actions and frustrated desires. Prime witness to this was offered by a man named George Ritchie, who was given a firsthand look at them:

In Ritchie's near-death experience, Jesus took him to a large city on earth where he observed earthbound souls stalking the living for one reason or another. One earthbound soul begged in vain for a cigarette. A young man who had committed suicide begged his parents in vain for forgiveness. In a house, Ritchie was shown the soul of a boy following a living teenage girl and begging for forgiveness despite the fact that the girl was completely unaware of the boy's presence. Jesus told Ritchie that the boy had committed suicide and was chained to every consequence of his act.

These are the ghosts of unpaid karma. It's worth remembering that hellish experiences don't depend upon dying. People have seen Satan in dreams, visions, imagination, and even in the flesh (or *inside* the flesh, if you believe in demonic possession and Satan's ability to take up his abode in a person's body until he is somehow exorcised).

NDE investigators are among the few in our society whose job is to think about the afterlife, and when they consider any experience of hell or tormented souls, certain factors create these visions of torment. Our minds put us in hell, and they can take us out again. Whether suffering is created here on earth through physical pain or in the afterlife through psychological torment, the causes remain the same, since they can be traced back to the workings of Karma. Every culture believes that bad deeds are inescapable in the afterlife, but the rishis opened the picture to describe how torment can be escaped in general.

On the material level it's not self-evident that "as you sow, so shall you reap." Wrongdoing escapes notice, much less punishment, all the time. We all harbor a fantasy of a life where we can get away with anything. It's strong enough to turn bank robbers into heroes, for example, at least in movies.

By saying that bad karma will one day catch up with wrongdoers, are we guilty of wish fulfillment? Skeptics would certainly say yes, because if a karmic debt is paid outside the material world, it isn't being paid at all. The matter can't be easily settled, but in spiritual terms we can observe the difference between someone who is mature—and by implication has paid off some debts—and someone who is immature, loaded down with unpaid debts. The spiritually mature person pursues a meaningful life through the following:

Self-worth: I matter in the divine plan, I am unique in the universe.
Love: I am deeply cared for and care for others deeply.
Truth: I can see past illusions and distractions.
Appreciation and gratitude: I cherish the fits of creation.
Reverence: I can feel and see the sacred.
Nonviolence: I respect life in all its forms.

To live outside these values is painful, and if intense enough, perhaps the pain puts a person in hell. So the value of a meaningful life demonstrates the hidden side of karmic debts: when you are free of them, your life becomes fulfilled and deeply worth living.

Religious Christians will object that I have painted a psychological picture of hell that leaves out Satan. To leave Satan out is to ignore biblical text, which tells us of the angel Lucifer, closest to God among all the angels, who disobeyed God and fell through the sin of pride until he reached the farthest place in creation, hell. That millions of people believe literally in this myth says a great deal about our refusal to take responsibility for the afterlife. We prefer to objectify a Prince of Darkness, an all-powerful opposite of God, who then becomes the agent of all evil.

Taking responsibility for hell sounds awful, but not taking responsibility is the same as giving up on ourselves. Hell is farthest from God because it represents the low ebb of consciousness. The causes of hellish experiences here on earth aren't merely psychological. They don't just involve being depressed or guilty. When we become disconnected from ourselves, a sense of deserving to suffer begins. Hell is the suffering you think you deserve. When connections are repaired, we no longer believe we deserve punishment: we are back in the flow of life with all its healing properties.

Everything Satan stands for is included in our own self-judgment. Indeed, he is a massive reflection of self-judgment. Satan is a creation of consciousness, and as such he waxes and wanes, he evolves, and he changes in significance.

Satan is real under the following conditions:

- People feel they deserve punishment instead of healing.
- A culture believes in the Satan myth.
- Believers pay attention to that myth and give it value.
- Guilt is projected outward onto demons instead of healed inside.

- Wrongdoing accumulates without a means for finding forgiveness, atonement, or purification.
- Children are put in fear of demons and told that they have supernatural power.

Satan is unreal under the following conditions:

- People feel they deserve healing instead of punishment.
- A culture is aware of how myths are made.
- People are self-aware and take responsibility for their own emotions.
- There is a belief in forgiveness, healing, and atonement.
- Outlets for negative energies are found (through therapy, sports, open dialogue, healthy family dynamics, education, etc.).
- Children are not conditioned to believe in demons and other supernatural enemies.
- Society promotes the evolution of consciousness.

Our culture has largely moved beyond Satan, because despite religious literalists, we have a century of secularism behind us. Whatever its faults, which can be glaring, secular culture has promoted therapy, discouraged superstition, given people responsibility over their own destinies, and encouraged open-minded dialogue in every area once considered taboo. These are considerable achievements; they bespeak tremendous growth in consciousness. Evil, however you define it, remains even after Satan is gone, but removing our attention from Satan has diminished him greatly, just as the ancient gods of Mount Olympus, once so powerful that they served to explain every natural phenomenon, are now relegated to history.

Like the Greek gods, Satan has outlived his usefulness. When people find a better explanation for any phenomenon, the old explanation withers away—meteorology replaces Aeolus the god of wind, and thermodynamics replaces Promethean fire. We have the power to make Satan grow or diminish. In fact, we have the power to make him real and unreal, which is far more crucial.

As consciousness evolves, Satan will become more unreal. Already I believe there are millions of people who are ready to stop talking about demons, sin, and cosmic evil as the root cause of suffering. They are ready to talk in terms of consciousness. They are ready to talk about being disconnected from themselves. We have spent centuries calling upon God to rescue us and fearing Satan as the supreme enemy. Perhaps this was necessary to our evolution, but now we can turn to the deeper, more humane wisdom of the rishis, which speaks of one reality, not a fractured universe with heaven and hell at opposite poles.

Good and evil, the rishis tell us, is a direct function of being connected to the soul. The soul is the most real aspect of the self. When we break our connection with the soul, we lose touch with reality.

THE SOUL IS DISGUISED WHEN . . .

- You are too tired or stressed.
- You are pulled outside yourself.
- Your attention is dominated by externals.
- You let others think for you.
- You act out of compulsion.
- You are influenced by fear and anxiety.
- You struggle and suffer.

These conditions have to change before the soul connection can be reestablished. Death provides access to the domain of the soul, but Vedanta declares that the soul has a great deal to offer before death. Life is conducted under the gaze of the soul. Your portion of pure consciousness has certain universal qualities:

- It is constant.
- It never loses sight of you.
- It is connected to every other soul.
- It shares God's omniscience.
- It is untouched by change.
- It lives beyond time and space.

So it isn't only tender, loving, quiet moments that reveal the soul. Rather, it's those moments when the soul's own qualities come to the surface that are most important. Such moments occur too rarely in modern lives, but the soul never stops revealing itself.

THE SOUL IS REVEALED WHEN . . .

- You feel centered.
- Your mind is clear.
- You have the sensation that time has stopped.
- You suddenly feel free of boundaries.
- You are keenly self-aware.
- You feel merged with another person, either in love or silent communion.
- You feel untouched by aging and change.
- You feel blissful or ecstatic.
- You have an intuitive flash that turns out to be true.
- You somehow know what is going to happen.
- You sense the truth.
- You feel supremely loved or absolutely safe.

If there is only one reality, as the rishis declare, then life is not a struggle between good and evil, but a tangled web where all actions, good and bad, move us closer to reality or deeper into illusion. Karma spins the web. Karma isn't a prison, it's a field of choice. Karma keeps our choices honest. We sow what we reap, but this is far from saying that we are trapped by the forces of cosmic good and evil. Hell, like every other location in consciousness, ultimately reflects the state of our own awareness, and freedom from hell is won, like every other achievement, by coming closer to the reality of the soul.

❧

GHOSTS

"I AM DEEPLY grateful for all that you have taught me," Savitri said. It was getting late, and in truth she was beginning to lose hope of returning home. "I am resigned to living alone, and perhaps I can visit you to learn more."

"Is anyone ever alone?" Ramana said. The forest was enfolded in purple shadows, and Savitri couldn't read the expression on his face clearly.

"I feel alone," she said.

"Often feelings aren't trustworthy," Ramana pointed out.

Suddenly there was rustling in the bushes by the side of the path. Savitri jumped back. "What was that?" she exclaimed, feeling the return of her anxiety.

"Ghosts." Ramana had stopped short. "It's time you met them, for having traveled beyond this life, ghosts and spirits have much to teach."

He stood still and beckoned her to keep quiet. Savitri froze in place, and a chill passed over her skin. After a moment someone emerged from the dimness of the forest—a little girl no more than two years old, toddling toward them but not looking their way.

"Don't!" Ramana warned, anticipating that Savitri would want to run and hold the baby.

The baby looked around blankly, then it crossed the path and disappeared into the woods again.

"Did you recognize her?" Ramana asked.

"No, how could I? Is she lost?" Savitri felt confused and disturbed by what she'd witnessed. Instead of answering her directly, Ramana said, "There are more. You're attracting them." At that moment a second ghost appeared, this time a girl of four. Savitri was dumbfounded. "Do you know that one?" he asked.

"It's me!"

At that, the ghost peered her way for a moment before wandering away. "And the baby was also me?"

Ramana nodded. "Every former self you have left behind is a ghost. Your body is no longer the body of a child. Your thoughts, desires, fears, and hopes have changed. It would be terrible to walk around with all your dead selves holding on. Let them go."

Savitri could say nothing. One by one apparitions of herself appeared. She witnessed the girl of ten who sat by her mother's side in the kitchen, the girl of twelve blushing to talk to a boy, the ardent young woman obsessed with Satyavan, her first love. The last ghost was the most startling, because it was like a mirror image, exactly her age and wearing the same shawl that Savitri had thrown on when she fled her hut.

"You see, even the self you had today is a ghost," said Ramana.

When this last apparition had faded back into the forest, Savitri said, "What do they have to teach me?"

"That death has been with you every moment of your life," Ramana replied. "You have survived thousands of deaths every day as your old thoughts, your old cells, your old emotions, and even your old identity passed away. Everyone is living in the afterlife right now. What is there to fear or doubt?"

"But they seemed so real," Savitri said.

"Yes, as real as dreams," said Ramana. "But you are in the here and now, not in the past."

Savitri had never seen herself in this way, and the sight gave her new courage. "I am still determined to defeat death, for I want Satyavan in my arms again. But if Yama is victorious, I won't cling to ghosts. At least I have won that much wisdom."

THE FIELD OF DREAMS

When people wonder if the personality survives death, the answer is that the personality doesn't even survive while we are alive. We are not the same person we were five, ten, or fifteen years ago and it would be a sorry state if we were. Our personalities are constantly evolving, transforming, growing. If the question becomes, Does the individual survive death?, the answer is, What's an individual? In reality what we call "me" is different from day to day, week to week, year to year. Which individual are you talking about, the young person who was in love and full of romance and desire, or the child who was full of innocence and wonder? Perhaps we must wait for the one who is senescent and dying. Which one would you survive as?

Perhaps none. Vedanta tells us that the afterlife brings the opportunity for a creative leap. As our choices continue to expand, we will experience a new reality that is far richer than the conventional notion of heaven. Heaven is an end point, whereby definitions, all transformation, stops. Souls lounge around in a blessed state that sounds, frankly, like eternal assisted living. Why should consciousness become inert? In the afterlife survival would be meaningless unless we continued to respond.

The biggest difference is that in the afterlife the input of the five senses no longer stimulates us. The furniture of the mind has been cleared away, leaving a space that is both inside and outside ourselves. This is why Jesus wasn't being paradoxical when he sometimes talked about heaven "within you" and heaven "with the Father." When you empty a room of furniture, the space left behind is empty, but the Vedic rishis say that mental space is different. It is full of possibilities. Anything can be born there. They called this pregnant space *Akasha*. The closest equivalent in English would be "dream space," or at least that's a good place to begin.

A dream is like a blank screen on which anything can be projected: any event, place, or person. Akasha is the same. When Vedanta says that every world is a projection of the mind, it is describing an Akashic dream. "Worlds come and go like specks of dust in a beam of sunlight," declares a famous Vedic saying. In Akasha we realize the transience of all things and the immensity of the unknown. The Akashic dream is cosmic, unlike the personal dreams we have at night.

NDEs tell us that the stage of "crossing over"—the temporary realm preceding the full experience of the afterlife—still feels personal. People report seeing their deceased friends and relations, for example. The dying person continues to see the room in which his body lies, and memories and associations keep tying him back to physical existence. The possibility of taking a creative leap has yet to be realized. As long as you continue to feel like the person you were, you can't experience the unknown. Let me give you an example.

On a speaking engagement a few years ago I met Gerald, a man who told me that he had become fascinated by the healing powers of shamans in the Southwest. What kind of healing did he need? I asked.

"I don't want to give you any background just yet," Gerald said. "I flew down to New Mexico and found myself in a group outside Santa Fe, about twenty of us. I'd never met a shaman before. Ours was Hopi, but he didn't wear any religious symbols. He was just a very pleasant older man with shoulder-length hair. He greeted each of us as we entered the meeting room in a motel."

The shaman began by asking everyone to pick a partner. "We were asked to pair off with the person in the room whom we felt most comfortable with. I picked a guy about my age who was standing next to me. I was as comfortable with him as anyone else, considering how bad I felt anyway."

Gerald now revealed that he had been through a debilitating course of treatment for prostate cancer, including surgery and chemotherapy. He had been cancer free for two years but was haunted by fears that the doctors hadn't gotten everything. His anxiety kept on growing even though he kept being reassured that he was in the clear. Finally, on the advice of a friend, Gerald reluctantly sought out a shaman.

"Once we'd picked our partners we formed a circle. The shaman walked into the middle and began to chant. He didn't ask us to do anything but observe. After fifteen minutes he turned to the first pair, a man and a woman. The shaman looked into the man's eyes and muttered something. Immediately the man's body began to tremble, then he fell down in a kind of mild seizure.

"In an insistent voice the shaman said, *Speak to me!* The man's eyes had gone blank. He began to mumble about being freezing cold, lying on the ground in winter. He'd passed out from alcohol and was dying.

"The shaman nodded. He turned to the woman, who looked pretty shaken. 'Are you an alcoholic?' he asked. 'Is that why you've come here?' Turning red, the woman nodded. 'Well, you have a spirit in your family line, someone who died of alcohol. We need to free him.' He helped the woman's partner to his feet and told him he'd done a good job. And that's how it went, one pair at a time going around the circle."

Gerald watched as each partner was used to invoke a departed spirit. In each case the spirit would talk about a problem—depression, cancer, addiction—which turned out to be a perfect match for the problem that the other person in the pair had come about. No one had talked to the shaman before meeting in the motel. Gerald was astonished when his partner brought in the spirit of Gerald's grandfather, who had died of lung cancer when Gerald was a small child.

"Not everybody recognized their spirit, and it wasn't always a close relative. In my case I had heard a lot about my grandfather, who had been a prominent citizen. It was spooky hearing him beg to be released from his pain, very spooky."

For some of the people in the room clearing the departed spirit, which the shaman proceeded to do, marked the end of treatment. Gerald stayed in the Southwest and underwent a series of medicinal sweat lodges, accompanied by rituals and chanting. After several weeks the shaman told him that his grandfather's spirit was now at peace.

"When I got back home I almost went back for a medical checkup, but I had stopped feeling anxious. I quit having nightmares or waking up in a sweat. It was over, just like the shaman said."

I'm recounting this story to open our perspective. Being raised in a Christian culture doesn't automatically mean that a dying person will see himself arriving at the pearly gates greeted by Saint Peter. (This isn't one of the common scenarios reported by near-death patients, either.) One might find oneself in the spirit world of Native Americans instead. The soul's passage follows links that we don't foresee.

Gerald's story has a curious addendum. A month after returning home he went with his wife on vacation to the upper Midwest where his family originally came from. "We checked into a renovated Victorian hotel. Our room was done up in flowery wallpaper and a four-poster bed. But what caught my eye was a framed newspaper hanging on the wall. It was from the turn of the century and showed a picture of a volunteer fire brigade. Right in the middle staring out at me was my grandfather as a young man."

"Did that shake you?" I asked.

"No, to me it was a sign that the shaman was right. I'm glad my grandfather was set free, wherever he's gone."

Akasha

In all the tales of ghosts who want to be set free, what holds them back is memory. They continue to remember what physical life was like, and the unfinished business of those memories has a grip. The unsettled spirit can't escape into the next stage of existence. What this means, strangely enough, is that when the afterlife has become real, the physical world has become the dream. It's just a matter of perspective. When you are in a physical body your perspective makes physicality real. When you are dreaming at night, the dream state is real. When you are "crossing over," both waking and dreaming are unreal, and Akasha—the field of consciousness—is real. What causes this change of reality? Vedanta holds that consciousness is convinced by its own creations. Therefore, nothing we can see, hear, and touch, whether in waking, dreaming, or beyond both, is ultimately real. They represent shifting perspectives.

To be completely free means waking up from all dreamlike states, and reclaiming who you are: the maker of reality. One cannot say that all dying people will achieve this kind of absolute freedom. They may glimpse it only for a fleeting second; they may sense the possibility of breaking away from one dream and yet be seduced into the next one that comes to mind.

I knew a woman who as a child had come home from school, and as she entered the door she saw her young cousin from Chicago standing in the corner waiting for her. Both were about eight at the time. The cousin didn't speak, and the girl ran to tell her mother that they had a visitor.

When she entered the kitchen her mother was crying. The little girl asked why, and her mother said that there had been a sudden death in the family. It was the cousin from Chicago, who had died that morning. Did the girl see her cousin as a vision, a premonition, or merely as a coincidental act of imagination? As she tells the story, she saw her cousin "for real." Yet what do we mean by "for real" except that something is convincing? This encounter with a departed relative can be judged as either hallucinatory or deeply spiritual, depending not on the event itself but on who is looking at it.

In the afterlife a person wakes up from one extremely convincing perspective—physical existence—and faces the possibility of freedom. Akasha isn't any particular perspective; it's a wide open playing field waiting for players to enter it. Who will the players be?

- They could be the same players we are already used to.
- They could be players we have imagined and are eager to see.
- They could be otherworldly beings.
- They could be emanations of ourselves.
- They could be embodiments of abstract ideas.

In world culture all these variations have been reported. Christian heaven is a specific Akashic play, a drama of redemption with otherworldly beings in it, along with familiar people from the past and an abstraction that we call God. To the extent that all these images materialize in the mind, a dying Christian accepts that she has arrived in heaven. Vedanta says that the deeper truth is that the dying person has arrived in a creative space, Akasha, which produces whatever is wanted.

But how does a person know what he wants? The answer gets complicated. Let's take it back down to earth and ask the same question. How do you know what you want right now? Until your next desire appears, you won't know. It's certain that you will want something, because the mind is a continuous stream of desires. However, this doesn't make the mind predictable. You may be a creature of habit who always wants two scrambled eggs for breakfast, while I may be restless and want a different breakfast every day. Both of us could be thrown out of our accustomed pattern by a sudden stress, such as having a death in the family, losing our jobs, being diagnosed with heart trouble. Suddenly we aren't hungry; our minds want to grieve, not eat. The unpredictable tug-of-war between old patterns and new situations makes it impossible to pin down desire.

In the same way, Akasha is elusive because it's so open-ended; it's as unpredictable as a dream and just as convincing. Even so, the Akashic field can be navigated. In fact, it must be navigated if we are to take advantage of the creative leap that the afterlife opens up.

Navigating the Field

We have a chance to open up the possibilities beyond what our culture has conditioned us to believe. One experience can't fit everyone. Our eyes continue to see what they expect, even when we use the eyes of the soul, but the Akashic field isn't a swirl of random images. It is more structured than a dream; it has a kind of invisible landscape. The structure of Akasha cannot be described in physical terms, yet if we look inside ourselves, the seemingly random flow of our minds also obeys a kind of invisible structure.

Let's say someone walks up to you and greets you by name. The person is smiling; there's an expectant look on her face. How do you come up with a response? Your mind does several things at once. It consults its stored picture files for familiar faces. It looks for a name to attach to the right face. If neither can be found immediately, the mind doesn't feel stymied yet—it has backup resources. It rummages through faces that could fit this person but are younger or fuzzily recorded. It tosses up sample names that might jog your memory. It runs through recent events that this apparent stranger may have played a part in. If all this doesn't work, the mind starts thinking of what to say to cover up your memory lapse.

We're all familiar with such situations, and we are so accustomed to matching names and faces that we don't marvel at how astonishing the whole process is. Not only can the mind Google itself for information with incredible swiftness, it performs multiple operations with backup plans if they fail. This implies an amazingly complex but invisible structure.

In the afterlife the same structure continues to exist. In near-death experiences the dying person, suddenly confronted with an unknown situation, searches inside for familiar landmarks: deceased relatives, recognizable voices, a divine light, the presence of a fatherly (or motherly) God. In other words, we all have a built-in map that we consult. This map prepares us to convert any unknown experience into something meaningful. (As I was writing this chapter a TV special about heaven came on, and one woman being interviewed was certain that she had been to heaven. Her near-death experience occurred when she was giving birth, had a crisis, and fell briefly into a coma. Describe heaven, the interviewer said. The woman's face grew rapturous at the memory. She described an endless stairway going up to the sky, and along the stairway happy animals pranced around. She added that the blue of the sky was like no color that could be found on earth. To me, she chose to interpret her experience by drawing from a scrapbook of childhood images.)

Psychologists have conducted experiments that illustrate how we automatically create meaning. In one, a group of subjects sits in a room before a tape recorder. They are told to listen to a tape of someone talking and to take notes on what's being said as best they can. They are also told that the voice on the tape will be very soft, since the experiment is testing how well the brain can register the faintest spoken words.

The tape is turned on and is barely audible. The subjects crane forward and take their notes, which are then collected. What they haven't been told is that the voice is speaking nonsense. Only random words are coming out of the machine. Yet each subject will take notes that make sense, because an expectation of hearing meaningful words leads to the *creation* of meaning.

In the afterlife the creative possibilities are enormously expanded. Instead of asking one question—*What is the voice on the tape saying?*—the mind has a host of questions to ask: *Where am I? What's happening to me? Who have I become? What lies ahead?*

In the afterlife the mind is multidimensional. Akasha takes us out of all time-space limitations. In truth we always were multidimensional, only we were so convinced by inhabiting the material world that we conformed to its rules. Now we need to adapt ourselves to Akasha, where there is structure without rigid rules and creative possibility without cultural dogma.

THE INVISIBLE THREAD

TO TELL THE truth, the things that Ramana had told Savitri didn't come as a total surprise. She had been raised to believe in the soul. She had heard about how the higher self, the "inward dweller" as Lord Krishna called it, was immortal. But these lessons had seemed remote.

"How do I know I have a soul?" she asked.

"You cannot know by seeing it or touching it," Ramana said. "Your soul might whisper to you, but even then you could just be hearing echoes of your own voice."

"So the soul may be a fiction?" Savitri asked, with a sinking feeling.

"The soul isn't a fiction just because it's invisible," Ramana said. "Look."

Suspended in a shaft of light was the outline of an intricate spiderweb anchored between two bushes. It gleamed and rippled with the slightest breeze.

"A spider made this web," said Ramana. "You see his work but you don't see the spider. He holds a tiny thread that tells him when anything lands in the web. Where has the soul gone? It doesn't matter as long as the connection exists."

Savitri couldn't help being stubborn. "I still may be imagining I have a soul."

"Ah, but that's the wonder."

Ramana's face was suddenly aglow with inspiration. "Nature imagines spiders. Big ones were imagined and small ones, smooth ones and hairy ones, those that live in the air, water, and earth, those colored white and black and every shade in between. Think of baby spiders that fly on gossamer threads in the spring while giant water spiders dive to the bottom of a pond and catch fish. We are foolish to think the spider is a thing. It is a shifting whirl of qualities, ever changing and fascinating. The soul is like that, too. However you imagine it, it will take on that quality and still have infinite potential left over. When you ask, 'Where is my soul?' the answer isn't a place but a potential. The soul is wherever it is, has been, and will be."

Ramana's eyes remained fixed on the web rippling in the sunlight, and through his fascination Savitri began to be fascinated, too. She couldn't know for certain if the spider that made this web was white, yellow, or red, big or small, male or female, yet that didn't stop her from knowing that it was real. She had no idea of what her soul looked like, either, or what lay across the boundary of death. All she had was an invisible thread. Would it be enough?

"Yes," Ramana said. "You have listened well today. You are learning."

Savitri smiled a bit doubtfully. Suddenly she was quite tired. She sank down on a billowy bank of moss and closed her eyes. Her mind slowed down, bit by bit, until she forgot where she was or the dangers she faced. It was enough just to sleep.

A WEB OF WORLDS

The Akashic field has been interpreted by every culture to make it meaningful to that culture. In and of itself, the field is pure potential. But the great spiritual guides of the past wanted to reassure their followers that space wasn't the same as a void. We know this because our own inner silence isn't a void. It doesn't take dying to go beyond thoughts and images. When someone meditates deeply enough, thoughts disappear and leave only the experience of silence. One could say that this silence is nothing, emptiness, but the Vedic sages tell us that it's a very rich silence indeed.

We've been following the soul's journey into the highest stage it can attain, which is the Akasha itself, the source of creativity. Different spiritual traditions envision this end point in different ways. Here are seven versions that continue to shape how people experience their spiritual journey:

Paradise
The Godhead
The Spirit World
Transcendence
Transmigration
Awakening
Dissolution

These are seven settings for the soul, and each possibility is self-created. A dream begun on earth continues until it reaches its conclusion. Its ingredients are taken from the mind's invisible structure, then combined in such a way that makes sense of the Akashic field.

SEVEN DESTINATIONS FOR THE SOUL

1. *Paradise:* Your soul finds itself in a perfect world created by God. You go to paradise as a reward and never leave. (If you are bad, you go to Satan's home and never leave it.)

2. *The Godhead:* Your soul returns to God, but not to any particular place. You discover the location of God as a timeless state infused with His presence.

3. *The Spirit World:* Your soul rests in a realm of departed spirits. It rejoins your ancestors and those who passed on before you, who are gathered with the great Spirit.

4. *Transcendence:* Your soul performs a vanishing act in which this expression person dissolves, either quickly or gradually. The pure soul rejoins the sea of consciousness from which it was born.

5. *Transmigration:* Your soul is caught in the cycle of rebirth. Depending on your karma, your soul moves from lower to higher life-forms—and even may be reborn in objects. The cycle continues eternally until your soul escapes through higher realization.

6. *Awakening:* Your soul arrives in the light. It sees with complete clarity for the first time, realizing the truth of existence that was masked by being in a physical body.

7. *Dissolution:* Eternity is nothingness. As the chemical components of your body return to basic atoms and molecules, the consciousness created by the brain disappears completely. You are no more.

There is a good deal of cultural overlap here as one tradition feeds into another. The Muslim vision of eternity as a paradise garden, complete with the sexual attractions of *houris* and exotic fruits, owes its existence in part to the Garden of Eden. Spirit worlds are common all over the globe. The ancient Greeks expected to meet the shades of the departed across the River Styx in Hades, but filtered through time and Christianity, Hades became a punishing hell presided over by Satan while the Greek place of blessed spirits, the Elysian Fields, became heaven.

There are invisible spirit worlds found in the ancestor worship of Japan and China. In a prehistoric age aboriginal peoples drifted from South Asia to Australia and the islands of the South Pacific, bringing their spirit worlds with them. With them also came a kind of "dream time" that infused ordinary time, in which material events could be seen as depending upon spiritual events. But spirit worlds didn't hold in India, where the dominant belief gathered around three other afterlives: transcendence (rejoining the sea of consciousness), awakening (discovering that one's true nature is Atman or the soul), and transmigration (the eternal cycle of rebirth).

Being born in a certain culture, however, doesn't always determine where your soul finds itself after "crossing over." Eternal life, it turns out, is also very personal.

Expanded Awareness

The standard assumption is that no one really knows what happens after we die. But the rishis asked the question, Why don't we expect to know? Instead of being unknowable, perhaps the afterlife is something we haven't looked at hard enough. And if so, why not?

For one thing, the mind is addicted to repetition. We pursue the same desires today that we had yesterday. Even our thoughts today are generally about 90% the same as the thoughts we had yesterday, according to some studies. Habit rules our actions; a fixed roster of likes and dislikes governs our taste. If you are afraid of being poor today, it's likely that you've had that same fear since childhood. If you think about losing five pounds, it's likely that this reflects a bodily obsession that goes back years. On the positive side psychologists point out that the pursuit of pleasure and the avoidance of pain motivate us every day, and generally to good effect. We're reassured by what we know. In fact, the Vedic rishis declare that habit is what makes a person feel real. (In the business world, when someone suddenly loses his job, the loss can be psychologically devastating—not to mention that a sudden layoff greatly increases a person's risk for heart attack, cancer, and stroke.)

At the same time that it reassures us, repetition has a deadening effect. By keeping out what's new, it forces reality into the strait-jacket of the old. Each of us lives behind a wall, beyond which lies the infinite potential of the unknown. Only the smallest gates are built into the wall, and we stand guard at these, allowing one experience to enter but excluding another, calling this experience good and that one evil. As long as we keep on taking in reality so selectively, freedom is a remote possibility.

In this regard death is a great gift, because it throws open all the doors and windows. Dying forces us outside the wall. Instead of seeing the familiar things we've assiduously collected and labeled as reality, we must start over. However, the rishis assert that we don't enter the Akashic field empty-handed. Whatever our dream is right now, *that dream continues.* Consciousness is tied by thousands of threads to old memories, habits, preferences, and relationships.

Whenever someone really presses the issue of what happens after we die, my response comes in the form of a question: "Who are you?" You have to know where you are right now, in order to know where you will be tomorrow, and the afterlife is just a special kind of tomorrow.

Here are the things necessary to knowing "Who am I?":

1. *What is your story?* Your story is more than just a list of the events in your life. It's about your self-image, how you see yourself, what shaped your mind, which memories imprinted themselves on you. Taken altogether, your story tells you where you are in the cycle of life.

2. *What are your expectations?* Expectations are seeds. Once planted, they manifest into those things we gain from life, or lose. When you become aware of your own expectations, you discover the unspoken limits you have set on yourself. There is a huge difference between those who expect great things and those who don't.

3. *What is your purpose?* This is the meaning you are trying to find. Purpose runs deeper than the superficial things we hope to get, which mostly center on money, possessions, status, and comfort. If you know your purpose, you know the deeper project to which your life is dedicated.

4. *What is your destination?* This is about fulfillment. Human goals are endless; they unfold, not like a road that has an end but like a river that flows to join the sea, merging with ever larger possibilities. If you know your destination, you can envision your highest fulfillment.

5. *What is your path?* Having identified your purpose and your destination, there must be a way to get there. "Path" has been adopted as a spiritual term, but in fact everyone, spiritual or not, follows certain ways to get where they want to go.

6. *Who are your adversaries?* Forward motion is never without obstacles. On your path you will find yourself blocked. At times the adversary is external, but if you examine yourself deeply, you will find it is always internal as well.

7. *Who are your allies?* We all bring others with us on our journey. Just as your adversaries did, you may identify these allies as external, but they only reflect your own inner strength, just as an opponent reflects your inner vulnerability.

None of these questions asks anything about the afterlife. They don't touch on your beliefs about heaven and hell or about your soul. That's because what we know right now is immediate and personal: how we feel, what we want, whom we love. And that's enough. The decisions we make determine how life proceeds. We don't go through life simply making good choices and bad ones. We go through life making who we are. Choice is the hand that shapes the raw clay of a person.

With a little thought each of us can answer questions about who we are and our purpose in life. All we need to do if we wish to choose what happens in Akasha is to extend the same questions over the threshold of physical death.

What do you want your story to be after you die?
What do you expect will happen next?
What does the afterlife mean to you personally?
Where will your last breath take you?
How will you get there?
Who will block your way?
Who will help you along?

Notice how strange these questions would sound if you hadn't first encountered them in the context of every day. We are caught between two levels of existence. Let me give an example:

Recently I met Lydia, an older woman who has been devoted to a Zen *roshi,* or master, for over thirty years. This particular roshi was Italian rather than Japanese and a woman. Lydia mentioned these unusual facts without explaining how she happened to choose her teacher. "We were always very close. It's not something one can intellectualize about. It has to come from in here." Lydia touched her heart lightly.

"I spent time with my teacher in Rome, and over the years my practice became central to my life. Every winter I go to Rome to stay with her, and I practice Zen with the small group she's gathered there."

"You've found your path," I remarked.

She looked doubtful. "Have I? The last time I was packing to go, part of me kept wondering, *Why am I doing this? What's the point?* My doubts seemed ridiculous at first, but then I began to wake up at night in a panic, my mind racing."

I asked her what the panicky thoughts were about.

"Always the same thing. I imagine I will be lost over there, lonely and with no real confidence in what I'm doing. But I know every-thing is going to turn out all right once I get with my Zen group, so I go back to sleep."

After decades of meditation and other spiritual practices, Lydia knew herself well, but these panic attacks had recently grown worse. She asked me what I thought they were about.

"A lot of things are possible," I said. "Maybe you're just going back and forth to Rome out of habit, and your real commitment has come to an end. Maybe you haven't gotten what you expected from Zen Buddhism. Maybe you've reached a stubborn level of resistance that refuses to let you move on."

Lydia nodded eagerly. "All of that. I sometimes get so disgusted with myself and all my stubborn habits and judgments that I think I haven't gotten anywhere. Is that possible?"

"Of course you've gotten somewhere," I assured her. (In fact, Lydia had a strong presence that made itself felt the moment she entered the room.) "But the things we've accomplished spiritually get put on the shelf, and the things we still have to work on loom large, like spots on a tablecloth that attract attention even when the rest of the tablecloth is clean."

Lydia liked the analogy, but she remained doubtful. "Maybe something inside me wants to be judgmental and depressed, or what-ever negative thing it is I can't move past. If so, then what?"

I offered several ways to look at it. They apply generally to exis-tential doldrums.

"You are a deeply spiritual person, and that means you're allowing your deepest issues to come up to the surface instead of hiding them.

"Being spiritual isn't about being comfortable all the time.

"You may be in transition, anxiously awaiting a new phase in your journey."

"I didn't realize I had that many choices. I thought I was just . . ." Lydia's voice trailed off.

"Failing?" I said. "Not at all. Most people spend huge amounts of time and effort on one thing: avoiding the painful truth about themselves. You're doing exactly the opposite."

She felt better, and she had something to think about. Many people resist a commitment to being spiritual once they discover that it brings a state of ferment. Everything serious and difficult gets postponed, often to their dying day. But the rishis taught that self-exploration is the most important thing one can do to prepare for the afterlife. All the tactics we use to avoid ourselves must be dissolved. Which puts someone like Lydia in an unusual position. In effect she is experiencing the Akashic field as her own inner silence. Buddhism sometimes describes its practices as conscious dying. One dies to old memories, conditioning, habits, and self-denial, all the things that the mind uses not to see itself.

To experience the Akashic field requires an expanded state of awareness. Contracted awareness keeps us anchored in daily affairs. I told Lydia that her mood swings and lack of decisiveness were symptoms of swinging back and forth between expanded and contracted awareness. When her mind wasn't in the Akashic domain, she was centered in her ego personality. Everyday desires and impulses took control. But at other times her mind would slip outside its boundaries. Seeing herself with expanded awareness, she'd drop her ego—as much as anyone can.

"It's the price you pay," I said. "Everyone feels wobbly who walks the path with your kind of dedication."

Lydia was lucky, in that she was used to the swings between contracted and expanded awareness. Many people find negative words for expansion. They say "I'm just spacey," "I've lost my bearings," "I hardly know who I am." Sometimes those labels may apply, but moments of transcendence are being overlooked. By the end of our conversation, Lydia affirmed what she had learned from long years of practice: The dramas we live out take unexpected turns, and as we make new choices, the life of the soul takes shape. The critical thing is to *have* a life of the soul, and that comes about only through expansion.

A Variety of Choices

Akasha is the home of the soul and therefore cannot be limited in any way. The mystery, strangely enough, is how we manage to restrict the unbounded potential of our own minds. But we do. The choices we make build invisible barriers that only we can take down. There are constant forks in the road that shape the invisible structure of the mind depending on the road we choose. The key words for such choices are

EXPANSION	CONTRACTION
Expression	Repression
Self-knowledge	Denial
Comfortable with uncertainty	Crave security
Personal insight	Received opinion
Spiritually oriented	Materialistic
Self-accepting	Guilty, self-denying
Individualism	Conformity
Altruistic, selfless	Ego-driven

These qualities don't describe types of people but qualities of your own mind, which expands and contracts depending on many factors. The mind isn't a single thing moving in one direction. We may share a tendency to be more expressive when young, more repressed in old age, but we may also have gained personal insight to replace the received opinions that give young people a sense of belonging. From day to day the mind fluctuates, even when we feel we are committed to a single path. It's natural for life to be open-ended, and so it will continue in the afterlife. In the Akashic field we will meet both sides of ourselves, the individual who wants to be free and the conformist who wants to be secure. The Akashic field is nothing more than our own potential. Will this idea take root?

For centuries Eastern beliefs have had little effect on the West, despite some evidence that the Old Testament, for example, considered reincarnation possible. The Gnostics, a sect of early Christianity, espoused reincarnation before they were wiped out as heretics. Jesus seems to refer to it once. The followers of John the Baptist believed that he was either the Messiah or the return of the prophet Elijah, called Elias in the New Testament. This was important because of the belief that Elias would "first come" before the Messiah. When Christ's disciples questioned him about this, he replied, "'Elias must truly first come and restore all things. But I say unto you, That Elias has come already, but they knew him not, but have done unto him whatsoever they liked' . . . then the disciples understood that He spake unto them of John the Baptist" (Matthew 17:9–13). However, in Catholic theology reincarnation was condemned as a heresy by A.D. 553. This disparity with Jesus' comment has given rise to dark muttering that all references to reincarnation have been systematically removed from the Bible. True or not, the East was resisted.

Once the Vedic scriptures began to be translated at the turn of the nineteenth century, their ideas began to crop up in strange places. The Atman, for example, became the immensely popular Oversoul that Ralph Waldo Emerson spread throughout New England before the Civil War. Drawing from Indian ideas, Emerson's circle began to redefine inherited Puritan beliefs, discarding sin, damnation, and the absolute boundary between life and death that can only be crossed through faith in Christ. This launched the Transcendental movement.

Now we face a polyglot blend of East-West beliefs. The New Age movement is an outgrowth of many traditions, but the main one is

Theosophy, a spiritualist movement that began with séances in Victorian parlors but was deeply transformed by Hinduism. (Mahatma Gandhi, in fact, first became acquainted with the Vedic scriptures through English translations produced by the Theosophical Society in India.) It was primarily through the spiritualism of the late nineteenth century that reincarnation began to be embraced by popular culture.

By contrast, some versions of the afterlife have no wish to overlap with any other. When Mel Gibson was being interviewed about his controversial movie, *The Passion of the Christ,* with its emphasis on ultra-violence and its almost total neglect of Christian love, he freely admitted his belief in an exclusive heaven. Gibson was being interviewed by the *Herald Sun* newspaper in Australia when he was asked if Protestants are denied eternal salvation. "There is no salvation for those outside the Church," Gibson replied, referring to the Catholic Church. "Put it this way. My wife is a saint. She's a much better person than I am. Honestly. She's, like, Episcopalian, Church of England. She prays, she believes in God, she knows Jesus, she believes in that stuff. And it's just not fair if she doesn't make it, she's better than I am. But that is a pronouncement from the chair. I go with it."

Fundamentalism is often criticized for its inflexible and literalist interpretations of Scripture. The great advantage of believing in this kind of exclusivity, as millions of devout Christians, Muslims, and Jews do, is its unalloyed simplicity. Dying is as cut-and-dried as winning a football game—or losing it, in the case of hell—and just as irrevocable. Good and bad deeds are added up with a specific weight assigned to each one. A petty theft or adultery can be offset by penance of equal value, while some sins, such as murder, cancel all good deeds and buy a ticket directly to eternal damnation.

In traditional Hinduism, however, the arithmetic of good and bad deeds is infinitely flexible. For every act that earns bad karma, sending the soul downward in its next rebirth, there is a chance to balance the scale through good karma. Reincarnation also allows a soul to experience one heaven or hell after another without limit until *Moksha,* or liberation, is achieved. Moksha ends the entire cycle of heaven and hell forever, at which time the soul returns to its original state as pure consciousness, a drop of bliss in the ocean of bliss. Here, the quarrels of religion end. Like all earthly attachments, they fall away.

According to Vedanta, eternity isn't a smorgasbord. If "God is one" as so many faiths declare, there must be a deeper layer to the Akashic field where disagreements and multiple choices end. Consciousness is consciousness no matter who is interpreting it. Akasha exists beyond choice, beyond mind. This state of unity attracts the dying person toward it. Through the magnetism of the soul, one is drawn to the next stage of a personal dream that is universal at the source.

SEEING THE SOUL

THE MOMENT SHE woke up, Savitri saw that they were back at the banyan tree where they'd started. She sat up, squinting at the sun overhead. How could it be so high in the sky? Then she saw Ramana standing over her. He wore a mysterious look.

"We haven't left yet," he said. "There are still hours to go before Satyavan returns home."

Weakly rising to her feet, Savitri gazed at the monk as if he were a magician. "What did you do?"

Ramana shrugged. "You were exhausted. You slept. I'm not responsible if you had a productive dream." Without another word he picked up his flute, exactly as he had before, and set off. This time Savitri followed him without hesitation. They did not take the trail up the mountain but the path down, and after a while Ramana said, "When I was young there was a traveling fortune-teller who set up his tent by the Ganges. Every devout person wants to die in Benares. Their families come to the funeral, and a fortune-teller can make a good living, particularly this one, since his specialty was predicting the day that a person will die. But I refused to go."

"Why?" asked Savitri.

Ramana laughed. "I was different, even then. I used to say it's easy to see the future. I'll go to the fortune-teller who can see the present. The most difficult thing is seeing what's right here."

"Can you explain?" Savitri asked.

"Have you heard of Maya?"

"Of course. She is the goddess of illusion."

"Just so," said Ramana. "But what is illusion? A kind of magic that hides reality from us? Maya is more subtle. Let's say I show you a piece of ice, a cloud of steam, and a snowflake. Have you seen any water? If you say yes, then you have overcome Maya—the forms of ice, steam, and snowflake didn't fool you. You went to the essence, which is that they are all made of water.

"If you say no, then you fell for illusion. The ice, steam, and snowflake grabbed your attention, and you lost the essence. It didn't take magic to fool you. You allowed your mind to be distracted. So it is with the soul. We look at people and see everything on the surface. This one is ugly, that one beautiful, this one poor, that one rich, this one I love, that one I hate. Yet each is Atman, the same essence in infinite forms."

"Is that what you see?" Savitri asked.

"Yes, and so did you when you fell in love with Satyavan," Ramana said. He gazed at her deeply. "I know all about you, princess."

Suddenly Savitri's cheeks burned. Somehow Ramana had uncovered her secret. She had been born a princess, the most cherished daughter of a rich and powerful king. When the time came for her to marry, Savitri had insisted on finding the right man herself, and so her father, despite his worries, sent her with a band of nobles to find the husband of her heart's desire. Savitri and her guards traveled through the dense forest, and by chance they came upon a woodcutter's hut. As soon as she set eyes on Satyavan, who was humble and poor, Savitri resolved to marry him, whatever the obstacles.

When she announced her choice, Savitri deeply disappointed her father. However, after meeting Satyavan and recognizing his good heart and generosity as well as how deeply he loved Savitri, the king reluctantly accepted his daughter's choice. Then something disturbing happened. On the three nights before her wedding, Savitri dreamed of Lord Yama, and each night he said the same thing: Satyavan would die when they had been wed exactly a year.

"So you already knew," said Ramana. "And yet you decided to marry someone who was doomed. Why?"

"Because I loved him," Savitri murmured.

"And what is true love but recognizing someone else's soul? If you can see past all the illusions laid in your way by Maya, you will always commune with Satyavan's soul. This connection can never be lost, no matter what happens to his body."

Ramana touched Savitri's forehead, and instantly she saw bodies burning on the funeral pyres beside the Ganges, their ashes escaping on the wind. "The eye can't help but see this," Ramana whispered, "yet it never saw the soul in the first place, so the act of seeing nothing makes us believe in death." He let these words sink in. "Do you think you can stop believing your eyes now?"

Savitri nodded, and for an instant she felt Satyavan's soul merge with hers, just as she had on the day they met.

THE DIFFERENCE BETWEEN LIFE AND DEATH

Believing what we see is addictive—we can hardly do without it. I know a man in his sixties, a retired broker, who lost his wife in a tragic accident. She was driving home around sunset and got distracted somehow. Her right front tire slid up over the curb, and one jerk of the steering wheel caused her vehicle to overturn into oncoming traffic.

She died of massive internal bleeding in the ER three hours later. Her husband went into shock. He couldn't comprehend suddenly losing her. Even after several months he was in severe psychological pain; he became obsessed with the idea that he had to talk to his departed wife or live in grief permanently.

"They say that when you love someone long enough they become part of you," he said.

"I think that's true," I replied.

"The moment Ruth left I felt a hole inside me. That's how I would describe grief—and it hurts like hell." We were sitting in his house, which felt far too big for one person. He must have realized this himself, because he had taken to shutting off several bedrooms and retreating to an overstuffed chair in the study.

"I was grieving, like a sick dog, for months after Ruth died," he said. "Then I decided it just hurt too damn much. I mean, some part of my mind was telling me, over and over, that Ruth wasn't really gone. I began to have conversations with her. Yet I wasn't one of those fortunate people who feel the presence of the departed. I was talking to—what? The air? A figment of my imagination?" He paused for a moment before going on.

"I made up my mind to see a psychic about this. You'd be amazed how many people you can find in Southern California who can talk to the dead for you."

I murmured something about a survivor's need to know what happened to their loved ones.

"Yes, I agree. The psychic I found had only good intentions, I'm sure. I walked into her place feeling nervous. She didn't live in a gypsy's tent or anything. It was a town house, and to look at her, she could have been anybody standing in line at your local supermarket."

The psychic was reassuringly down to earth. She found him a comfortable chair with pillows, put some bottled water by his side, and sat on the opposite side of the coffee table. She closed her eyes and asked that they both sit quietly. He could meditate if he knew how. The man didn't, so he sat with his eyes closed, peeking at the psychic when it seemed she was taking a long time to speak.

"But then something happened?" I asked.

"She said a woman wanted to talk to me, and that she was getting images: two children, one far away now, a cabin in the mountains, a great field of white (snow? a frozen lake?). We do have two grown children, and our daughter lives in England. And Ruth and I liked to ski, sometimes renting a cabin near the slopes. All at once I was paying attention."

"A lot of people like to ski," I remarked.

He sighed. "I know. That's how it went. The psychic kept hitting on things that felt real to me, but if you weren't there—"

"I didn't have to be there. You definitely thought it was Ruth."

"Right then I did. Maybe because I wanted it to be her so damn much." He went on to say—as thousands of people do in such situations—that the psychic came up with many arresting details. Whoever is contacting the psychic draws a picture through convincing small touches, such as pet names and quirky events that stick in the mind.

I said, "Ruth told you she was in a good place and not to worry. She was safe and kept telling you she loved you. Right?"

"I know it sounds trite," the man said hesitantly. "But it felt genuine. I was very emotional the whole time, close to tears. The session lasted maybe forty-five minutes. The psychic hugged me. It had been emotional for her, too; it was weird to think we had been total strangers an hour ago."

"And what has been the fallout?" I asked.

He shrugged. "I immediately felt better. But then doubts crept in. Why was Ruth talking only about things I already knew? Was the psychic just reading my mind, or my aura, whatever that is? Was she tuning in to some desperate wish of mine? Now I'm not sure how much good it really did."

What this man didn't know was that I had had a similar experience myself. Several years ago I was asked to participate in a university study to explore whether communication with the dead is real. I sat in a sealed-off room and was told to say nothing—all contact with the psychic would occur through the experiment leader. In fact there were three psychics connected to us by telephone, each in a different part of the country, and they were unable to hear or talk to one another.

Two of the three psychics said, "Do you have Deepak Chopra in the room?" They had not been told who I was, or even that I was a man. They didn't hear my voice.

All three said that someone departed wanted to talk to me. Two immediately knew it was my father, who had died suddenly two years previously. One took a bit more time circling around the relationship with me, then hit on it being my father. This "father" knew my childhood nickname in Hindi. He said he was happy and not to worry. All three psychics came up with these generalized, positive sentiments. The whole thing lasted two hours.

Like the man who contacted his dead wife, I thought this was a genuine experience. I also came away with doubts. My "father" knew things I knew, but nothing more. The experiment had strict guidelines, which I came to regret. I couldn't blurt out questions or react to what I was hearing. I wondered why the departed don't say more about what dying is like. There are also questions about whether "Ruth" and my "father" should be considered ghosts, departed souls, or not quite either. To the Vedic rishis they were wisps of memory in the Akasha, information floating around until it found a place to attach itself. "Ruth" and my "father" were as real as anything else in the Akasha, but to give them quasi-physical status remains a problem. I prefer to view the "father" who talked to me as aspects of his consciousness that had such a close association to me that we could still communicate.

Skeptics would point out that we are in the habit of seeing and hearing other people, a habit we are loath to drop even after death. Therefore a ghost is a holdover created by the mind. Believers would contend the opposite, that ghosts are real and almost physical, the embodiment in shadowy form of people who cannot find a way to leave this world. But in both cases habit and memory are at work. Was it my habit or my father's that brought us together? I think a bit of both, because anyone whom you relate to through love and intimacy shares your consciousness. We are inside one another, as shown by how easily I can call up my father's voice, face, mannerisms, speech patterns, and ways of thinking. To some extent I have adapted some of these as my own, which further blurs the line between us.

When we speak to the dead we are using a familiar connection, then, and it can be strong or weak. When it's weak, we see and hear the deceased in our minds; when it is strong, we see and hear them more vividly, as if outside ourselves. But neither I nor my father is outside the field. That's the point the rishis emphasize over and over, and my experience tells me it's true.

The Powers You Need

To successfully navigate the "other side" means mastering the powers that are needed there. If the "other side" isn't merely an imitation of this side, those powers must be different from willpower, physical strength, and the other familiar supports of life in the material world. Yet our subtle powers, being part of ourselves, can't be totally foreign, either. For most of us our primary world is physical, of course, but we are using subtle powers all the time, and these may support us in the afterlife. If the rishis are correct in saying that everyone inhabits the Akashic field, both in life and after death, then subtle powers of consciousness unite both.

THE POWERS YOU NEED

Self-awareness: The power to know yourself. This power keeps you centered.

Willingness: The power to open your mind. This power allows reality to be seen despite old conditioning and beliefs.

Intention: The power to manifest desires. This power connects you with your purpose.

Discrimination: The power to make fine distinctions. This power guides you in the subtleties of understanding.

Acceptance: The power of nonresistance. This power enables you to integrate reality into yourself.

To truly know something as deep as what happens after death, your mind must call upon these powers. That's the only thing, really, separating us from the Vedic rishis: they used their subtle powers to the fullest; we call on them to a much lesser degree. We are postponing the soul journey until we die. Yet our subtle powers are needed every day—for ourselves and for those relationships that expand our horizons.

You have to be centered and *self-aware* so that you don't manipulate others or allow yourself to be manipulated.

Your *willingness* to see beyond your own ego creates an open space for the relationship to grow.

Instead of allowing the relationship to fluctuate as mood dictates, you *intend* for it to become richer and deeper.

Your partner is constantly filling you with a stream of desires, needs, and opinions (you are doing the same back). You must *discrim-*

inate how much of this outside influence is positive for you, neutral, or outright negative.

Having paid attention to all of the above, you can fully *accept* your partner without posing a threat to your integrity and personal growth.

Now substitute the word "soul" for "relationship." All the things that make a relationship work apply to your soul. Those skills will be crucial if the afterlife brings you into the soul's domain, as every spiritual tradition says it does. You and I can already identify with every experience that occurs in the afterlife because they are familiar. As I grow, so do my powers.

I will become more self-aware as the boundary between "me" and "not me" dissolves. The self will begin to encompass much more of reality as the boundary dissolves. I will feel free.

I will become more willing to change and evolve. My old beliefs will be tested and allowed to change if need be. I will feel curious and fascinated.

I will trust in my intention to know the truth, whatever it may reveal. I will feel in control.

I will find that I can discriminate very fine layers of nature. Subtle worlds won't be hidden from me because they are inside my self already. I will feel connected.

I will accept my own truth as it unfolds. This brings a final end to fear and doubt. I will feel fulfilled.

I've placed so much emphasis on feeling because for most of us the reason to be alive is so that we can pursue the feelings of being safe, loved, happy, and fulfilled. We connect to the soul through these desires, and we are motivated to move into the subtle realm of the soul for the same reason. For some people that's motivation enough, but most of us require a breakthrough or a turning point before we can fully put our subtle connections to work.

"My husband and I were having problems," a woman in her forties told me; I'll call her Kate. "He promised to work less and spend more time with his family, but that didn't improve things much. He kept moping around the house, and instead of sneaking off for a drink he'd sneak off to check his voice mail. Just for peace of mind I agreed to a friend's suggestion and learned the same meditation technique she was using."

This involved sitting alone in a quiet room twice a day for ten to twenty minutes and repeating a mantra, Kate said. The first few times she fell asleep, but her teacher reassured her that this was a positive sign. She had a lot of stress to release from her body.

"The second week went better. My mind got quieter and I stayed awake. My breathing settled into a soft, slow rhythm. It surprised me one day when I had the feeling that I wasn't even breathing at all. Even more surprising was the time I had the impulse to sit on the floor in a modified lotus position. I had never taken a yoga class; my body seemed to know what it wanted to do."

Kate felt good about all this, and she began to feel more centered in her daily life, less subject to flashes of anger and irritation. Things settled down considerably in her marriage.

"Then one night as I was falling asleep, I noticed a faint blue glow. My eyes were closed, and at first I thought it was just an afterglow from the bedroom lights, the kind you see when a photo flash goes off in your eyes. But this was different. The blue I was seeing felt magnetic. I couldn't keep my attention off it. Then I opened my eyes in the dark, and the whole room was filled with the same blue glow. There were sparkles or flecks of gold in it."

I told Kate that this was not an uncommon experience for Yoginis. She was perceiving the light that emanates from a subtle level of perception. I asked her how it felt.

"Soothing. Safe. But mostly the light was fascinating. It drew me in until I felt I could gaze at it forever."

"Which shows," I said, "that you were being fascinated by your own awareness. The soul, it is said, shows itself to our subtle senses as a pearlescent lustrous glow."

"Is this something I should try to repeat?" Kate asked.

"There's no realistic way to do that," I said, "since your experience was spontaneous. It's like trying to repeat a first impression or a first kiss."

When she looked a little crestfallen, I told her that one of the classic traps for spiritual seekers was the temptation to repeat a moment of heightened experience. We harbor that impulse. Have you noticed this yourself? The surprise of a breathtaking sunset, a delicate moment of intimacy, even a superb meal, all beg to be repeated. But it's never quite the same, because what makes the moment special isn't the sunset, the loving gesture, or the fine food. It's a sudden crossing over into the subtle world.

I told Kate about the continuum of experience that leads from happiness to bliss, from physical intimacy to oneness with the soul. She had given herself permission to move more fluidly along this continuum. Meditation is a gentle way to unloose our moorings. It isn't so forceful that it pushes your perception into a new domain; instead there is a gentle arrival into subtler sensations—like the blue glow Kate saw—attended by subtler feelings and insights. I congratulated her and promised that there would be more breakthroughs to come.

Through our brief voyages into the subtle world we can anticipate how gentle the afterlife will be. There, subtle power feels natural. Peace and fulfillment come through direct communication with the soul.

❀

TWO MAGICAL WORDS

"LOOK, DO YOU see that?" said Ramana. He pointed ahead, where Savitri could make out a wisp of smoke above the trees.

"A cooking fire?" she guessed.

"Follow it and find out. I'll stay here until you return." Ramana made himself comfortable on a stump.

So Savitri headed toward the smoke alone. Soon she noticed that trees had been burned down, and saw wrecked oxcarts and other signs of destruction. Eventually she found herself in a deserted village. Soldiers had invaded from a nearby kingdom and had laid waste to the countryside. In this village all the houses were reduced to smoldering ashes except for one, which was untouched.

Savitri walked up to the door where an old woman sat. "Everything all around is destroyed," Savitri said, bowing to her. "How did your house come to be spared?"

The old woman replied, "All the men of our village were away fighting. When the soldiers came with their torches to rob me and set fire to my house, I told them, 'Come, come, for no one else is brave enough to enter. Everyone inside has scarlet fever. Help me tend to my sick family.' At that the soldiers were so frightened they refused to come a step closer and ran away."

Savitri reached into her sari and found a small coin, which she gave to the old woman. She retraced her steps until she found the place where Ramana was waiting.

"Why did you send me there?" she asked.

"The old woman turned away an army with two words: *scarlet fever*," he said. "The wise know that Death can also be turned away with two words: *I am*."

"I don't understand." She was even more confused when she looked at the sky and saw that the wisp of smoke had disappeared.

"That village was just a symbol," said Ramana.

"For trouble and sorrow?"

"No, for impermanence. Heed this, Savitri. There is no permanence in this life. Possessions come and go, as do other people. Somehow we cope with so much loss. How? By clinging to the notion that *we* are permanent, that our world is forever.

"But that is the wrong way. Death is greedy and wants to destroy everything as wantonly as an invading army. Just hold out your arms to him and say, *I am*. Death will retreat because there is nothing for him to destroy. *I am* has no possessions, no expectations, nothing to cling to. Yet it is everything you are and everything you will ever need, in this world or the one to come."

Ramana spoke with calm authority, and this helped Savitri.

"The old woman lied when she said *scarlet fever*. You must tell the truth when you say *I am*. I think that you are nearly ready," Ramana said gently.

"How can I make it the truth?" asked Savitri.

"It's not difficult. When you are happy, go inside and feel the one who is the experiencer of happiness. When you are sad, go inside and feel the experiencer of sadness. They are the same. There is a still, small point that watches all, witnesses all. Be with that stillness whenever you can. Notice it instead of sliding past it. Familiarity is your greatest ally. *I am* is your being. There is nothing foreign about simply being.

"At first the still, small point will not be much of an experience, yet it can grow without limit. When you die and finally have nothing to hold on to, *I am* will fill the whole universe. The wise have repeated this truth over and over, in every age. But you mustn't buy a truth secondhand. Find the *I am* inside yourself, and it will expand to fill you. When that happens, you are safe. Your being will be the same as your soul."

ETERNITY

When all images have disappeared at the subtle level, the dying person arrives at eternity. Eternity is the source of the soul. The rishis say that at last illusions have ended and reality begins. The fact that we can't see eternity while we're alive, as it extends in all directions around us, is a limitation the rishis strove to overcome.

The more boundless your vision, the more real you are.

As inspiring as this sounds, it also makes us uneasy, for we are used to living inside boundaries. "Years ago I became interested in spirituality," one woman told me, "but I hated all this talk about the One. I couldn't relate to it. I knew that the way I was raised, believing in a grandfatherly God sitting in heaven, was very narrow. But at least I could understand it. I can't understand the One." I find this a very natural reaction. At the end of the journey there are no loved ones, no physical destination, no memories of the material plane. Even the Buddhist phrase "Clear Light" is only a metaphor, since eternity is neither light nor clear.

Imagine what this means. As you get closer to eternity, you won't experience being dead or alive. You won't be male or female.

A moment will be the same as a century, and before will merge with after. Have we wound up in a place that is too incomprehensible to understand? If that were so, it would be too incomprehensible to matter, either.

Eternity gives you more freedom than the mind can conceive. The absence of images means you don't need images anymore. The absence of loved ones means you don't need relationships anymore. You are back at your source, but with a difference. *You've experienced it all.* Creation has shown you everything. The mind we possess now may recoil, thinking that this must be the ultimate nightmare. But the rishis, who called this stage Moksha, or liberation, celebrated it. Only the liberated soul can choose *anything.* There is no tug up or down, and the whole mechanism of pleasure and pain grinds to a halt.

What would it feel like to find yourself free? Boundless? Nameless? If you try to apply any word to the eternal soul—good, holy, loving, truthful—the rishis respond with *"netti,"* the Sanskrit word for "not that." In fact, in some schools of Vedanta, the spiritual path is called *"netti, netti,"* by which you keep repeating "not this, not this," until by a process of stripping away you arrive at essence. That's also what the afterlife journey is about. The dying person realizes, step-by-step, "This used to be me, but it's not anymore."

As it happens, one person who reported his near-death experience in great detail came close to describing eternity. The account, now famous in near-death literature, comes from an artist named Mellen-Thomas Benedict, who died of a brain tumor in 1982. That he could be dead for an hour and a half, only to return to life, is not credible by Western standards. In Tibetan Buddhism he would be considered a delog, and Benedict's experiences are as detailed as any given by delogs. I will recount it in detail because Benedict's journey practically provides an encyclopedia of the afterlife.

He found himself out of body, aware that his corpse was lying in bed. His perception was greatly expanded—he could see over, around, and under his house—and he sensed that he was enveloped in darkness, but soon a brilliant light became evident. He moved toward it, aware that if he entered the light, he would be dead.

At this point Benedict made a startling decision. He asked for the experience to stop, and it did. That he found a way to control what happens after death would not surprise a rishi, but it is almost unique in NDE literature. Benedict called a halt so that he could talk to the light. As he did so, it continually changed shapes, sometimes resembling Jesus or Buddha, other times turning into a complex pattern like a mandala or archetypal images and signs, as he puts it. The light told him (or, to be precise, transferred information to his mind) that a dying person is given a "feedback loop" of images that fits their own belief system: Christian images are seen by Christians, Buddhist images by Buddhists. Being a loop, the dying person can enter into the experience and shape it, as Benedict found himself doing. (The light explained that he was a rare case: most people proceed ahead without question.)

The fact that Benedict saw so many shifting images may have to do with his immersion in world religions and spiritual traditions after he was diagnosed with cancer. Next Benedict became aware that what he was actually seeing was the Higher Self matrix, which he describes as a "mandala of human souls"; that is, a cosmic pattern of consciousness. Each person, he realized, has a Higher Self that serves as an oversoul and also as a conduit back to the source. These terms, with almost no change, sound like pure Vedanta. This gives an opening to doubt, since Benedict may have been strongly influenced by his recent reading in Indian scriptures. On the other hand, the experience unfolded, from his perspective, as entirely spontaneous and real.

Gazing at the matrix of souls, Benedict became aware they were all connected; humanity formed one being; each of us is an aspect of this wholeness. He was drawn into the matrix, which he describes as ineffably beautiful. It radiated a healing, generative love that overwhelmed him. The light conveyed to him that the soul matrix formed a subtle energy level that girded the earth and bound people together. Benedict had spent a decade involved in nuclear disarmament and ecology, disturbing issues that had made him deeply pessimistic. Now he was confronted, he says, with the pure beauty of every human soul and was dumbfounded.

He was particularly astonished that no soul contained evil, and the light informed him that souls cannot be inherently evil. Underlying all human action is the search for love, and when people are driven to evil actions, the root cause is lack of love. When he asked if this meant that humanity could be saved, there was a "trumpet blast" accompanied by spiraling light, and Benedict was told never to forget the answer: human beings were already saved, no matter how dire the current predicament looks.

Benedict was experiencing profound ecstasy as he was absorbed deeper into the light, reaching another realm that was subtler but also much more vast. He beheld an "enormous stream of light, vast and full, deep in the heart of life." When he asked what it was, the light told him it was the river of life and that he should drink from it to his heart's content.

Fueled by limitless curiosity, he now asked the light to reveal the entire universe to him "beyond all human illusion." He was told to ride the stream of life, and as he did, he passed through a tunnel hearing "soft sonic booms" on the way. His speed accelerated beyond the speed of light as he left the solar system, passed through the heart of the galaxy, and became aware of many worlds and many life-forms, all in a dizzying rush. At this point Benedict made a critical discovery, that what appeared to be travel through space was in fact the expansion of his own consciousness. The appearance of galaxies and star clusters racing past was his own consciousness streaming past one boundary of spacetime after another.

Benedict describes entire galaxies disappearing into a point, of all life-forms making their presence known, of a second light that contains every vibration in the universe. According to the Vedic rishis, these are the primordial vibrations from which creation emerges, which means that Benedict was actually witnessing the operation of consciousness itself. Benedict finds his own language for this stage, saying that he was interfacing with the hologram of the universe.

Passing into the second light, he experienced a profound shift into silence and utter stillness. It came to him that he could see to infinity. He was in the void, or pre-creation as he calls it, and his consciousness was limitless. He was in contact with the absolute, which wasn't a religious experience but one of unbounded awareness. He perceived all of creation generating itself without beginning or end. Instead of one Big Bang, a singular event that created the universe, Benedict perceived millions of Big Bangs constantly generating new universes. Since he was beyond time, this was happening simultaneously in all dimensions.

After reaching this cosmic epiphany, Benedict's journey reversed itself, step-by-step, and he woke up in his bed at home with the unshakable realization, now so familiar in the NDE literature, that death was an illusion.

Benedict assumed that his return to earth would be as a baby, in a new incarnation. When he opened his eyes, however, he still had the same body, one that had been dead for over an hour according to the hospice worker who was present (there was no monitoring machinery or doctor). The hospice worker, who had been crying over him, assured Benedict that he had shown every sign of being dead, including a growing cold stiffness in his body. An amplified stethoscope revealed no heartbeat. (In and of itself this claim is medically so outrageous that it would lead a skeptic to discount every other part of Benedict's story.)

Although severely disoriented at first, Benedict felt better than he had in his life. It took him three months to chance a new brain scan, being understandably nervous about his tumor—but it proved to be great news. All traces of malignancy were gone, which his oncologist explained as a spontaneous remission, a rare example of a malignancy disappearing on its own. This sidesteps the issue that remissions through death are not found in medical literature, and remissions of advanced brain tumors, so far as I know, are the rarest of occurrences.

My own view is that every end point is also a starting point. For Mellen-Thomas Benedict pure consciousness became the ultimate end of a fantastic journey. For the rishis it is the starting point for living in the present. One of the most genuine things about Benedict's experience is that he wound up finding the greatest value in the present: "People are so busy trying to become God that they ought to realize that we are already God and God is becoming us. That's what it is really about." His sense that the void is everywhere, that the invisible domain contains everything, that God has gifted human beings with every possible advantage, rings true spiritually.

Traveling in Three Worlds

A staunch materialist may consider it impossible to travel to non-physical worlds, but we travel to other states of consciousness all the time, in fact. According to the rishis, we move between three levels of awareness that account for all experience:

Consciousness filled with physical objects.
Consciousness filled with subtle objects.
Consciousness filled with nothing but itself—pure consciousness.

In each state the soul looks different. In the physical world the soul is centered around emotions and idealism. It connotes warmth of heart, love, devotion to God. We look to our souls to remind ourselves that we have a divine spark inside, and yet we don't base our lives on it. The soul flickers in and out.

In the subtle world the soul is spirit, denoting holiness, closeness to God, and freedom from the burdens of physical existence. The soul no longer offers mere comfort; it is the bliss that pain was disguising. The soul is constant now; its guidance can be clearly followed without confusion. The primary feeling is magnetic: one is being drawn inexorably toward the divine.

In the domain of pure consciousness, merging is complete. One sees that self and soul are one. Since there is no here and there, the soul has no location. It exists everywhere and nowhere at the same time. One no longer seeks the soul's goodness, holiness, or purity. It simply is.

After death a person experiences the subtle dimension automatically, yet to the rishis every dimension is enfolded into the others. The appearance of angels on earth is possible, even though they are properly consigned to the domain of subtle objects, and so is the sojourn of the prophet Mohammed to heaven on a white horse. Each involves a shift in awareness. At the same time, each state of consciousness has its own particular qualities and is perceived as its own separate reality.

THREE WORLDS: A MAP OF ETERNITY

1. *Consciousness of physical objects:* This is the world of concrete things that we verify through the five senses. It obeys linear time. We appear to ourselves as physical bodies separated in time and space. A life span occupies a limited number of years between two absolute events, birth and death.

The **laws** obeyed in this dimension are strict. Gravity, the speed of light, and the conservation of matter and energy (which can be neither created nor destroyed) form the foundation of every other natural law.

If this is your primary world, you have certain *powers* that allow you to explore it. These include physical strength, willpower, reason, emotional expression, sexuality, and personal authority. To the extent that you use these powers fully, you will be more and more successful. At the same time, you are more likely to become attached to this dimension of consciousness as the only reality.

In this world Akasha feels like physical space filled with an infinity of material things.

The *soul* feels personal but is seen only in short glimpses.

2. *Consciousness of subtle objects:* This is the world of dreams, imagination, and inspiration in all its many forms. We verify this world through intuition, detecting qualities like love and beauty, feeling a subtle presence within and without that is not available to the five senses. A life span in this dimension lasts as long as it can be imagined.

The *laws* of the subtle world are fluid. Events can happen forward or backward. Invisible structures may persist for a long time (for example, as myths and archetypes), but even then, time doesn't bind them as strictly as in the physical world. Gravity and the speed of light are no longer absolutes.

If this is your primary world, you will have certain *powers* that allow you to explore it. These include imagination, memory, artistic ability, spiritual sensitivity, healing abilities, and intuition. The more you exercise these powers, the more successful you will be. However, you may also find yourself detached from the physical world and unable to navigate it as well as someone without intuition and spiritual sensitivity. This will worry you until you discover that the subtle world is capable of supporting you.

Akasha feels dreamlike, filled with memories and images, archetypes and gods, spirits and etheric beings.

The *soul* feels like a guiding force leading back to the source. It is sensed constantly.

3. *Pure consciousness:* This is the world of awareness being aware of itself. There are no objects, gross or subtle. We verify this world through "I am." Existence becomes its own end, its own reward. As an experience, pure consciousness begins with a silent mind; this grows in richness and meaning the longer a person has the experience.

The *laws* of this world apply to creation itself. The seeds of every object and event gestate here. Here is the possibility of time, space, and physical things. There is also the possibility of mind, as yet without thought or images. Although totally free of anything visible, pure consciousness is eager to give birth; mystics tell us it is pregnant with All That Is.

If this is your primary world, you need no powers to navigate it. The flow of time and the expansion of space are neutral events to you; they come and go within your being. You witness them without attachment, although if you wish, you can call upon any quality— love, compassion, strength, truth—and experience it in fullness.

In this world Akasha feels uncreated. Concepts like birth and death, life and death, have no relevance. There is only existence. To be is an all-enveloping experience.

It must always be kept in mind that the afterlife is not as "after" as we assume. All three dimensions of consciousness are ever-present space.

Akasha enclosing the world of physical objects is three-dimensional. Our eyes can survey the landscape to tell us where we are. Up and down are fixed directions to orient us physically. Before and after are fixed points in time to orient us as to where we are in our lifetimes.

Akasha enclosing the world of subtle objects has much vaguer boundaries. These can change in an instant to freefloating dreamspace. In the absence of fixed dimensions, experience is measured in terms of intensity. Emotions are heightened, dreams become more vivid, and the presence of angels and other etheric entities is felt directly. With experience this becomes a comfortable space on its own terms, as it already is for artists, intuitives, and deeply spiritual people.

Akasha enclosing itself is pure existence. It feels incredibly secure because there is unity with everything. Any experience comes from within, a single point from which creation emanates like an energy beam or a flower opening infinitely.

The *soul* is impersonal. It is Being, with no added qualities.

Shifting Your Allegiance

So far, we've used the metaphor of a journey to describe what happens in the afterlife. Most people expect to give up the physical world for a "higher" world. The Vedic rishis would point out that the real shift is one of allegiance. When we die we give up our allegiance to "consciousness filled with physical objects" and move on to "consciousness filled with subtle objects." In Vedanta this is what going to heaven actually means.

A shift of allegiance looks easy from the perspective of the rishis. However, it proves terribly difficult for most people, East and West, because the physical world is so convincing. Doubt arises when we think about the other world, despite the fact that we inhabit it in our dreams all the time. A perfect example of such doubt and the anxiety it brings is Shakespeare's Hamlet.

In Hamlet's most famous soliloquy, "To be or not to be," he won-
ders whether he should commit suicide in the face of overwhelming
misery. He cannot bring himself to obey his father's ghost and kill the
usurper to the throne, his uncle Claudius. He is trapped by agony,
and undone by many things—his conscience, his sense of cowardice
and failure, his disgust with his mother's sexual betrayal, and a depth
of depression bordering on madness. Even though committing suicide would end his suffering, Hamlet pauses to reason out things log-
ically, breaking down the problem as the rational mind is used to
doing.

> . . . *To die, to sleep;*
> *To sleep; perchance to dream: ay, there's the rub;*
> *For in that sleep of death what dreams may come,*
> *When we have shuffled off this mortal coil,*
> *Must give us pause.*

Leaving aside the greatness of the poetry, the Prince of Denmark
is caught between the physical world and the subtle, and he can't
convince himself that he trusts either one. To put the argument into
modern English: Is dying the end, or is it akin to going to sleep? If
it's like going to sleep, will it mean the end of my troubles, or will I
be engulfed in nightmares? Maybe these dreams are worse than being
alive, even when life is at its most painful. I can't speak with anyone
who has come back from the dead, so I can't resolve this problem. I'm
left with doubt. And doubt is enough to make me cling to life.

This is what Vedanta means about shifting your allegiance; if
you aren't successful, you will be caught up in bewildering doubt.
The secret is that *you have to master the subtle world in order to let go of the
physical.* Right now you rely on rational thought. You proceed from
event to event in a linear way. Your physical strength enables you to

manipulate objects and feel secure that you can defend yourself. Your willpower and force of character support you in accomplishing long-range goals.

None of these powers are relevant in the subtle world and therefore provide no support in the afterlife. And the threshold between physical and subtle reality is very disorienting. We already experience this in dreams. In a dream you can lift a house as easily as a feather, leap backward in time, or feel totally helpless in a frightening situation no matter how hard you struggle to get out of it. The long saga of Carlos Castaneda's apprenticeship with Don Juan, the Yaqui sorcerer who became his spiritual master, is basically an education in learning how to navigate the subtle world, in which Castaneda portrays himself as full of anxiety and doubt.

In one episode Don Juan takes Castaneda's hand, and together they jump over a tall tree. When they land on solid ground again, Castaneda feels sick and disoriented, on the verge of vomiting (queasiness is the most prevalent condition the apprentice finds himself in, along with fear). Don Juan asks, What is the difference between jumping over a tree as we just did and jumping over a tree in a dream? Then he answers his own question. In a dream you can comfortably jump over a tree because it's natural in the dream world. You know that you are going to wake up, and when you do you realize that all the events in your dream were just neural impulses in your brain. There was no "real" tree; you look back on the whole dream world as an illusion.

The reason you can't jump over a tree in the physical world is that you don't realize you can wake up. A sorcerer is someone who has learned to wake up completely, so to him jumping over a tree is natural. It all happens as neural impulses in the brain. There is no "real" tree. But if you buy into the tree being real, you must accept the limitations of such a world.

One suddenly realizes the immense challenge of shifting one's allegiance away from the physical. Does it involve being able to leap over trees? That would be an extreme case (although not unheard of: Catholic and Hindu lore are filled with levitating saints, and a nun in Egypt even had to be coaxed down from her perch in the air above the tree). The fact that so few of us ever explore the mystery of life after death is testimony to our fixed allegiance. Yet there are moments when we realize that we already have the power to shift from one level of consciousness to another without the illusion of dreaming. Let me illustrate.

"Thirty years ago I found a switch inside my head that can change reality." The man speaking is Harold; he is around sixty and a retired freelance editor. We met at a large New Age book convention two years ago. "I was born with a congenital heart defect that put me at risk for dying young," Harold went on. "This was something I'd grown used to growing up. But after college my defective heart landed me in the hospital as a prime candidate for a pacemaker.

"Unfortunately, there were complications—an infection, all kinds of trouble. One night during the worst of it I was lying in my hospital bed. The nurse came in to take my temperature, and as she left she forgot to turn off the light. I was irritated, but I was too sleepy to get out of bed. Then the lights went off.

"At first I didn't think this was unusual, even though I had a direct view of the light switch and hadn't seen anybody. A few seconds later the lights went on again. Then off, then on. I didn't freak out but just lay there, staring at them. It was obvious that no one was flicking the switch, but I could even hear the buzzing of the fluorescent bulbs going off and on. Suddenly I had the strangest idea: *It's me.*

"At that moment I wasn't sleepy anymore; I felt a sense of extraordinary clarity. Have you ever heard of such a thing? Turning the lights off and on with your mind?"

I told him I've heard of much stranger things. Did the episode repeat itself?

"Not for a long time. Fast forward to last month. A hot summer night in New York. My plane was four hours late, and I was seething. I'd missed all my connections and was just standing there waiting impatiently for my bag to come off the carousel. All at once I had this thought: *they've lost my bag.* Sure enough, everyone grabs their luggage, but my bag never shows up.

"So I march into the lost baggage office, and I begin to grumble at the clerk, who couldn't care less. Yawning, she phones somebody to see if any bags have been left behind, then in a bored voice she tells me to fill out a claim. Nothing unusual so far."

On the verge of losing his temper, a faint notion entered Harold's head. *It's just as easy to be happy as angry. You can make this a positive situation.*

"What I saw in my mind's eye was an invisible switch. And I knew if I flipped the switch, everything would change. So I did. The clerk smiled at me and said she'd phone to find out about my bags. I mean, she acted as if she hadn't already done that. She phoned, and then she told me that my bag had been located. I felt a strange sense of accomplishment. Then a pretty girl standing in line behind me said that her bag was lost on the same flight. Inside I had the idea, *You should get your luggage, too.* And the next instant the clerk said that they'd found another bag besides mine. It was the girl's, of course."

"And you connect this incident to what happened in the hospital thirty years ago?" I said.

"Wouldn't you? After the airport incident I used the switch a couple more times. Once to get a seat on a completely full flight, another time to get my room changed in a hotel when they said I couldn't."

"Don't things like that happen all the time without the involvement of special powers?" I asked. Harold looked bemused. This was different. He could tell that he was causing it.

Several things are striking about his experience. It involved a deliberate change of awareness. It felt special, even eerie. It made Harold see himself in a new light. It expanded the possibility of what the mind can do, yet somehow "flicking the switch" felt normal at the time. Finally, once the experience was over, it faded away and was basically forgotten. Can we say, then, that Harold took a trip into the Akashic field? Vedanta would say that Harold experienced a shift in consciousness, and when that happened, the world "out there" shifted with it. This is also how moving into the afterlife works, via an internal shift that creates a different external environment.

It's important to grasp that the domains of physical objects, subtle objects, and pure consciousness are actually one domain—Akasha—seen in three aspects. This becomes evident in a phenomenon like faith healing, which brings together pure consciousness (God), a subtle event (prayer), and the physical body. The light so often seen by those who are healed is a subtle energy, which can also be perceived as an electrical or nervous charge in the body, a seizure, rapture, or dizziness. In her book, *The Healing Touch of Mary,* Cheri Lomonte recounts the following story:

Dawn J. was a devout Catholic who as a young woman had prayed for a vision of the Virgin Mary. Soon after she left her parents' house, she experienced an actual visitation. This created a sense of awe and humility; she hardly felt worthy to behold the Mother of God in the flesh. But Dawn came to feel that she had been chosen as a messenger.

Soon thereafter she was asked by a coworker to help with a personal matter. The coworker was worried about his wife, who had begun to visit a house in the Bronx where a statue of Mary had begun to spontaneously exude scented oil. Dawn agreed to intervene and paid a visit to the house. When she walked in, however, she was greeted by the powerful scent of roses, and when she was shown the small statue, exuding a continual stream of oil, she became convinced that this was a genuine miracle.

Subsequently she paid several visits to the house, each time experiencing a divine presence in the scented oil. On one visit the woman of the house told her that the walls and furniture had now begun to exude oil, which she wiped up with cotton balls. Dawn was given a bag of these to take home. Sometime later she heard that a friend's three-month-old baby was gravely ill with spinal meningitis and had been hospitalized in intensive care. Dawn felt a strong impulse to use the holy oil as a healing. With the parents' permission she entered the hospital room and found the baby listless and nearly unconscious, its body incubated for feeding and medication. It was a piteous sight.

Dawn took an oil-soaked cotton ball and gently stroked the baby's spine with it. She left, and the next day was informed that the infant was out of danger. Within two days it was sleeping and nursing normally and had been sent home with its parents. The doctor in charge of the case considered this recovery miraculous. Dawn attributed it to the healing touch of Mary.

Of course, Catholic lore is filled with thousands of similar tales, but what are we to think of this one in particular? To me, it shows that the three domains of consciousness don't merely overlap; they are actively involved with one another. The physical plane is represented by the statue, the oil, and the baby's body. The subtle domain is represented by the vision of Mary, Dawn's faith, and the divine presence felt in the oil. The domain of pure consciousness is represented by the divine itself. I'm not offering this story as established fact; the author who repeats it went through no process of investigation to prove its truth. She relied on the sincerity of people who came forward, with nothing to gain, describing their own experiences. My only purpose here is to open the possibility that there is a unifying principle, the Akashic field, that embraces a wide range of phenomena.

Somewhere in Akasha angels might look around and say, "This is real." The same might be perceived by departed spirits, great spiritual beings, and souls "crossing over." The landscape of the afterlife can be as complex as anyone might desire, so long as we remember that ultimately gods, goddesses, spirits, and souls become only one thing: consciousness creating within itself.

SURVIVING THE STORM

SAVITRI TRUSTED RAMANA, but as the hours grew long, once again she began to worry about the time. Her mind was filled with a vision of Satyavan's strong body turned cold and lifeless with a glance from Yama. *I would lose everything,* she thought.

Ramana turned to her. "Does that make you afraid, to lose everything?" He seemed to have no trouble reading her thoughts.

"Of course," Savitri said miserably.

Ramana pointed up ahead. Alongside the path was a rustic shrine that someone had erected in the forest. The pine boughs of the altar sheltered an image of Vishnu. Knowing that Vishnu was the aspect of God that sustains life, she quickly ran ahead, gathering some wildflowers to offer at the altar. *This must be a sign,* she thought. Ramana hung back, as with bowed head Savitri begged Vishnu to help her. *I will do anything,* she implored.

When she raised her eyes, the god Vishnu was actually standing before her. Savitri was awestruck. "You will do anything for me if I save your husband?" he asked. Fervently Savitri said yes. "Then go to the river and fetch me a drink of water," said Vishnu.

Savitri ran off to do as she was bade. Ramana was nowhere to be seen, but she remembered passing the river and knew it was close by. Kneeling beside it, she wondered what she could carry water in when her eye caught sight of someone else along the bank. It was Satyavan! Overjoyed, Savitri ran to him, bursting into tears. Satyavan embraced her and asked what was wrong.

In between sobs Savitri told him the danger he was in. "Then we shall not return home at all," Satyavan declared. He took Savitri tenderly by the hand. They walked along the river until they spied a boatman tied up to shore.

The boatman greeted them cordially and said that he had been out fishing. He pointed to an island in the middle of the river. "That's my home," he said. Quickly Satyavan made a bargain with the boatman to become his helper. He and Savitri were carried to the island, where they began a new life.

Savitri became sublimely happy, for after a few days it was apparent that Yama had not pursued them. Her husband learned to be a fisherman, and together they lived in peace on the island. Years passed. They had two children, which were the joy of their hearts. Then one night a great storm crashed down on the island. The winds howled, and the river rose higher than it ever had. By morning everything had been washed away. Savitri had been saved by tying herself to a tree with a rope. At sunrise, she saw that Satyavan, their house, and their children had been swept away into the river.

She managed to find a boat and rowed to shore, but Savitri was so devastated that all she could do was lie on the sand moaning. Suddenly she felt a shadow looming over her. She looked up to see Lord Vishnu. "Did you remember my drink of water?" he asked.

Savitri looked down and was amazed to see she was wearing the same sari as the day years ago when Vishnu first appeared to her. As she bent to get him some water, her reflection showed her the same young woman. "What happened?" she asked in bewilderment.

Vishnu replied, "With me there is no time, for I am beyond

death. Time is the field of gain and loss. As long as you are in time, it is an illusion to think that you can prevent loss, which is just another word for change."

"Then Satyavan may still be alive!" Savitri exclaimed. "Can he be saved?"

Vishnu was already beginning to fade away. Savitri grasped at his image, but all she held was air. When she turned around, she saw Ramana standing behind her on the path.

"You see," Ramana said, "whatever you are afraid to lose is unreal. Death cannot touch what is real. In a way that is a gift from Death."

"I don't see that," Savitri said dejectedly.

"When you die, you will be forced to lose everything, yet something will remain. It is the soul, which is real. Therefore you should celebrate loss. The trappings of existence can fall away at any time; the essence will always remain. And that essence is you."

LIVING BEYOND BOUNDARIES

The afterlife is not just a mystery to be solved. It's an opportunity to expand life beyond boundaries. As the rishis described it, awareness begins in an unbounded state with pure consciousness and then cascades, plane by plane, until it reaches the physical world. Each level is in you. At any given moment you could place yourself anywhere; the choice of boundaries—or unboundedness—is yours alone. Therefore journeys to heaven and hell are daily occurrences, not far-off possibilities. This is hard for many people to accept, because they want a fixed, reliable "me" that will bring stability to an unstable world. But there is no separation between observer and observed. The inner and outer worlds are changing constantly.

After death experience shifts to the subtle realm, which presents its infinite variety. Yet we are already touching on subtle experiences every day. Here are some of the labels we apply to our voyages in the subtle world:

Dreams
Imagination
Myths
Archetypes
Epiphanies
The "shadow"
Collective consciousness
Numinous creation (angels, demons, saints, bodhisattvas, deities)
Sacred visions
Desires and wishes
Inspiration

Somewhere on this list falls everything the rishis called "consciousness filled with subtle objects." You cannot see yourself as a complete person without taking these subworlds into account. They are destinations in the future but are also in the here and now. The "shadow" may be an unfamiliar term; it refers to hidden forces that influence us as if beyond our will. The shadow self in Jungian psychology is a region of the unconscious where we store energies that become our version of dark, evil, shameful, or adversarial beings. It's hard to imagine how the shadow can occupy the same space as beings of light, which are numinous and include angels and deities. We're tempted to allot separate places for each, but there are no physical divisions in the subtle domain and therefore no barriers between heaven and hell, light and shadow. Access to the entire subtle world is always open. If you can imagine and dream, you can also experience departed spirits, angels, or gods.

Therefore, the first step for anyone who wants to enter the subworlds of consciousness is to drop one's inflexible rules about what is real and unreal. Many cultures have viewed the barrier between life and death as permeable. We insist on making it into a wall, and behind this insistence lurks a good deal of unspoken fear. We equate the entire subtle domain with the realm of death, which is far from the case.

"My son died when he was just twenty-two," a woman told me recently. "It was a brain tumor, and I was staying at his home the day he passed away. With me were his sister and his new wife. Tom's passing was peaceful, and that evening we three women stayed up late talking about him. We must have talked too late, because we fell asleep together by the fire.

"The next morning his wife was quite excited and told us that Tom came to her in a dream and reassured her that he was all right. His sister blurted out that Tom had also come to her in a dream saying the same thing. They turned to me, and yes, I had had the same dream. We all felt that Tom was so vividly present that it had not seemed like a dream—it was really him."

In this example one sees a bleed-through between several levels of the subtle world: dreams, departed spirits, and collective consciousness. In this case "collective" means an awareness shared by three people, although the term can be expanded much, much further. This kind of blending is more common than we think. Boundaries, after all, are arbitrary. Einstein, whose reputation rests upon rational thought, declared that the germ of the theory of relativity came to him while daydreaming. Shall we call that a dream, a vision, or inspiration? Shall we call Tom's reassurance to his family real or illusory, inspiring or merely a projection of grief that needed an outlet?

Sorting out the subtle world was a project that the Vedic rishis set for themselves. By going deeper into their explanations we can begin to navigate this level of reality that is closest to the soul. We have arrived at the suburbs of immortality, as it were, which are not quite eternal yet not bound by time and space, either.

Near-death experiences, Tibetan Buddhism, and the Book of Revelation agree on one thing: when we die we will look beautiful. The "golden body" of the Tibetan Bardo and the perfect body rising from the grave at Judgment Day are untouched by age and decay. When people are visited in dreams by the departed, they usually appear in the prime of life, somewhere around thirty, rather than as children or disembodied ghosts. Apparitions of the Virgin Mary never seem to be of someone in old age but of a luminous, lovely young woman. On the other hand, in near-death accounts of hell (much rarer than going into the light), the damned never look young and healthy. They are old, withered, sick, scarred, deformed, or some wretched combination. Visions of reward and punishment deliver totally opposite images.

The rishis weren't satisfied with such simple, idealized images. Seeing the entire subtle world as a projection of consciousness, they focused on the *Koshas,* or divisions of pure consciousness. *Kosha* translates to mean sheath, layer, or envelope, but it's easiest to think of pure consciousness as a point that wraps five bodies around itself like layers of an onion. (One can also think in terms of vibrations, moving from grossest to highest.) The five layers are:

1. Physical body
2. Prana (subtle breath or life force)
3. Mind
4. Ego and intellect
5. Body of bliss

The five Koshas, operating in unison, give rise to the self, or to put it more accurately, the self system. You and I are multilayered because we are inseparable from our five Koshas. The fact that each sheath has its own rules provides us with a structure for the subtle world. The afterlife is a journey only in the sense that a dream is—in both cases we are taking our attention away from one Kosha and placing it on another. Our travels remain within the self system.

The Koshas are also shared. The universe has its own layers. Experiencing an angel or departed spirit, for example, is made possible by the countless generations that helped create that subworld. Shared reality isn't mystical. You claim your physical body as uniquely your own, but even that is shared—the air you breathe today contains millions of atoms of oxygen that were breathed out in China, for example, just a few days ago. You absorb ideas floating around in the mass media, and at moments you may have an inspiration only to discover that someone else has had the same idea simultaneously. (As a writer I am ruefully familiar with the occasions when a brilliant book or script idea was anticipated by two or three other writers within days of one another.)

So the analogy of the onion built up in layers breaks down at a certain point. A Kosha isn't an individual possession. It's a dynamic realm with its own laws and experiences, a realm we can enter alone or with others.

Annamaya Kosha (physical body): The physical body is the most separate aspect of the self system. At birth most babies are very much alike physiologically, but by age seventy no two people's bodies are remotely alike. Time has made each of us unique. This material fact underlies a great deal of the separation in the world, as people struggle to grab their share of food, money, possessions, and status. They want to promote the well-being of their physical body, to enhance its charm and beauty, and to protect it from the threat of injury and death.

At this level first consciousness is biology. It operates silently, without a voice, as it organizes the myriad functions of the body. Yet even here, if we look at what is happening at the cellular level, it turns out that consciousness transcends boundaries. Cells cooperate, communicate, exchange functions, perform acts of self-sacrifice, remain in balance, keep aware of their environment, adapt to change, and know that they survive by being part of a greater whole.

Every Kosha reveals wholeness and separation at the same time. If we look upon *Annamaya Kosha* as the physical world, it's obvious that our bodies are isolated from one another, which keeps us in separation by giving rise to the illusion that we must struggle and compete with every other isolated body. Yet this Kosha *brings us closer to wholeness* through cooperation, physical security in social groups, and shared desires for food, shelter, sex, and physical comfort.

Pranamaya Kosha (subtle breath or life force): Prana means vitality. In the individual, Prana is the breath that sustains life by rhythmically joining us to Nature. We inhale all that is necessary to remain alive, then exhale it back to wherever it is needed next. There is no equivalent in the West for Prana, except a tradition called vitalism that centers on the "life force." Whatever name you give it, a subtle, flowing intelligence sustains, the physical body.

At this level consciousness is the binding force that keeps Nature intact. Humans recognize that we are united with all living things. Consciousness doesn't recognize higher or lower levels of life; it orchestrates diversity into a wholeness. When you feel connected to the life-forms enveloped in the ecosystem—to pets, an old shade tree, the full moon, a thunderstorm—you are feeling the flow of vitality that binds Nature together. When you become aware of the incredible intelligence that knits every cell in the body, it is no longer possible to say "I own this." You cannot own life, yet you cannot help but be at its center also. Yet in this level separation still seems to dominate over wholeness, which is why human beings continue to depredate the ecosystem without realizing that they are destroying part of their own self system.

This Kosha *keeps us in separation* through imbalance, a disrupted ecosystem, pollution, and urban overcrowding.

This Kosha *brings us closer to wholeness* through vitality, kinship with other living things, balance in the ecosystem, and empathy.

Manomaya Kosha (mind): The root of the mind is individual ideas and thoughts. You know who you are by what you think. This is the level where you process the raw data of the world to make it meaningful. Mind includes emotions, sensations, memories, and other uses of the brain. The rishis understood that mind is organized into its own invisible body, a body of personal memories and beliefs that we guard from harm as fiercely as we guard our physical bodies.

At this level consciousness finds itself at play in the cosmos without boundaries, for the mind can fly anywhere, imagine anything. Your mind is free to interpret the world any way it wants, and unfortunately some of those ways include ignorance of the self. It is impossible to restrict the mind, yet many people fear its gift of freedom. At this level we come up against the self-created boundaries of belief, fear, and prejudice. Blake's "mind-forged manacles" create separation and repression where none need exist.

Mind is more collective than individual. I may say "my mind," meaning my unique thoughts and memories, but 90% of our thoughts are picked up from society and its many outlets. A great many memories are shared, and the very stuff of thought—language—is a collective creation. Therefore the rishis say that mind is the first Kosha where wholeness dominates over separation.

This Kosha *brings us closer to wholeness* through shared beliefs, social conditioning, religion, received opinions, and common values.

This Kosha *keeps us in separation* through divisive beliefs in politics and religion, prejudice, "us versus them" thinking, nationalism, and arbitrary mental boundaries made of fear and hatred.

Vigyanmaya Kosha (ego and intellect): This is the level of identity dominated by "I, me, and mine." Society places positive value on someone with high ego drive and will to succeed, but in spiritual circles the ego's reputation is low. Spiritual seekers often feel it is their duty to "kill the ego" and control its impulses. However, if we look at "I-ness" without prejudice against the ego, this level of the self brings identity into being, not all the external things that ego drive makes us pursue.

Identity isn't a blank slate for long. It becomes filled with attachments and associations depending on what we choose to identify with. Vigyanmaya Kosha is that level where myth and archetypes operate, giving us stories and models to identify with. The gods play out our primal desires, quests, wars, and loves. Ego also gives us knowledge about identity itself, what it means to be human: I cannot know who I am without family and society.

At this level consciousness is self-centered, brought to a focus upon "I." Nothing is more universal, yet ego drives separate us when one person's desires clash with another's. To be fair, this clash develops in the mind, not in the ego itself. When we say ego, we usually mean the ego-personality, which is full of individual desires, dreams, beliefs, likes, and dislikes. Vigyan is closer to unity than that. At this level wholeness dominates over separation, as can be seen from the world's shared archetypes and myths.

This Kosha *brings us closer to wholeness* through a sense of one humanity, heroic quests and mythic exploits, and the need for self-respect, dignity, and inner worth.

This Kosha *keeps us in separation* through personal alienation, separation anxiety, loneliness, and repressed emotions that give rise to shame and guilt.

Anandamaya Kosha (body of bliss): To the rishis bliss was more than a feeling of ecstasy. It was the basic vibration, or hum, of the universe, the ground state from which all diversity springs. It's possible to imagine an afterlife where one no longer has a body, where there is no need for breath, where the mind doesn't process data anymore. But there must be a faint sense of both ego and bliss. Ego says, "This is happening to me." Bliss says, "I feel the spark of creation." Ananda is the possibility for creation to manifest, and as long as you inhabit the body of bliss, bliss is an intense, dynamic experience and not just a potential.

At this level consciousness is the joy of being. Instead of focusing on anything in the external world, our attention comes to rest on the numinous presence that has been described as a golden light suffusing every particle of Nature. In bliss you perceive that separation is only a thin veil. Behind the veil shines the light of pure consciousness. Devotional practices that increase a person's sense of joy can reach as deep as the level of ecstasy. But bliss itself is far from the feeling of happiness or even joy, though in diluted form it can be experienced as both. It is the vibratory connection that allows pure consciousness to enter into creation.

This Kosha *reveals wholeness so entirely*—through love, joy, and ecstasy—that separation no longer holds any attraction. One could say that Anandamaya Kosha is pure Being mixed with just a touch of individuality, just enough to allow someone to live in physical form, and whatever form the afterlife takes. Without this gossamer sheath you would dissolve into Being and become bliss itself, without an experiencer.

It's not difficult to see yourself in multidimensions once the Koshas are described.

The *physical dimension* contains action. You live here whenever you see yourself as a body separate in time and space.

The *Pranic dimension* connects you to other living things. You live here when you see yourself as part of the web of life, a creature of Nature.

The *mental dimension* organizes reality through thought. You live here when you see yourself as the sum of your thoughts, desires, wishes, dreams, and fears.

The *ego dimension* defines your unique identity. You live here when you see yourself in terms of "I, me, and mine."

The *dimension of bliss* holds out ultimate fulfillment through love and joy. You live here when you see yourself blending into everything through the power of love, or when you have no other sensation than ecstasy.

Making these dimensions more familiar doesn't automatically bring them together, however. Each Kosha, as we saw, can pull you closer to wholeness or increase your tendency to remain separate and isolated. The rishis considered wholeness to be the only reality, compared to which every experience in separation is a dream. The goal of life is to find unity, or Yoga, and this can be accomplished, they said, by focusing on each Kosha.

Physical body: Yoga uses physical postures (called *Asanas*) that combine balance, strength, and body awareness to bring us to physical consciousness.

Pranic body: Yoga uses exercises in soft, self-aware breathing (*Pranayama*) to bring us to consciousness of the flow of Prana.

Mental body: Yoga uses the whole field of discrimination (*Viveka*) to bring us to consciousness of how the mind works. Manomaya Kosha is therefore the level of evolution in consciousness, both for you and me and for human beings as a whole. We carve out individual niches in collective consciousness, and as a wave of evolution passes through humanity, each of us can decide to catch the wave or ignore it, to embrace it or defend against it.

Ego: Yoga uses mindfulness in all its various forms, such as contemplation and meditation (*Dhyana*), to bring a person to consciousness of the "I am" that underlies all experience.

Body of bliss: Yoga uses sustained periods in a deep state of silence (*Samadhi*) to bring the subtle vibration of bliss to the surface of the mind, making a person conscious that the "hum" of the universe is present in every experience.

I've outlined very briefly the contours of yoga as a way of life, but a typical modern person cannot be expected to suddenly shift his or her allegiance so drastically. This makes the "after" in the afterlife too far away to work with; we must create more unity in the "now." Yoga was not meant to be specifically Indian or to belong primarily to ancient times, but, unfortunately, this is how things transpired, leaving us with a new challenge. How do we take the fact that we live in five worlds and use it to redefine life as a whole?

At Home in Consciousness

You and I may seem to live primarily in the physical world, yet our awareness began in pure consciousness, and as we traveled into this life layer by layer through different dimensions, each one gave us a new sense of self. We possess an entire self system. The rishis studied this system and came to various conclusions:

- Pure consciousness is always present in everything, no matter what world it occupies or form it takes.
- The physical world has the least amount of pure consciousness because it is dominated by physical things and the illusion of separateness.
- The closer you get to pure consciousness, the more powerful it becomes.
- Changing one's consciousness on subtle levels brings change to all the Koshas at once.

If we follow these principles, we can gain the same mastery enjoyed by the sages, or at least a fair share of it.

I posted opinions on the Internet to this effect, saying that basing one's life on consciousness is the best route to mastering the physical world. Responders were quite skeptical, however. Many said, in effect, "Talk about consciousness all you want, but we have to get people to stop destroying the planet." Or "Consciousness is all well and good, but it won't end war and terrorism." Or "Good luck using consciousness to stop a bullet." In other words, they were putting the physical Kosha first, assuming that material things can only be influenced through direct action.

How can one prove that the best way to change reality is through consciousness? On the physical level action seems separate from consciousness. The Buddhist concept of nondoing seems quite mystical until you realize that it means "action in consciousness." Action in consciousness takes many forms. The passive resistance of Gandhi was an outward form of nondoing that had a huge effect on consciousness; it brought an entire historical era to an end. Powerful ideas are also in consciousness, and there is no doubt that have changed the world, from the Greek invention of democracy to modern theories of relativity. As we move to subtler Koshas, *all action takes place in consciousness.*

Let me simplify things by making some suggestions about action in each of the five Koshas:

Annamaya Kosha, the physical body: Nourish and respect your body. Appreciate its incredible inner intelligence. Do not fear it or taint it with toxins. Take time to really be in your body. Take it outside and let it play.

Pranamaya Kosha, the vital body: Go out into Nature and sink into the feeling that this is your home. Respect and nourish the ecosystem. Do not harm other living things. See Nature without fear or hostility. Reverence for life is the key here.

Manomaya Kosha, the mental body: Develop positive uses of the mind. Read and appreciate what is finest in human expression.

Become aware that you are a wholeness, and allow ideas to come in that support wholeness over separation. Resist us-versus-them thinking. Examine your automatic reactions and secondhand beliefs. Find every opportunity to welcome signals from your higher self.

Vigyanmaya Kosha, the ego body: Find a vision; go on a quest. Fit yourself into the larger pattern of growth. Seek ways to evolve personally. Celebrate the vast traditions of spirit and wisdom that unite cultures. Be as humane as you can in every way, following the dictum "The world is my family."

Anandamaya Kosha, the body of bliss: Develop your own practice for transcending and finding bliss. You already know the phrase "Follow your bliss"; now put it into practice through some kind of "alpha wave" exercise like meditation and deep relaxation. Devote yourself to discovering what Samadhi, the silence of deep awareness, is really like. Experience your own being as a reason to be here.

GUIDES AND MESSENGERS

"HAVE I LEARNED enough now?" Savitri asked. She was beginning to change, she could feel it. Many things she once considered
real now seemed like phantoms, while the most profoundly real
things were invisible.

"I think so," said Ramana. "Go home."

"Will you come with me?"

He shook his head, smiling. "I wouldn't want to scare Yama to
death."

Savitri's heart skipped a beat. "But how do I get back? I don't
know where I am."

"Or so you imagine." Ramana pointed into the darkest part of the
forest, and Savitri saw a swarm of lights that might have been fire-
flies, only it was midafternoon. Ramana nodded toward them. "Go,"
he said. "I know you think I won't be with you. That's just another
bit of imagination." Seeing her reluctance, Ramana bowed his head.
"Everything will be as it will be."

Savitri remembered that those were Yama's exact words to her.
She lingered for a moment until Ramana's form disappeared into the
heart of the forest. Then she walked toward the hovering lights. They

grew larger, and she knew she was seeing a band of *devas*. (A deva is the same as an angel, but it can also be a Nature spirit.)

"Who are you?" she asked. "Are you tree devas?" In India devas inhabit every level of Nature to infuse them with life.

But instead of answering, the lights darted away. Savitri had the distinct feeling that they were afraid of her. In her gentlest voice she begged them to come back. One of the lights said, *Why should we when all you want to do is kill us?* The voice was not outside Savitri's head but inside.

Savitri was shocked. "Kill you? I would never do such a thing."

The light replied, *You are doing it right now. We are the devas assigned to you, yet look how feeble we are.*

Savitri said, "Tell me how I did this, because if I ever needed you, it's at this moment."

The light said, *You have been full of secret sorrow. You are anxious about death. You think nothing of us, and you never call upon us. That's how you are trying to kill us.*

Savitri had never thought of devas that way, that they needed attention. But now the very mention of death drew her mind back to fear, and when it did, the lights grew smaller and dimmer.

She exclaimed, "Wait! Don't let me kill you."

To which the light replied, *You can't. We are immortal. The danger isn't that you can really hurt us but that you can break our connection to you. We need your love and attention, and in return we will help you.*

"How?"

Through inspiration. We bring messages. We can let you see us, as you do now, and that will help you see your place in the divine plan.

"Is it in the divine plan for Satyavan to die?" Savitri asked. The devas had been coming closer, but now they scattered and moved away from her. Savitri caught herself and took a deep breath, asking for hope and courage. The lights cautiously drew closer.

The divine plan is life itself. It includes all creatures in their proper place. The proper place for humans is, first, in eternity and second, here on earth. Death, like the pause between two breaths, is how you cross from one home to the other.

Savitri felt a rush of gratitude, which brought the lights even closer. They began to gleam, lighting the way. Savitri found that she wasn't lost. In fact, her hut was close by, and with determined steps, led by a flickering host of lights, she headed home.

HOW TO MAKE AN ANGEL

Drawing a sharp line between real and unreal ignores how consciousness really works. If you say to me, "I have a guardian angel," I can interpret that statement through several states of awareness. You could mean:

> I imagine I have a guardian angel.
> My religion teaches me that I have a guardian angel in heaven.
> I have read eagerly in the mythology of angels, and the one that
>   attracts me is the guardian angel.
> I see my guardian angel and experience its presence.
> Having a guardian angel is my cherished wish.
> I saw my guardian angel in a dream.

Certain states of awareness, such as dreams and imagination, are accepted in our society, but they press close to other states that modern people often relegate to superstition, such as seeing departed spirits and having holy visions. Yet I've met too many people who tell me soberly of having saints appear to them in meditation, and others who have been visited by gurus, the archangel Michael, Jesus, Buddha, ancient Tibetan lamas, and incarnations of themselves. Access will not be denied.

Other cultures have felt more comfortable navigating the subtle dimension than we do; our tendency is to wall this region off from the physical world and to make arbitrary judgments, like the following:

People who see angels are imagining things.

Dreams are illusory, so every other subtle phenomenon is an illusion also.

If you see or hear anything that isn't physical, you must be hallucinating.

Seeing a god or angel is the equivalent of seeing a UFO. Both are outside normal experience.

Sacred visions are the result of organic diseases like epilepsy or paranoid schizophrenia.

Yet, to create in consciousness is our greatest gift, and what we create continues to evolve. If you open yourself without judgment to your role as a creator, you gain much more freedom. Genesis doesn't have to be a far-off event that put the universe into play. It can be a constant event that renews itself at every moment.

A great work of art can begin in a dream, a vision, or an inspirational moment. It gestates in the invisible reaches of the imagination, but then the artist begins to shape it in clay or on a canvas. The *Mona Lisa* needed an audience, and that audience had to think that painting was important. The painting had to inspire viewers with its beauty, and as it did, it gained fame, appreciation, and understanding. Eventually, if an artwork is supreme, a whole culture adores it. The word "angel" could be substituted for "Mona Lisa" without much change. Being a work of art, a human product, the *Mona Lisa* doesn't stir our skeptical nature, but since we can't observe ourselves creating angels,we aren't as accepting of the process. The next step, then, is to unfold that process in detail.

The mechanism by which angels are created is called projection. In the field of psychology this term is often used pejoratively, as a synonym for hanging a subjective state on an object outside ourselves. Instead of being able to accept their own negative emotions, for example, people frequently project them onto others. Consider these familiar exchanges:

> *I don't think you love me anymore.* You're just projecting. Of course I do.
>
> *There's a noise outside. I'm sure it's a burglar.* You think every noise is something dangerous. You're just projecting.
>
> *If I go to the party next week without losing ten pounds, everyone will think I'm disgusting.* Stop projecting. You look fine.

Projection can get complicated. A society that feels endangered can project wild fantasies. Muslim fundamentalists project a West that is corrupt, unholy, and decadent, while Christian fundamentalists project an Islam that is barbaric, fanatical, and godless in return. Projection is "successful" when we no longer can see reality but have created a false version based on fear, hostility, anxiety, or insecurity—any negative emotion for which we refuse to take responsibility. Projection also can be positive, as it is when a smitten lover sees perfection in the object of his love, although to friends and family the beloved remains an ordinary creature of flesh and blood.

Vedic rishis said that projection is the mechanism by which consciousness created reality. We are all familiar with this because the movie business depends entirely on projection. In Hollywood, a star is an actor who has crossed the dividing line between reality and projection. When Tom Cruise stops to help a stranded motorist change a tire, or when Jennifer Aniston goes out on a date, it's worldwide news.

Why? Because stars are projected into a superhuman dimension. Their smallest gesture is significant beyond reason. If you or I help someone change a tire, it's not a feat of heroism; if a young woman goes out on a date, the Goddess of Love hasn't entered the world. Projection is a recipe for turning the human into the superhuman, and the natural into the supernatural. Here are some of its ingredients:

Symbolism: Our projection must stand in for something deeper and more significant.

Desire: Our projection must fulfill a wish or need that cannot be fulfilled directly.

Fantasy: Our projection must operate in the realm where physical constraints don't hold sway.

Myth and archetype: Our projection must be universal in meaning.

Idealism: Our projection must connect us to higher values.

These requirements can be met only in the consciousness of a creator. A fireman who rescues a child from a burning building isn't a hero. He's just a man in a fireproof coat who runs into flames as part of his job. Heroism is created by projecting the necessary ingredients:

The fireman *symbolizes* a protecting father.

He fulfills our *desire* to be rescued from peril.

In *fantasy* he is more powerful than the fire. He defeats it in personal combat.

He fits the *myth* of the great warrior and the prince who rescues the maiden in distress.

We *idealize* him as heroically masculine. Firemen don't just do a job—they live up to our manly ideal.

Without projection we wouldn't see firemen the way we do, and they wouldn't see themselves that way either. This is a good example of how we first create the projection and then participate in it. Society is constantly caught up in the rise and fall of its projections. Sports figures who take drugs become fallen heroes; soldiers in battle step into hell; movie actresses are goddesses until their next extramarital affair, which turns them into home wreckers. People we deem larger than life have learned how to manipulate symbols, fantasies, ideals, and myths. The most successful products in the marketplace do this as well.

However, these superficial examples of projection hide a profound power inside all of us. Our entire culture has been built upon projection, and at this moment you and I are continuing the process. *Projection creates meaning.* By themselves, events are meaningless until we give them value. Think of the many deaths we see on the television news. Some deaths feel meaningless to us because they seem so remote. But if we attach value to a person, everything changes. Certain phrases—"somebody's child," "cancer victim," "a soldier who loved his country"—cause us to project a positive meaning. Other phrases—"insurgent," "escaped convict," "gang member"—flip meaning to the negative side. It could be the same death in question, since everyone is someone's child, for instance. We react to information (which often comes prepackaged with spin included) so quickly that we lose sight of the power we are exerting as creators.

Everything that is real at one level of consciousness is unreal at another.

If you want to make an angel, you must project it, but to do that, you must be in a state of consciousness that accepts angels as real. In India there's a specific region called *Devaloka,* where angels abide, but it's not the same as heaven. Devaloka is often portrayed like heaven— a place in the clouds where ethereal beings float—but it's understood that all Lokas, or other worlds, are layers of consciousness. Therefore angels are part of the whole self system.

The rishis tell us that any one projection affects all the Koshas. While we are creating in the material world, we are affecting every level of consciousness and therefore every level of creation. Meaning is never isolated. Angels exist because they have been projected in consciousness. Just as a movie requires an image, a projector, and a viewer, so do angels. In terms of Vedanta three elements are involved:

The seer or observer is *rishi.*
The process of projecting is *devata.*
The thing projected is *chhandas.*

In a movie house the audience is the rishi, the machine run by the projectionist is the devata, and the images on the screen are the chhandas. It's not so important to remember these terms, but ancient sages hit upon a universal rule of consciousness, called three-in-one. If you occupy any of these roles—seer, seen, or the process of seeing— you occupy all of them. These modest-sounding words have the potential to revolutionize the world.

If you are blankly looking at the world, it has power over you, because you are passive and the world is doing everything to you. If you engage in a process—going through a divorce, driving to work, cooking a meal—you are a bit closer to power, but the process has its own momentum and can overwhelm you. If you are the object being seen—a rich man, a beautiful woman, a preacher, a criminal—those objective labels give you status and meaning, but you have given yourself over to others, the ones who make labels and stick them on people. Only in the unity of all three roles do we achieve our complete power as creators.

At the soul level all three roles are enfolded into unity. That's why, paradoxically, God is the Creator and his creation. Once he projects his creation outward, unity turns into diversity. This is Vedanta's equivalent of the Big Bang. When the creator begins to look at himself, instantly there is a three-in-one state. An observer (rishi) beholds an object (chhandas) through the process of observation (devata). As soon as the three emerge, the entire universe emerges with them; the matter dispersed by the Big Bang is only one facet of an invisible mechanism in which the creator suddenly sees what's possible, and in that seeing the possible comes true in infinite variety. We shouldn't be surprised that the entire universe contains only 4% visible matter and energy, the remaining 96% being so-called dark matter whose function seems to be that it holds the visible universe together in some mysterious way. The "Creator" doesn't have to be a person; it can include the invisible field from which everything visible is organized and upheld.

The three-in-one state wouldn't matter if it didn't affect everyday reality, but it does. Seeing is enough to create. The "observer effect," as it is called in physics, literally creates matter: It takes an observer to turn the invisible energy state of an electron into a specific particle located in time and space. Before the observer effect takes place there is no electron; there is only the possibility of one. Our eyes cannot detect it, but we are immersed in a sea of possibilities. Every possible electron that could ever exist is here right now. We pluck electrons out of the sea of possibilities simply by looking. Somehow the Vedic rishis understood this astonishing fact. How? Because they watched the process firsthand, not with electrons, but with the rise and fall of events, which are so fluid that to them it was no more than a dream.

Is this really believable? The spookiest thing about the observer effect is that when you see a single electron, all other electrons are affected. This makes sense only in a universe where there are no single electrons, only a vast, all-encompassing web of charges, positions, spins, and points in—which is exactly the view on which theoretical physics is converging. The Vedic sages called themselves rishis (seers) because to them everything comes back to the observer, the seer. Seeing is the ultimate creative act.

The Devata Effect

The mystery of creation lies in the gap between the observer and the observed. Angels exist in this gap; they are the processors of consciousness, and thus, to use a biblical term, the servants of God. Devata, the Sanskrit word for this process, has its root in *deva,* which means angel. Devas are more than messengers; they are agents of creation. They carry out the bidding of the creator, and since the creator does nothing but observe, devas stand for the active aspect of seeing, which is hidden. It would be fair to say that everything we've ascribed to projection belongs instead to the devata effect, the ability of consciousness to turn invisible impulses into physical reality. The devata effect regulates every level of reality, and angels therefore appear in all the Koshas.

In the *physical dimension* angels appear as visitors and guides. They deliver messages from God or offer help in times of crisis.

In the *vital dimension* angels sustain Nature by breathing life into creation. They serve as builders of form; they give each living thing an essential connection to Nature.

In the *mental dimension* angels appear in visions and dreams. They embody the mind of God and connect it to our thoughts.

In the *ego dimension* angels serve as personal guides and guardians.

In the *dimension of bliss* angels surround God and praise Him constantly. They embody joy in its most exalted state.

All five levels share the need for communication. The creative impulse must cascade from one level to the next. Angels are really symbols for how information gets passed along and organized. The reality beneath the symbol is the devata effect. Let me offer a concrete example that might get us closer to understanding this hidden reality.

I know a woman who earns her living from angels. Her name is Lily, and she first became aware of angels at a birthday party when she was three or four. "My mother turned off the lights so I could blow out the candles on my cake. I looked around and noticed these people standing around the edge of the room. They weren't there when the lights were on. I pointed to them, only to discover that nobody else could see them. But I remember that they made me feel very happy."

Lily's first encounter was the most physical one. After her mother discouraged her from seeing "people" where there were none, they quickly disappeared. Lily was still aware of their presence, however, and as she grew up she learned to adapt to this presence. Eventually "the guys," as she called them, became images she could see when she closed her eyes, and voices she could hear when she asked questions.

"They weren't constant voices," she says. "I never considered them hallucinations. I had to consciously call on the guys, and when I did I felt a comfort, a guiding wisdom. I know most people don't make contact with their own guides, but I can see theirs, too. We all have them."

This ability, which the rishis would say belongs in the world of "consciousness filled with subtle objects," came and went in Lily's life. A great deal seemed to depend on where she found herself. Right after college she had a brief marriage to a man who discouraged Lily from contacting "the guys," and after their divorce Lily held an office manager's job for fifteen years that needed little inner guidance. But eventually she was led to think about the issue of healing.

"The guys told me that I could heal people emotionally, and that they'd help. At first this made me nervous. But I kept noticing how painful it is for many people when they are faced with their old wounds. The guys told me it didn't have to be that way. They would show me how to move the trapped energies of pain and trauma. I could learn to do this without the person feeling anything stressful. That appealed to me deeply."

By the time she turned forty, Lily had begun her healing work in earnest. She started out with friends with whom she could freely talk about "the guys." As the work deepened, she began to use the phrase "higher guides and angels" to fit what she saw.

"I'm a conventional person in many ways. When I'm not tuning in to the level where I do my work, my life is completely ordinary. It took me years to think of the guys as angels, but then they showed me the archangel Michael. I brought in the presence of Christ to help me. I tell people that they are energetically connected to God. It's become very natural now because I can see everything I talk about."

Outside the boundaries of the reality, on which we generally agree, people like Lily exist and always have. Lily brings us to a critical point in our investigations. It doesn't matter if we try to settle the argument over whether angels are real or unreal, whether they are here on earth or far away in heaven. Our own consciousness regulates what is real and unreal; we have stepped into our own projection. If that projection consists of physical objects only, to the exclusion of subtle objects, it's nevertheless a self-creation. You and I exist not as observer, or observed or the process of observation but all three at once. To deny this is to deny our wholeness, and the power that is our birthright.

"I have various ways of seeing people," Lily says. "I see them physically, but even then I sense their energy. When I go inside, I see their energy as a field of light around them. That's the basic reality, but if I ask to, I can also see their angels and other etheric beings. Some of these are very negative. They've been drawn to the person by negative beliefs. I can see people as they were in other lifetimes, and to a limited extent I can see them in the future. It's all very fluid, but it's all accessible."

Twenty years ago I knew no one with subtle sight like Lily; now I've met many of them. Each has learned to ignore the boundary that society sets between one level of life and another. At the soul level we are free to do whatever we want with the potential given to us. Angels are not absolutes; they have changed over history as human imagination has changed. This creative project of ours goes back millennia, and it continues to this day.

When you die, how much of what happens will be your choice and how much will be left to outside forces? Lily herself is clear about this. She and "the guys" could work together without interruption by physical death. In this way Lily is doing consciously what we are all doing unconsciously. Thanks to the devata effect, we *are* the process of creation. Through us, gods, angels, and souls come in and out of being. Lily says, "When I started out on this work a lot of my vocabulary was Christian, because from early on I felt very close to Jesus. Then I began to experience him as the Christ presence, without any picture in my head. I discovered that there was an esoteric name for the universal Christ, which is Sananda, and the guys told me I could use that when I wanted to relate to the cosmic Christ. Now even Sananda has become more abstract, like a field of compassionate light."

I asked Lily what might come next for her.

"That's the big question, isn't it? At some level I know I don't really need the guys. They're just aspects of myself. If I wanted to, I could just ask myself what needs to be done and rely on my own abilities. That's the next stage."

If she knows it is all herself, I asked, what keeps her from moving on to the next stage right now?

"Habit, maybe some residual fear that I haven't faced. You've got to remember, the guys have been with me all my life. I imagine I'll hold on to them until I'm comfortable enough to be on my own."

We are all at some stage of taking responsibility for participating in creation. Gods and goddesses, angels and etheric beings exist because they have been drawn out of the raw material of consciousness. The workshop where this creation takes place is Akasha, the field of consciousness. The artisans in charge are those with enough awareness to do the job. I'd like to propose that even if you don't feel competent to make a god, you can at least teach yourself to make an angel.

I once interviewed a man who had remarkable healing abilities, and he was very modest about them. He told me, "I could teach you to do the same thing in a few days." When I replied that I doubted that, he said, "It's actually very simple. The hard part is removing your belief that you *can't* heal." The same holds true for almost everything. We spend our whole lives projecting a dream, stepping into it, and believing the dream is real. See yourself as the one who is doing all three, and suddenly the world of angels becomes as real as this world of solid things.

THE DREAM CONTINUES

HOW DOES SAVITRI'S tale end? The sun had already dipped beneath the treetops when she ran back into her hut and peered out the front window. Yama was still sitting in the dust, only now the long shadows of the pines completely covered him. Savitri braced herself, saying one last prayer, and went out to face him.

And then? In one version Savitri puts on a great show of welcoming Yama. The Lord of Death is so pleased that he grants her a boon. Savitri asks for the boon of life, which confuses Yama. "You are already alive," he points out. But Savitri insists, and Yama grants her wish. Savitri rises to her feet, saying, "You have given me life, but I cannot live without Satyavan." At which point Death is outwitted and must give her husband a reprieve.

But not everyone is satisfied with such a simple trick. I can tell you what I believe. Savitri had conquered all her fears, and so she went outside and danced for Yama. She danced so exquisitely that when she ended up with her head resting in his lap, she whispered, as one lover to another, "Time isn't long enough to satisfy my longing for you."

To which the enchanted Yama replied, "But we have eternity together." Savitri shook her head. "If you are all-powerful, add one second to eternity so that I can love you more than anyone has ever loved. That's all I ask."

Yama had never been offered any kind of love, certainly not by a young woman who had every reason to fear him. So he granted Savitri a single second more—and thus he was defeated.

How?

A second to the gods is a hundred years to mortals. In that extra second Satyavan returned home and embraced Savitri. They went inside their hut and lived as before. They had children and grew old together. In time Savitri's father, the king, relented and welcomed them both back to his palace. And in her old age Savitri wondered if she had asked for too much time, because she survived long after Satyavan left this world. She spent her final years in meditation and became enlightened, so when the extra second was up, Yama was amazed to find that Savitri hadn't tricked him after all. She actually did love him as one loves the wholeness of life rather than one aspect alone.

This ending is beautiful and consoling. I would like it to be read when I have no more days left. In the spirit of Savitri I've already written this note, which I will leave for my family to read. *No matter what, don't cry for me. I'm all right, and I'll go on loving you no matter what happens. This is my road to travel.*

Every once in a while I look at the words for a moment. Somehow, like Savitri, I've won nothing more than an extra second of existence. It will be enough.

REINCARNATION

Making an angel isn't the ultimate accomplishment of consciousness. Making a new life out of nothing is. This ability is known as reincarnation. The popular notion of reincarnation is simple: we die and come back as somebody else. But how does the soul clothe itself in a new personality in order to be reborn? In a culture like India, where reincarnation has a strong foundation, people want to know why they are born with certain karmic tendencies, and whole groups in society—astrologers, priests, philosophers, gurus—exist to explain the process whereby Karma attaches itself to a soul and gives rise to a new lifetime of experience.

Most people are aware that Tibetans expect their religious leaders, including the Dalai Lama, to reincarnate as a baby who will give signs of his identity. These babies are almost always born in Tibet, but there are cases where they can appear in Europe; for example, about a decade ago the search for a great lama led Tibetan investigators to a family in Spain. In India noted religious figures are often matched to illustrious predecessors; Mahatma Gandhi has been linked by his followers to great gurus in the past. Who is to say which match is valid? The subject becomes very complicated.

There are Native American tribes in which five or six children may be born who have vivid recollections of having the same mother in a prior lifetime. There are similar instances in Japan of children who remember identical experiences in a past life in World War II, as if a single soldier's soul fragmented into pieces, each of which was reborn separately. Experts in "soul regression," which takes a person back one lifetime after another, claim that memories blend and become absorbed. Thus a great personage like Cleopatra or Napoleon affects the recollections of an entire society, and people in later lifetimes remember being Napoleon when in fact their lives were simply touched by him in some powerful way.

People can become fascinated by the game of "Who was I in a prior lifetime?" or even "Didn't I meet you in a former life?" But I've known others who cover their ears when they hear the word "reincarnation," distressed by the notion that they might be reborn as a pig or a dog. Reincarnation offends Christian theology, which doesn't permit a second chance for redemption after this lifetime. Reincarnation is more forgiving. Mistakes can be corrected; whole lifetimes can be redeemed, not in heaven but by trying on a new body and repeating the same events that produced failure, sin, or lack of fulfillment the first time around.

Without reincarnation we might have the mistaken idea that the universe is ruled by death. Within a few milliseconds of the Big Bang 96% of the matter and energy that emerged from the void collapsed back into it. The remaining fraction still winks in and out of existence, but so rapidly that matter looks solid and permanent. In fact everything solid is transitory; every particle in existence is oscillating in and out of the void, giving the illusion of solidity because our senses aren't quick enough to catch the vibration. The new particle that emerges is never exactly the same as the one that vanished, which is how nature manages time, location, electrical charge, spin, and other basic properties that require stability and change simultaneously.

The same is true for you and me. We exist as a fluid product of change and stability. Our brains look the same from moment to moment, but the activity of neurons is never exactly the same— a brain is like a river where one cannot step into the same place twice. DNA reincarnates when the genes of one parent split in half in an act of creative suicide to join with the genes of the other parent. The very fact that DNA can replicate itself doesn't involve the death of the mother cell, but produces new genetic material that leads to new flesh, and the root word of incarnation means flesh, from the Latin *carneus.*

Humans have ambiguous feelings about the fact that we are made of flesh. It befits us as mammals but becomes more complicated when we consider the dimension of spirit. Seeing how the flesh ages and decays, how it betrays us with illness, one may not be happy to get a new body after death—for some of us one body may have been enough. Certainly Christianity takes that position, its rationale being that the flesh is innately corrupted by sin, and therefore it is far better to be clothed in the soul after death than to go through recycling.

The East has managed to live comfortably with reincarnation for several reasons. If the universe is constantly re-creating itself, we would be the only aspect that isn't involved, which doesn't make sense. And psychologically, if I can come back again into a new body, I may be able to fulfill desires and ambitions that were thwarted in this lifetime, which is consoling. Even more consoling is the possibility of meeting loved ones I've lost (or never gained, if my love wasn't returned). Reincarnation offers hope for social advancement: a slave in this lifetime might come back as a noble in the next. Finally, the cosmic system of birth and rebirth has an evolutionary impulse behind it: step-by-step, each soul rises higher in the soul's progress to God.

Perhaps it is not a question of belief, East versus West. Reincarnation may be a question of choice. Consciousness is useful. We shape it according to our desires. Rather than being the final word, the denial of reincarnation by Christianity could be simply a collective choice. Having considered all the relevant factors, a large sector of humanity says, "I don't want to come back to this place," while another says, "I do." All we can say for certain is that Nature depends on the mechanism of rebirth.

Choosing to Come Back

The rishis made every aspect of the afterlife a choice. What you choose becomes real, what you don't choose becomes unreal. But this sounds baffling. Does reincarnation take place, or doesn't it? Child psychologists are aware that there's a critical period, usually between infancy and eight to ten years old, when some children seem to remember prior lives. In a recent, highly publicized example, a boy became obsessed with fighter planes from World War II. He wanted to visit airfields to see them, he cut out pictures of them, and when he ran across a book about the fierce air battle off Iwo Jima in the waning days of the war in the Pacific, he announced to his parents that he had died then.

Startled as his parents were by the boy's absolute conviction, they assumed that he was exercising his imagination, until their son crossed a shadowy line and began to name people and dates. He remembered his former name and the moment when a Japanese machine gun shot his plane down. The parents tracked down the incident and discovered that indeed an American pilot by that name had been shot down in the manner described; survivors in the Air Force attested to the details recalled by their son.

Such recollections are more common in India, where a general belief in reincarnation removes the initial shock and disbelief that might lead people to keep such stories to themselves. One reads in the news of children who demand to be taken to a nearby village, which they recall vividly as their last home. Once they return, it's not unknown for the child to be reunited with relatives or even former parents. Psychologists inform us that this intense interest in former incarnations is temporary; beyond age ten the old memories fade and lose their obsessive quality. It's as if some souls take a while to get adjusted to their new place in time and space.

The most detailed study of such children comes from the psychiatrist Ian Stevenson at the University of Virginia. Working from more than 220 case studies of children who vividly remember past lives—the number is increasing all the time—Stevenson discovered that the most startling are those who carry physical characteristics from one lifetime to another. There are 14 examples of children who remember being shot to death in a previous life and whose bodies show a scar as if a bullet had entered the body, with an opposing exit scar. One child born in Turkey had vivid recollections, almost from the moment of being able to speak, of a notorious criminal who had been cornered by the police and committed suicide rather than be captured. The criminal had shot himself under the chin, and this child had a round red scar in exactly the same place. Stevenson was curious about an exit scar, and when he parted the child's hair he found a round, hairless scar on the scalp at the top of the head.

Children who remember past lives show a marked similarity in behavior, according to Carol Bowman, another researcher in the field. They speak of their past life very early on, sometimes from the age of two, and typically they stop around age seven. The children speak matter-of-factly about dying. They may be frightened of certain things associated with violent death, but usually their affect isn't emotional. They often sound like small adults and have quite detailed memories. They can make startling comments, such as the following reported to Dr. Stevenson by various children:

"You're not my mommy/daddy."
"I have another mommy/daddy."
"When I was big, I . . . [used to have blue eyes/had a car, etc.]."
"That happened before I was in Mommy's tummy."
"I have a [wife/husband/children]."
"I used to . . . [drive a truck/live in another town, etc.]"
"I died . . . [in a car accident/after I fell, etc.]"
"Remember when I . . . [lived in that other house/was your daddy, etc.]"

Such children talk just as matter-of-factly about the afterlife. About half of the 220 studied by Stevenson said that they didn't go directly to heaven but had to wait in another place first, which corresponds to the "crossing over" phase. They report making decisions about their next lifetime once they got to heaven, choosing a new family and new challenges. As one girl put it, "Heaven isn't easy. You have to work there."

Because they are often so young, children who report past lives are the strongest evidence that reincarnation isn't just a cultural artifact. There is also the convincing matter of convergence: all three categories of witnesses—children who remember past lives, people who have had an NDE, and people who have experienced being out of their bodies generally—agree on how the afterlife works.

Out-of-body experiences are much more common than we suppose, and a few people have mastered them to the point that they become "astral tourists." F. Holmes Atwater of the Monroe Institute is one of several researchers in the field, and his subjects often report experiences that take them into the Akashic field, including those domains we associate with dying. What they see is completely consistent with NDEs and children who remember a past life. One child told her parents that God doesn't speak in words or in a language like English or Spanish. This is consistent with the esoteric belief that communication takes place on the astral planes by telepathy. People returning from near-death also say that what they heard or learned came to them without speech, often through instantaneous insight or revelation.

Are these children exceptional because they remember a past life, or are the rest of us abnormal in not remembering who we once were? I think neither answer is right, exactly. The function of memory is closely attached to strong emotions. Few people can remember what they had for dinner on a Tuesday last month, but if that dinner was the occasion for proposing marriage to someone you loved, it can be recalled for years. Similarly, these children seem to remember being wrenched from their old life, and this powerfully negative memory carries over beyond the boundary of death. Dr. Stevenson records one instance where a child was born with a pattern of red dots on his chest and had memories of pain from a fatal shotgun blast.

On the other side, however, it would be emotionally barren if we remembered everything that ever happened to us. The pioneering

Soviet neurologist Alexander Luria had one such patient, a journalist he called S., who had total recall. He could sit in a crowded press conference and afterward remember every word spoken by each person in the room. But S. was an emotional blank and lacked the ability to understand poetry, symbols, and metaphors—for him, every event was a literal fact recorded on a mental tape. (When Luria asked him if sorrow ever sat heavy on his mind, S. replied matter-of-factly that sorrow doesn't weigh anything.)

Memory is erased in many ways, one of the most typical being retrograde amnesia. We see this phenomenon in victims of automobile accidents and war. A person who loses consciousness after being hit by a car or struck down by a bullet can remember everything up to the moment of impact, but not beyond. After waking up in the hospital wondering *What happened to me?* the patient or soldier tries to fill in a gap in time based on guesswork. *If I am in a hospital and my arm is broken, I must have been hit by a car.*

Reincarnation creates a similar gap in memory, except for those few who carry recollections over from one life to the next. In the space between lifetimes identity is reshaped; somehow we change completely, and at the same time we continue as who we are. The afterlife, then, is a kind of transformation chamber. On a cool fall day, if you stroll outside, you might find a chrysalis hanging from a twig. The pupa inside was once a caterpillar and in time it will reincarnate as a butterfly. To do so, every cell in the caterpillar must be transformed. In its pupal stage the insect is shapeless organic goo. That caterpillar melts and reshapes itself at the same time. Its old physical identity is erased entirely. All insects that move from larvae to fully grown adults do something similar, and just as caterpillars bear almost no resemblance to a butterfly, a dragonfly nymph stalking the bottom of a pond for minnows bears no resemblance to its final stage, nor a maggot to a housefly.

For insects, reincarnation is a creative leap that doesn't involve conscious choices, since the information encoded in the insect's genes produces the same transformation generation after generation without variance. Countless monarch butterflies are clones of the original butterfly millions of years ago. Human DNA, however, manufactures new people, each of whom feels unique. Uniqueness in physical structure is only the beginning. We emerge from the transformation chamber not just a bit unique, the way one chimpanzee or dachshund might differ from another, but totally free to create ourselves from the inside, using desires, hopes, dreams, beliefs, and aspirations, all the tools available in consciousness.

The Vedic rishis would argue that consciousness governs this whole machinery—reincarnation is just a variation on the theme of time and place, producing new talents and interests. As the rishis saw it, reincarnation is a creative leap that recombines old karma, good and bad, in a unique combination. The new lifetime and the old are joined inexorably by millions of karmic links, yet for the most part the person being reborn feels that he is something totally new.

This is where a creative leap comes in, according to the rishis. Think of it like money in the bank: you may have only $500, but you are free to spend it any way you choose. In karmic terms cause leads to effect, and as long as that chain holds, event A is forged to event B. A universe without cause and effect would be chaotic. If you drop a ball, gravity makes it fall downward toward the earth, and this result is so reliable that it can be reduced nearly to a certainty. If Karma were just as certain, there would be no need for reincarnation, because the karmic balance at the end of a lifetime would be as reliable as the cocoon that produces monarch butterflies from a larva, not monarchs one spring and swallowtails the next.

Karma isn't predictable, however. People perform all kinds of actions and reap completely different results from the seeds they sow. It's disillusioning that evil deeds go unpunished and virtue is overlooked, that bad things happen to good people all the time. The Vedic rishis did not mark this down to the vagaries of a whimsical Providence. Karma is unpredictable, they said, for the same reasons that consciousness is unpredictable:

Creativity is innate.
Uncertainty allows new forms to emerge.
The unknown contains infinite possibilities, of which only a
    fraction appear in the known world.
Nature is change and stability at the same time.

These are the basic tenets of Karma, and what's most fascinating is that we are held together not by inexorable mechanics but by a deep commitment to uncertainty and the creative leaps that result from that.

Reincarnation is how consciousness becomes new even as it uses materials that can never be created or destroyed. That is the wonder of it. Infinite change and infinite stability coexist—this is also the mystery we have to solve before reincarnation can be fully understood.

Karma on the Brain

Karma may turn out to be the key to understanding the brain itself. Neurologists are puzzled over what they call "the binding effect," a mysterious force that pulls different areas of the brain together. Recent advances in brain imaging show that it takes several regions of the brain to cooperate in any thought, feeling, or sensation. Say you walk into a room, recognize your mother, and ask her if she remembers the recipe for the birthday cake she made for your tenth birthday. Your brain isn't jumping from one area that recognizes who she is to another that wants to ask a question to a third that remembers your past birthdays. The whole brain assigns these tasks to several areas all at once, and the mystery is how this happens.

If the brain had a high-speed telephone system to send messages whizzing from place to place, the binding effect would be explained as a series of sequential commands. But neurons act simultaneously. Point A and point B light up at the same time, leaving no interval for a back-and-forth signal. Moreover, the brain is capable of infinite combinations that have little or no relationship with one another.

Every thought, then, is an activity of the whole brain. Even though a CAT scan might be able to visualize the exact clump of neurons in the brain where a murderous thought arises in a criminal mind and to a kindly thought in a saintly mind, it's the whole brain that differentiates a criminal from a saint. It takes an entire brain to oversee all the traffic that coordinates a hundred billion independent neurons, making sure that they all tie in to an infinite, teeming conversation. If I want to perform an act of kindness, my brain might provide me with a simple thought, such as, *I should donate to disaster relief.* This single thought requires the following:

A moral sense of right and wrong
Memories of what it's like to be helpless and victimized
Empathy with fellow sufferers
A feeling of compassion
A sense of duty to society

These interlocked elements reside in various parts of the brain and represent unique patterns of activity. At the same time, at a deeper level my brain has to remain aware of who I am, my history of kind and unkind acts, my unconscious guilt, my awareness of role models who were also kind, etc. What's truly amazing is that the brain knows how to mesh all these ingredients instantly. It doesn't go to the wrong memory or feeling. It doesn't forget who I am, or provide me with bizarre distractions, unless I am mentally ill, in which case I could become completely untethered. In my inability to recognize that my thoughts are actually my own, I might think God is ordering me to give money to disaster relief.

I may be aware only of a single thought, yet what my brain does in support of that thought spans a much larger extent. (Neurologists estimate that a person is aware of about 2,000 bits of information per minute being processed by the brain. This sounds impressive, but outside our awareness the brain is actually processing 400 billion bits of information per minute. Miraculously, it remains in control of each one and filters out all but the tiny fraction that we require to be in the world and follow our train of thought and desire.)

I've gone into some detail here because if it takes the whole brain to produce one thought, it also takes the whole universe to perform a single action. Like a neuron, electrons and atoms seem to be independent, yet a change of electron spin at one extreme of the universe will be mirrored, instantly and without sending signals, by a paired electron billions of light years away. So the "binding effect" is cosmic as well as personal; it exists "in here" and "out there." The net result is that *you* are an activity of the whole universe, an insight that sounds abstract, but just as a single thought requires your brain to perform a huge number of unseen calculations, so Karma performs unseen calculations to produce you.

As we now can prove, change and stability coexist in the brain; without both it couldn't operate. When you remember an old birthday, you can call it "my" thought, but you feel no personal connection to synapses and dendrites or the firestorm of signals passing over them. Brain cells work by totally predictable means involving exchanges of electrical charges between sodium and potassium atoms and simple oscillations between positive and negative electrical impulses. Somehow that mechanical stability produces free, creative, unpredictable thought forms.

The rishis asserted the same about Karma. It is infinitely flexible and infinitely inflexible depending on how you look at it. Unknown forces are free to reshape you without your knowledge. They do it all the time, since none of us has the slightest awareness of how our brains move from thought A to thought B. Neurology is witness to the event, but that's far from knowing the how or why. Two people can say the word "apple," and their brains will exhibit the same pattern of activity. This pattern, however perfectly mapped, has no predictive value in telling us the next word each person will speak—event B could be any word, sound, or gesture, perhaps just silence.

This opens the question of how much choice we exercise over our next lifetime. It's not useful simply to say that Karma is flexible and inflexible at the same time. In fact, the coexistence of opposites is a paradox, and unless we solve it we have no control over the afterlife; we are just caught in the meshes of a machine that can produce any outcome according to its own whims.

From This Lifetime to the Next

We aren't in control of the afterlife for the same reason that we aren't in control of this life. We don't yet have enough consciousness. The gaps of ignorance of our full potential are too large, and whatever the gap claims turns into the unconscious. In Tibetan Buddhism one lifetime is firmly connected to another. When a lama dies, it's expected that his reincarnation will be found. Signs are left behind that link the two incarnations. On his return, the baby will recognize his old toys, for example, and the adults around him can determine beyond doubt that the chain of identity hasn't been broken.

This is the same as saying that Tibetans don't fall into the gap when they die. Continuity is preserved. The famous Tibetan Book of the Dead elaborates every detail of conscious dying, in the belief that a dying person should remain as connected as possible to the uninterrupted flow of awareness. To a Western reader the book is baffling; it describes so many gradations of awareness, so many possible destinations in the Bardo that it would take a lifetime of Buddhist practice to absorb all the possibilities. This is precisely the point, for Tibetans don't want to wander outside their belief system; it upholds who they are and where they are going on the path to liberation.

That's one example of tightly patterned choice, compared to which a Westerner is a reckless gambler. We do not typically try to hold on to unbroken consciousness, and although we may harbor a wish to come back to a lifetime closely resembling the one we left, it's just as likely that we may yearn for something completely new. In any event, we don't usually assume that our wishes matter. The business of heaven and hell will take care of itself, which means, ironically, that Westerners are more resigned about Karma than most people in the East, who always keep in the back of their minds some notion that Karma follows a person from lifetime to lifetime. For them, every action in this life reverberates into the next, and apparently random events in the present have their roots in decisions made in the past.

What this implies is that there are many ways to relate to Karma. You can choose to be as aware as you like, or as unaware. Karma glues events together, but that isn't the same as being fatalistic. In the East this point is often missed, and people commonly assume that bad actions are like crimes with set punishments while good actions earn fixed rewards. Logical as that sounds, it denies freedom of choice.

"I used to think that karma turned me into a kind of puppet," a friend of mine once remarked. "Having made millions of choices in the past, each one with its own consequence, how could I be free of them? Each bad choice jerks me one way, each good choice another. Fate holds the strings."

"How did you break free from that way of thinking?" I asked.

"I couldn't," he said. "But then one day it hit me. What does it matter if I'm a puppet? I can't feel the strings. I can't see anybody manipulating them. For all I know, every decision I make is mine and mine alone. I may still be fate's puppet, but what does it matter if I can't tell the difference?"

It's hard to argue with such pragmatism. Only afterward did I think about its flaws. If Karma is akin to the invisible working of the brain, we can't ignore it just because it's unseen. Our brains produce all kinds of disturbing and distorted thoughts. They can become imbalanced and throw us into depression or outright madness. They are subject to false perceptions and hallucinations, not to mention crippling disease, which may be treatable. More basically, what we say and do changes the brain. The hard wiring of neurons is altered by experience, so that the brain of someone who has suffered a terrible calamity, for example, becomes different from someone who hasn't. Positive and negative experiences condition the mind to see the world in a particular way, and the brain then adapts.

Let's apply this to reincarnation. At death the visible and invisible aspects of karma mesh. The standard version recounted in India goes like this: When you die you leave your body but remain aware of who you are. You may continue to see the room you died in; you retain the sensations of possessing a physical body for a time (traditionally, bodies remain untouched immediately after death in the belief that the deceased would continue to feel anything done to them).

Next, like a drowning man seeing his life pass before his eyes, one's karma unravels like thread coming off a spool, and the events of this lifetime march in review across the screen of the mind. You re-experience all your significant moments since birth, only this time with a vividness and clarity that shows you exactly what each one meant. Right and wrong are also clearly revealed, with no excuses or rationalizations. You become responsible for everything you did.

As these judgments are made—they are all self-judgments, not divine edicts—you find yourself in various Lokas, worlds that reflect the kind of reward or punishment that your actions deserve. A single soul is not assigned to one Loka forever but stays only as long as Karma dictates. During this passage, which encompasses worlds of pleasure and pain, you will learn about yourself and come to your own conclusions. No external force tells you what your life meant or how to proceed to the next step. You may suffer in a hellish Loka for what seems like eternity, or you could leave immediately. Time is purely subjective, and what you're actually experiencing is your own awareness working out its dilemmas and conflicts. *Why am I here? What makes me suffer? Do I deserve to suffer? Is there a way out?*

People who are disconnected from themselves will be as baffled by the afterlife as they are by the present. For them, cause and effect aren't clear. Feelings of being alienated, alone, victimized, tossed around by fate, out of control, or abused by authority clash with one another. In this fog of confusion they cannot take responsibility for their own motivations and desires, and the afterlife may frighten or baffle them.

Being disconnected is an illusion from the soul's perspective, and however long it may take, the person eventually prepares to leave the region of Lokas. Understanding, symbolized by light, begins to dawn. In clarity you realize that "I am" is your basis, not the things you did. You no longer identify with being a certain person; you now identify with being conscious, and what fills your mind is fresh possibilities. The karma you brought into the last lifetime has been exhausted, and fresh seeds of karma are ready to sprout.

Being reborn enters your mind gradually. For a long period (speaking subjectively) you experience bliss, or Ananda; you have gained pure being, which brings its own fulfillment regardless of any karma, good or bad. You find yourself in the same gap as the one between two thoughts, only this time you are aware of uncountable possibilities from which to choose. How do you choose the next life? Through the same process as choosing the next thought. We do this all the time, yet we don't know how we do it; the next thought emerges from the gap, the purely unknown.

You will witness as the dream of a new identity begins to clothe you, and you will fall into your next life in complete surrender to past actions that you still know almost nothing about. But all of us can take a more active role in how we reincarnate. In the gap, when every possibility confronts us, choice lies among those possibilities. The elaborate rituals in the Tibetan Book of the Dead aren't designed to get a kind person to a nice heaven and a better next lifetime. They are designed to make freedom of choice real, to bring the person fully aware into the gap so that karma can be shaped, controlled, or even fully resolved.

Freeing Yourself

What will it be like to find yourself in the gap? I'd like to answer that from personal experience. A year ago I was sitting on an airplane in a bewildered state of mind. During a short layover in the Midwest I found myself without something to read. I'd looked over the airport newsstand, but nothing on the racks appealed to me. When I boarded my next flight, intending to pass the time by writing, I discovered that my notebook and handheld computer had been packed away in a suitcase. Something—fate, circumstance, a clumsy oversight—had placed me alone for four hours.

Without notice or permission, a subtle mental voice started to guide me. It gave me a glimpse into how my mind works when it has no distractions around. What I saw was very basic. There is a thought in the mind and then another, and then another and another. Thoughts can be gripping or pass by unnoticed; they can be strong or weak, momentous or casual, frivolous or serious. The guiding voice pointed all this out in a few seconds.

Now, what is the proper way to relate to your mind? the voice asked. Should you always do what it says? Clearly not, for we have all kinds of thoughts that are irrelevant or fantastic. Should we ignore what it says? No again, because the mind gives us all the desires upon which we build our lives. *There is no single way to relate to the mind.* You can't take a stance that will always work. When people decide arbitrarily to be optimists, they may miscalculate when it comes to serious crises, evildoing, wars, personal conflicts, etc. If they decide arbitrarily to be pessimists, they will miss many opportunities for joy, fulfillment, hope, and faith.

My mental guide showed me this, and I was intrigued. It would appear that being spiritual is one stance that works, yet there are situations where even being spiritual—tolerant, loving, accepting, and detached from materialism—won't work at all. A parent can't simply accept and love a child addicted to cocaine, for example; active intervention is called for. A thousand other examples come to mind. Love won't defeat torturers; tolerance won't stop the excesses of fanatics. A person must find an infinitely flexible way to relate to the mind; otherwise something gets lost. The most precious gift of the mind—its total freedom—is the source of our creativity.

Now, my mental guide said, look at the world. Isn't it the same as the mind? The same unpredictability prevails, and therefore you cannot take a fixed attitude toward the world that works. People who are congenitally optimistic about the future are as shortsighted as people who are congenitally pessimistic. Go one step further. Karma is also unpredictable, and it too cannot be approached single-mindedly. To fight your karma is just as frustrating as accepting your karma.

At this point the sun had set and the plane cabin was empty and dark. I could see the last band of blue-orange light circling the horizon. My mental guide wasn't an accident or a daydream. I realized that for a long time I'd wanted to know *how it all works*. The answer is that mind, the world, and Karma are the same thing, perfect mirrors of one another. Their complexity is impossible to fathom. Their infinite connections can never be mapped out, and even if they could be, the next tick of the clock will bring a new, equally infinite set of possibilities.

That realization is as close as I've ever come to being in the gap where a new lifetime is chosen. The gap is pure freedom, and when you see that you are completely free, choices change. Some souls want to remain completely unattached; they choose Moksha, or liberation from a physical body and the karma it acts out. Other souls cherish Moksha but want to enjoy it while possessing a body. They choose to reincarnate with complete self-awareness—we call them enlightened. The rest of us fall somewhere else. We cherish being free, but we also want new experiences. So we let Karma weave a new story for us. We keep some self-awareness and sacrifice some. We agree to acquire amnesia about "I am" in exchange for the drama of being a separate person with likes and dislikes, challenges and opportunities.

The new life we clothe ourselves in will contain its unique measure of connection and disconnection. This is hardly the perfect way to relate to mind, Karma, and the world. The perfect way is freedom. But in our imperfect way we become part of a mystery. We accept a role in this fascinating play of light and darkness, and once again the physical world becomes our reality. We return to a belief that death is a fearful thing, that struggle is necessary, that pleasure is worth pursuing and pain worth avoiding. We forget the knowledge that our souls have, or that we had when we were in the gap. We keep only a bit of the truth close by so that we have something to aspire to. I have a feeling that we also keep a measure of sorrow for the decision we made to leave truth behind. Our half-truth has one virtue, however. As long as we believe in it, the soul will never give up on teaching us the rest. For that purpose, the dream continues.

Part Two

THE BURDEN
OF PROOF

UNTIL THIS CENTURY the burden of proof in spiritual matters lay with disbelievers. Religion had such a powerful hold upon the human imagination that for whole cultures—the ancient Egyptians and medieval Christians come to mind—the material world was much less real than the world of the gods or God. Most modern people can barely fathom this worldview, because we are as immersed in materialism as they were in idealism—the belief that nature begins in subtle realms of spirit. In idealism the earth is a lower world while heaven is higher. Thus everything about earthly life—its physicality, appetites, sexual drive, disease, suffering, and old age—is further from God or spirit than heaven.

Science did not overturn this view by disproving it. Idealism was simply outmoded by a new worldview—materialism—that was more practical. Materialism brought about technology, with its attendant comforts, and it explained many phenomena that religion preferred to regard as a mystery known only to God. Like any worldview, the old one overstepped its bounds when it claimed, for example, that diseases were acts of God to punish sinners. Once germs were discovered, this explanation seemed pointless and ultimately irrational. But by the same token, the new worldview would overstep its bounds, as it has today, when science claims that without physical proof we can abolish all notions of God, angels, ghosts, spirit, the soul, and the afterlife itself. Just as religion had no competency in physics and chemistry, science has no competency in spiritual issues.

The burden of proof has shifted, and now it is the believer who must prove that God and the soul are real. For many people, the triumph of materialism is so complete that even showing *why* we should care about God and the soul is a tough challenge.

If skepticism carries the day in some circles, in popular culture the burden still lies with proving that the afterlife *doesn't* exist. Consistently polls show that 90% of people believe in heaven, and almost that many believe they are going there. Belief in hell suffers a sharp decline to 75% and only 68% believe in the devil. This leaves most people in a quandary, dividing their allegiance between faith when it comes to spirituality and science when it comes to the material world. No less than Sir Isaac Newton was a devout Christian who wrestled his whole life with the schism he saw between science and metaphysics.

There is another way, however. In this book I've tried to present a view of the afterlife based on consciousness, and issues about consciousness can be settled, at least partially, through science. The evidence we're looking for isn't photographs of supernatural phenomena (these already exist in abundance but only lead to more skepticism). The most helpful evidence would be in support of the major claims that underlie Vedanta, which is consistent on its own terms. The primary claim, of course, is that reality is created from consciousness. We will have our proof if we can answer the following questions:

Is Akasha real?
Does the mind extend beyond the brain?
Is the universe aware?
Does consciousness have a basis outside time and space?
Can our beliefs shape reality?

These are fundamental questions that science has touched upon, even though few researchers had the afterlife in mind when they made their findings. It's fair to say that physics never set out to prove that the universe is self-aware. But so many mysteries remain unsolved if the universe *isn't* self-aware that cutting-edge theories are starting to include that once unthinkable idea.

Looking at unsolved mysteries is our best hope, in fact, because only those things that science hasn't explained offer room for radically new thinking. At present, neurology doesn't know how memory works, or how brain cells turn raw data into complex thought, or where identity is located. If we knew these things, there might be no need to speculate about "extended mind," the notion that thinking can occur outside the brain. Fortunately or not, we find ourselves with a rich store of enigmas that provide room for the Vedic rishis and their deep understanding of consciousness. On the frontier of many mysteries lies the answer to one mystery.

1 3

Is Akasha Real?

THE USE OF the word "Akasha" has lingered around the fringes of physics for at least a century. The reason for this is that an ancient and supposedly outmoded belief refuses to die—the belief that empty space is not empty at all. Akasha, the Sanskrit word for space, has an English equivalent: the ether. Up until a few generations ago, if you had gone to school and asked what filled the infinite void between the stars, you would have been told, whether in ancient Greece or medieval France or Harvard at the time of Abraham Lincoln, that pure emptiness isn't possible. An invisible ether that can't be seen or measured allows light to travel from the stars, as water allows ripples to spread when a rock is thrown into a pond. Without a medium to pass through, light waves have no way to move from point A to point B.

The ether suffered a decisive setback in the 1880s when two American scientists, Albert Michelson and Edward Morley, proved that light traveled at the same speed no matter what direction it moved in. This was important because the so-called "ether wind" that was thought to sweep energy through the universe should have made light travel slower going upstream than downstream. When Michelson and Morley proved that this wasn't true, even Einstein became convinced that space was a void without activity, a belief that was also wrong, as it turns out. Physicists now believe that space is full of activity in the form of invisible fluctuations in the quantum field. These so-called virtual fluctuations account for matter and energy and also for distortions in time and space. Thus, in a curious way the disproved notion of the ether has been revived indirectly.

To find out where matter and energy come from, physics wound up positing a universal field that envelops not just what we observe but everything that could possibly exist. Modern physics finds it easy to make the material world disappear into nothingness, but that is deeply disturbing, almost as disturbing as the disappearance of a dying person. Here is how the disappearing act of a rock, tree, planet, or galaxy works:

First, the rock, tree, or planet disappeared from sight when scientists realized that solid matter is made up of atoms that cannot be detected by the naked eye.

Second, atoms disappeared when it was discovered that they are made up of energy, mere vibrations in the void.

Finally, energy disappeared when it was found that vibrations are temporary excitations in a field, and that the field itself doesn't vibrate but maintains a flat, constant "zero point."

Theoretically, to reach the zero point in Nature one could cool empty space down to absolute zero, and instantly everything would cease to vibrate. Yet the zero point also exists here and now—it provides the starting point from which everything in the universe springs. Since matter and energy are constantly emerging and then vanishing back into the void, the zero point serves as the switching station between existence and nothingness. Newton had established that matter and energy cannot be destroyed, but they can oscillate in this shadowy way at the subatomic level, as long as the sum total of matter and energy isn't altered.

It wouldn't be so disturbing if this vanishing act was due to occur only when the cosmos dies billions of years from now by cooling down to absolute zero. Nor would it be so disturbing if matter only collapsed into the void theoretically. Such isn't the case, however. Matter and energy *have* to disappear. If they remained stable, which is how rocks, trees, and planets look to the eye, chaos would break loose. Matter would exist only as randomly floating particles in interstellar space. Exploded bits of the Big Bang would be flying apart at millions of miles an hour without any relationship to one another. There would be no forms, no evolution, no organization—in other words, no universe as we know it. At best, gravity could possibly pull together larger clumps of matter, but gravity is also a wave function that fluctuates around the zero point.

The fact that chaos doesn't totally dominate remains a huge mystery, which may only be solved by Akasha. Here the needs of physics and the Vedic rishis begin to converge in startling ways. The rishis were focused on consciousness as a universal principle. But to have a thinking universe, they needed to explain how the cosmic mind works, how it holds itself together and organizes itself into thoughts. If the "mind field" was totally stable, it would be a dead zone, or at best filled with a constant, meaningless buzz. Physics also needs to know how the universe holds itself together and organizes into coherent forms. Otherwise, the inconceivable fireball that appeared at the instant of the Big Bang would have blown itself apart, the way dynamite blows itself apart, without bothering to create forms along the way.

Physics was drawn, step-by-step, into the void because nothing in the visible world was adequate to explain what had to be explained. The zero point became an all-inclusive "field of fields" that encompasses every unseen, or virtual, particle in the universe. It was calculated that the zero point contained 10 to the 40th power more energy than the visible universe—that is, a one followed by forty zeros. The void turned out to be a seething exchange of energy, not just between photons and electrons but in every conceivable quantum event. Suddenly the unseen has become incredibly more powerful than the seen. But in what way is the "field of fields" like a mind, the thing the rishis were looking for?

Thinking, the basic operation of the mind, organizes reality to make sense. The universe does this physically. It forms complex systems. DNA is one example, but genes didn't create life simply by stringing simple molecules along a double helix. There are spaces between each genetic bit, and this sequencing is all-important. An amoeba differs from a human being in the sequence of carbon, oxygen, hydrogen, and nitrogen along its genes, not in the atoms themselves. The fact that empty spaces, or gaps, between genetic material are so important brings us back to the void, where *something* is arranging random events so that they are meaningful.

Once a form has been created, it has to be remembered in order to stay together. The universe remembers what it has created and meshes it with older systems. The Earth's ecosystem is a good example. Life-forms constantly relate to each other in exquisite balance. The oxygen given off by plants during photosynthesis, for example, would eventually poison the entire atmosphere, killing off all vegetation that needs carbon dioxide, were it not for the evolution of animals, which consume the oxygen and return carbon dioxide back to plants. This extremely complex balance can be traced back to the void, where every single fluctuation of virtual energy is passed along and absorbed by a virtual particle in need of energy. (As one popular writer has put it, it's as if the cosmos were passing along a penny, so that every time one particle is a penny poorer, another gets a penny richer.) The basic pattern is very simple, but when trillions of energy exchanges are involved every second, as they are with life on

Earth, the ecosystem's ability to keep one form separate from another, yet in dynamic relationship, is mind-boggling.

There are other things the mind can do that are paralleled in the universe. The mind can keep track of two events separated in time— this is how we recognize a face today that we saw years ago, for example. Similarly, the universe keeps track of any two paired electrons. They will be paired for all time even if they travel millions of light-years apart. Uncannily, if one of the paired electrons should change in position or spin, its twin will change simultaneously without sending a signal that needs to travel through space. The Zero Point Field communicates without regard for time, distance, or the speed of light.

The very fact that we use a word like "communicate" indicates how hard it is not to see parallels between our minds and Nature "out there." Which brings us to a dangerous trap. Mind and matter offer two ways of describing the same thing, but they are not, in themselves, exactly the same. If one could show that the universe has a memory, for example, that wouldn't prove it had a mind. Remembering a face is a mental act. The ability of two electrons to match each other's spin across a vast distance is a material feat. The same trap works in reverse. If one could calculate every vibration of a violinist's bow while playing a Beethoven sonata, that wouldn't explain music or its beauty. Those are mental phenomena, not material ones. All we can do is draw parallels between two models in an effort to place them in one reality.

I've been speaking as if the universe consciously knows what it is doing when DNA creates an amoeba, for example, instead of a chimpanzee or a human being. This implies self-awareness on the part of molecules, and that in turn requires the Zero Point Field to act like a mind as it organizes every possible fluctuation in the cosmos. No matter how closely one draws the parallels, this premise can't be proven—or disproven—because the Zero Point Field, by containing everything, contains us. We cannot step outside it, and so we are in the same position as a fish trying to prove that the ocean is wet. Unless the fish jumps out of the ocean, water is everywhere; there is no contrast, and therefore no dryness that makes wetness possible.

We cannot prove that the universe has a mind, because we aren't mindless. Nobody has ever experienced mindlessness; therefore, we have nothing to base it on. The Vedic rishis were fortunate that they started out believing that consciousness was real and needed no proof. Physics doesn't hold that consciousness is a given. To speak of a self-aware universe puts one at the fringes of speculative thinking in physics. But for our purposes in looking for evidence of the afterlife, it is vital to show that consciousness is everywhere, because then there would be nowhere to go after we die that *isn't* conscious.

Mind over Matter

What if our minds could alter the quantum field? Then we would have a link between the two models, mind and matter. Such a link was actually provided by Helmut Schmidt, a researcher working for the Boeing aerospace laboratory in Seattle. Beginning in the mid-Sixties, Schmidt set up machines that could emit random signals, with the aim of seeing if ordinary people could alter those signals using nothing more than their minds. The first machine detected radioactive decay from strontium 90; each electron that was given off lit up either a red, blue, yellow, or green light. Schmidt asked ordinary people to predict, with the press of a button, which light would be illuminated next.

At first no one performed better than random, or 25%, in picking one of the four lights. Then Schmidt hit on the idea of using expert psychics as his subjects, and his first results were encouraging: psychics guessed the correct light 27% of the time. But he didn't know if this was a matter of clairvoyance—seeing the result before it happened—or something more active, actually changing the random pattern of electrons being emitted.

So Schmidt built a second machine that generated only two signals, call them plus and minus. A circle of lights was set up, and each time a plus or a minus was generated, a bulb would light up. If two pluses were generated consecutively, the lights would go on in a clockwise direction. Two minuses would light up in a counterclockwise direction. Left to itself, the machine would light up an equal number of pluses and minuses; what Schmidt wanted his subjects to do was to will the lights to move clockwise only. He eventually found two subjects who had remarkable success. One could get the lights to move clockwise 52.5% of the time. An increase of 2.5% over randomness doesn't sound dramatic, but Schmidt calculated that the odds were 10 million to 1 against this occurring by chance. The other subject was just as successful, but oddly enough, his efforts to make the lights move clockwise had the opposite result: they moved only counterclockwise. Later experiments with new subjects raised the success rate to 54%, although the strange anomaly that the lights would sometimes go in the wrong direction persisted. (No explanation was ever found for this.) Schmidt showed that an observer can change activity in the quantum field using the mind alone, which supports the case that at some deep level mind and matter are one. The rishis' assertion that we are embedded in the Akashic field seems more credible, which also makes it more credible that we do not leave the field when we die; if we did, we would be the only thing in Nature that isn't part of the field.

Inspired by Schmidt's results, a Princeton engineering professor named Robert Jahn developed much more sophisticated trials, involving a machine that could generate zeros and ones five times a second. In the Princeton experiments, each participant went through three types of tests. First he would will the machine to produce more ones than zeros, then more zeros than ones, and finally he would try not to influence the machine at all. Each test was repeated until there were between 500,000 and 1 million results, a staggering number that in a single day outstripped all the previous trials performed by Schmidt and all the other parapsychologists before him.

After twelve years of study, it was found that roughly two-thirds of ordinary people could influence the outcome of the machine, unlike in Schmidt's study. These ordinary people, like his psychics, could will material changes, evoking more zeros than ones, more ones than zeros, about 51 to 52% of the time. This again may seem like a slim margin, but it turns out to defy chance by a ratio of a trillion to one. The solidity of the outcome is particularly radical because random chance is a bedrock of quantum physics, Darwinian evolution, and many other fields. (A dozen related follow-up studies also came up with results in the 51–52% range.)

If we accept that our minds are embedded in the quantum field and can change it, where does that leave us? We could be influencing the field a little bit—no more than a matter of slight coincidences, such as thinking of a friend's name and having that friend suddenly call on the phone—or at the other extreme, perhaps everything we call reality is manifested by consciousness, coaxed out of the field by intention. After examining this research in detail in her excellent book *The Field,* Lynne McTaggart sees the possibility of a complete revolution in consciousness theory: "On the most profound level, the [Princeton] studies also suggest that reality is created by each of us *only by our attention.* At the lowest level of mind and matter, each of us creates the world."

Jahn and his colleagues remained resolutely technical, however. They were baffled by their results, because if ordinary people could influence a machine, which part of the complicated machinery did they affect? Would we have to say that the mind actually changes the rate at which electrons are emitted? Just as important is the question, "So what?" If an ordinary person can make a machine generate more zeros than ones, does that really impact the big issues in science? In fact it does, in profound ways.

Does Akasha Explain Everything?

Akasha can be interpreted as the field through which the mind operates. Ervin Laszlo, a prominent Hungarian theorist on science and consciousness, has taken the bold step of introducing Akasha as the unifying answer to everything. After forty years of delving into cutting-edge theories in philosophy, biology, cybernetics, and physics, Laszlo found himself embracing the antiquated and discredited idea we discussed earlier: the ether. Physics had proven that light, unlike waves rippling across a pond, doesn't need a medium to travel in. When a photon starts at point A and moves to point B, the journey can be accomplished by the vanishing act discussed earlier: the first photon winks out of existence, changes its location somewhere in virtual reality (the Zero Point Field), and reappears intact in the second location. It doesn't slow down due to friction the way a rock skipping over the water's surface does. Moreover, in the instant that it is gone, the photon can "speak" to every other photon in the universe, coordinating its activity with every form in creation. I'm giving the scenario without any technical jargon in order to describe why physics threw out the ether—it simply wasn't needed in quantum calculations, not for half a century or more, during which time physics made enormous progress.

Then, according to Laszlo and other systems analysts, physics hit a wall. It couldn't explain *how* the universe managed to be so precisely coordinated. When matter and energy disappear into virtual reality, as they do thousands of times per second, things happen out of sight in some uncanny way. Time gets regulated; objects in space communicate their position, and seemingly random matter stays in touch with them. The Big Bang, which contained so much energy in a space millions of times smaller than an atom that billions of galaxies still express only 4% of it, occurred within a tiny window of possibility. If the expanding universe, moving at millions of miles per minute, had been off by a fraction of a second, the formation of stars and galaxies would have been impossible, because the momentum of the explosion would have exceeded the ability of gravity, the weakest force in nature, to halt it. Only the most delicate balancing act kept the push-pull of two forces so close together that they can dance together instead of tearing each other apart.

Randomness is a feeble explanation for such precision, Laszlo claims. (In the Princeton experiments, anyone who relied on randomness would be right only one in a trillion times.) Something so precisely organized requires a principle to hold it together and a medium to carry information from one end of creation to the other. The old notion of the ether doesn't suffice, but Akasha does. In his 2004 book, *Science and the Akashic Field,* Laszlo explains that Akasha is necessary, not as a medium for visible light but as a medium for invisible light, and invisible energy in general. Think of a jump rope nailed at one end to a wall. As the jump rope is turning, which stands for vibrating energy, follow the rope closer and closer to the wall. Every fiber now vibrates in a smaller and smaller range, until you reach the end point where the rope is nailed. That point isn't moving at all; it is the zero point, the beginning and end of energy. Zero isn't satisfactory, however, since quantum calculations already show that empty space is packed with infinite amounts of virtual energy, more per square centimeter than inside a star.

So think again about the point where the jump rope meets the wall. If you put a super-sensitive stethoscope to the wall, the rope's vibration is shaking the whole wall, and in return the wall is sending some of that vibration back out again. This, according to Laszlo, is also happening at the zero point. Every vibration is sending signals throughout the field, and in return the field is sending signals back. The universe, it turns out, is constantly monitoring itself by somehow coordinating every vibration that occurs anywhere in the visible or invisible domain.

Imagine two photons floating through the vastness of interstellar space. By chance they collide with each other and bounce apart. Did anything happen that's different from two grains of sand hitting each other as the surf crashes on the beach? Yes, Laszlo says: they exchange information and they begin to relate to each other. Systems theory, as summarized by Laszlo, helps to explain this interaction. When two particles touch, they are carrying information, and as they meet, they "speak" to each other: *Here's how fast I'm going, how much I weigh, where I've been, and where I'm going.*

This conversation doesn't happen in isolation. The field is listening in, and on hearing what's happening, it stores the information for reference, since it needs every single bit to run the cosmos. "Bit" is a technical term in information theory, referring to a single mathematical unit—either zero or one—with which any kind of information can be expressed. When the two particles separate, their future is changed because of the information they just exchanged.

This exchange brings to mind the possibility that these photons *know what they are doing.* Most speculative thinkers, including Laszlo, can't quite bring themselves to claim that the field is conscious; he speaks instead about "the roots of consciousness." From a physicist's standpoint, atoms don't need to think, much less be alive. They meet, they interact, they separate. If complicated things happen, they may be mysterious, invisible, and fiendishly difficult to calculate, needing far more computing capacity than all the mainframe computers in the world. Still, as long as numbers explain how matter behaves, there is no need to drop something alien like consciousness into the equation.

Well and good, but leaving out mind doesn't work, since you are leaving out yourself. Imagine that someone wanted to figure out the rules of football and had a silent videotape to work from. With no knowledge of the game, it would still be possible to watch enough plays and come to reliable conclusions about what's going on. All you'd need to observe is the way the ball flies and how the players hit each other, or don't. Every time the quarterback is knocked down with the ball still in his hands, for example, both teams line up to start a new play. Seeing this happen a few times would lead a scientist to conclude that the quarterback must either throw away the ball or run with it.

Yet it would be impossible to make sense of the game if you assumed that the players were mindless, inert objects. They are too coordinated, they form too many complex patterns, they repeat and remember those patterns, and the scoreboard makes sense—somebody wins, somebody loses. To go a step further, it would be a mistake to start your research by saying that football ipso facto cannot be based on the existence of mind or consciousness. You would wind up with wildly wrong conclusions if you insisted that no matter what the videotape shows, football cannot be a game; it must remain a random collision of objects.

In trying to figure out the apparently random activity in the quantum field, we've come to see that there is incredible timing, coordination, memory, information exchange, and self-interaction. But what is the point of it all? The observer effect adds the missing link. The observer effect is related to one of the cornerstones of quantum physics, called "complementarity," which holds that it isn't possible to know everything about a quantum event. When an observer looks at, or measures, an electron, whatever is being observed is limited. Each and every electron has a probability of appearing anywhere in the universe.

Only under observation does an electron jump from virtual reality into the visible universe, and as soon as the observer stops looking, it falls back into the field again. Erwin Schrödinger, the great German physicist, devised Schrödinger's equation, one of the foundations of quantum theory, which precisely calculates what these probabilities are, and yet the notion that an electron is everywhere until an observer calls it into existence defies logic. For those readers who haven't read about Schrödinger's cat, a famous paradox that grows out of the observer effect, here it is:

A cat is placed in a closed box with a fatal device inside. The device will release poison cyanide gas if it is triggered, and the trigger is a bit of radioactive matter. If the radioactive matter releases a single electron, that will be enough to trigger the device, release the poison, and kill the cat.

Here is the paradox: according to quantum physics, an electron has no visible reality until it is observed. It occupies a "superposition," meaning that it can be in more than one place at the same time (a fact that has been verified experimentally with subatomic particles that do in fact occupy multiple positions at once). Being in a closed box, the cat is outside the field of observation; it could be dead or alive, so according to quantum theory, it must be both. Only when the box is opened and the observer determines the situation will we know which state, dead or alive, has been decided upon. Until then, both must coexist.

Many physicists have escaped the paradox of a cat being dead and alive at the same time by pointing out that what is true on the micro level isn't true on the macro level: superposition holds for electrons, not for everyday objects like cats. But this begs the question, since the observer effect is alive and well in the Schmidt and Princeton experiments, where the mere attention of an observer altered the quantum field and the material world at the same time. The crux of the paradox is that you cannot know any outcome in the quantum world until you observe it (i.e., it is impossible to know if Schrödinger's cat is dead or alive until you look, and the looking *makes* it one or the other).

Akasha solves this problem by making every event participatory at every level. All observers are inside the Akashic field, and whatever they do causes the whole field to respond. Therefore, we are not falsifying the universe to describe it as behaving like ourselves. The predictable and the unpredictable coexist. A cat can be dead and alive at the same time without shaking up how the world usually works. In fact, it is through the unpredictable universe that we know ourselves and vice versa. The Vedic rishis realized that time and eternity have to be related, and their conclusion was that time is an illusion while eternity is real. This turns the tables on the five senses, which must operate as if time is real, since every event we participate in occurs in spacetime. The rishis declare that dying allows us to see eternal reality clearly and to participate in it more fully. In Laszlo's formation, the Akashic field does exactly the same for all matter, energy, and information. Their interactions in the visible universe are reflections of far more important invisible relationships taking place offstage.

Here's an analogy. Imagine that you are a scientist who's been assigned to measure the minuscule explosions of light that take place in a field; in this case, it's the screen of a television set. These explosions take place on the atomic level, so as you move in close you are confronted with millions of photons firing in random patterns. You would describe the TV screen as a field undergoing random excitations, exactly as physicists describe the electromagnetic field. As you move farther out, however, the patches of red, green, and blue begin to cluster; they start to appear organized. Moving out still farther, you begin to notice vague shapes. You feel like an astronomer using a radio telescope to determine if the background noise of the cosmos might contain patterns. Patterns are mathematical, and it takes intelligence to use a mathematical code.

So you begin to come up with a mathematical explanation for the patterns seen on the TV screen. Moving farther and farther out, you eventually see that these patterns are actually pictures of human life, and that the random firing of photons had a purpose. This would be startling enough to cause you to revise your entire theory; you would have to suppose that randomness was an illusion covering a deeper reality, which is the picture. Only consciousness can fully explain the reason why the bursts of red, green, and blue are being emitted.

We find ourselves at the point where many explanations based on randomness no longer satisfy, and a shift must be made to a more conscious explanation. Why do photons fire in a television? Because they turn into a picture. Why do photons fire in the cosmos? For the same reason. Preceding quantum physics by centuries, the Vedic rishis said that time and space are projections on the blank screen of consciousness, the screen of Akasha.

In other words, when you got up this morning, drove to work, and spent your day at the office, *nothing really happened* as you experienced it. Time didn't pass, nor did you move through space. This conclusion confounds common sense but is thoroughly accepted in physics. Let me explain. If you dream at night of flying to Paris and walking the streets, nothing of the sort actually happened; not only did you go nowhere physically, your brain didn't even make pictures that correspond to Paris. The dream resulted from brain activity that can be broken down into bits of information: tiny electrical switches were either on or off, polarities of certain molecules were either positive or negative. Your whole dream and everything in it was just a zero or one game.

The same is true of the people we watch on television. A character may seem to live in a house and mow the lawn. But the house is actually a flat image on the screen, and the movements of people are just phosphors switching on and off. Again, a zero and one game. Nothing moves on a TV screen. If someone appears to run to the left, it's only a pattern of signals that light up on the left and turn off on the right—the same as provided by blinking Christmas tree lights that seem to move around in a circle when in fact all that is happening is that the string of lights is going on and off in a pattern that makes it seem as if motion is occurring.

You move through time and space in the same way, as does the Earth in its orbit and the stars in the sky. Quantum impulses switch on and off, and a change of position occurs because energy gets excited a bit to the left or right from the last excitation. In reality not a single quark or photon changes position in spacetime. But doesn't it amount to the same thing? If an object appears to move, why not say it moves? In fact, we can't. The Earth appears to move around the sun, yet if that were really the case, it would eventually spiral into the sun and be destroyed. In fact, even though the Earth encounters friction in its orbit—in the form of interstellar dust and the solar wind—our planet never gets any closer to the sun or slows down. This is because every atom of Earth winks out of sight and comes back with the same energy and mass that it has always had. The zero point, it turns out, projects the Earth as surely as a television screen projects its pictures. (A skeptic would ask how anything changes if the Zero Point Field constantly replenishes the visible universe. That is a riddle, but its answer may lie in two factors: the slow decay of protons, which takes billions of years, and the expanding universe, which is carrying dispersion of energy, or entropy, as the original heat of the Big Bang becomes dissipated. But folding these two factors into quantum theory is far from being achieved.)

How does all this relate to the afterlife? Ask yourself a simple question. When you're watching TV, which is more real, the picture you're seeing or the station that's sending the signal? Of course, the station is more real, the picture is only an image. Likewise, Laszlo says, the Zero Point Field—Akasha—is more real than the visible universe. Akasha organizes and coordinates all the projections we call time, space, matter, and energy. If this is correct, then we have established a foundation for several key assertions in Vedanta:

The material world is projected from a nonmaterial source.
The invisible world comes first. It contains the seeds of time and
    space.
Reality increases the closer one gets to the source.

To put it in human terms, we do not have to fear that death is a vanishing act because life has always been one. What we most value in ourselves, our capacity to think and feel, didn't come about from entering the physical world. It got projected into the physical world from a source, the Zero Point Field, that is the root of consciousness, extending back billions of years and ahead into the foreseeable future. Far from being a religious vision, this model explains the universe better than any other, and gives us what the rishis and modern physi cists both demand: a bridge between mind and matter.

THINKING OUTSIDE THE BRAIN

IF I DIE and the information contained in my brain survives, does that mean I will survive? Survival means remaining intact at some level—mind, personality, memory, or soul—that is "me." To a materialist, when the brain dies, so does the person. Fortunately, over the past two decades some ingenious experiments have raised hope that the mind extends outside the brain, and that the qualities that you and I cherish, such as love and truth, may be embedded permanently in the field.

The closer we can get to showing that the field is intelligent, the more credible it will be that our own intelligence can survive after death. One way to approach this issue seems strange but turns out to be very fruitful: animal telepathy. Many pet owners will attest to the ability of a dog or cat to know what the owner is thinking. A few minutes before going on a walk, a dog gets excited and restless; on the day when a cat is going to be taken to the vet, it disappears and is nowhere to be found. These casual observations led the ingenious British researcher Rupert Sheldrake, a trained biologist now turned speculative thinker, to conduct controlled studies to find out if dogs and cats can actually read their owners' minds. One study was very simple: Sheldrake phoned sixty-five veterinarians in the London area and asked them if it was common for cat owners to cancel appointments because their cats had disappeared that day. Sixty-four vets responded that it was very common, and the sixty-fifth had given up making appointments for cats because too many couldn't be located when they were supposed to come in.

Sheldrake decided to perform an experiment using dogs. The fact that a dog gets excited when the time comes to go for a walk means little if the walk is routinely scheduled for the same time every day, or if the dog gets visual cues from its owner that he is preparing to go out. Therefore, Sheldrake placed dogs in outbuildings completely isolated from their owners; he then asked the owner, at randomly selected times, to think about walking their dogs five minutes before going to get them. In the meantime, the dog was being videotaped in its isolated location. Sheldrake found that when their owners started thinking about taking them for a walk, more than half the dogs ran to the door wagging their tails, circling restlessly, and keeping up this behavior until their owners appeared. No dog showed anticipatory behavior, however, when their owners were not thinking about taking them for a walk.

This suggests something intriguing, that the bond between a pet and its owner creates a subtle connection at the level of thought. Polls show that about 60% of Americans believe they have had a telepathic experience, so this result is not completely startling. The next leap is quite startling, however. After writing up his results with telepathic pets, Sheldrake received an e-mail from a woman in New York City who said that her African gray parrot not only read her thoughts but responded to them with speech. The woman and her husband might be sitting in another room, out of sight from the bird, whose name is N'kisi, and if they were feeling hungry, N'kisi would suddenly say, "You want some yummy." If the owner and her husband were thinking about going out, N'kisi might say, "You gotta go out, see ya later."

Greatly intrigued, Sheldrake contacted the owner, an artist named

Aimee Morgana. The situation he found was remarkable. African gray parrots are among the most linguistically talented of all birds, and N'kisi had a huge vocabulary of over 700 words. More remarkable still, he used them like human speech, not "parroting" a word mindlessly but applying it where appropriate; if he saw something that was red, he said "red," and if the object was another color, he said that color. But Aimee had even more astonishing stories for Sheldrake. When she was watching a Jackie Chan movie on television, during one scene with Chan perilously perched on a girder, N'kisi said, "Don't fall down," even though his cage was behind the television with no line of sight to the picture. When an automobile commercial came on next, N'kisi said, "That's my car." Another time Aimee was reading the lines, "The blacker the berry, the sweeter the juice," in a book when simultaneously from another room the bird said, "The color is black."

Sheldrake wanted to confirm this for himself. On his first visit, Aimee gave him a taste of N'kisi's telepathy: she looked at a picture of a girl in a magazine, and with remarkable clarity from the adjoining room the parrot said, "That's a girl." The next step was to conduct a formal experiment. If N'kisi could understand words and also had telepathic abilities, could the two be tested together? Sheldrake proposed that Aimee would look at pictures that corresponded to words her parrot already knew. She would sit in one room while N'kisi remained isolated in another. The bird would have two minutes to utter a "key word" that matched the picture. If he said the word within that time, it would count as a hit. If he didn't say the word, or if he said it after the two minutes were up, it counted as a miss.

To ensure neutrality, someone besides Aimee chose both the pictures and the key words that matched each one. (This proved somewhat unfair to the bird, since the neutral chooser picked some words like "TV" that N'kisi had only said once or twice before; the bird didn't utter these words at the right time during the experiment, nor did he say them at all.) After all the trials were over, the tapes of what N'kisi had said were played for three judges, who wrote down what they heard; unless N'kisi distinctly said the right word, as transcribed by all three judges, a hit wouldn't count. The results were beyond ordinary comprehension. For example, when Aimee looked at a picture showing scantily clad bathers on a beach, N'kisi mumbled for a bit, then all three judges heard him say, "Look at my pretty, naked body." He didn't say other, irrelevant key words in between saying the right words, the bird only whistled and made tones. When Aimee looked at a picture of someone talking on the telephone, N'kisi said, "What'cha doin' on the phone?" Perhaps his most intriguing response came when Aimee concentrated on a picture of flowers. Instead of simply uttering the key word "flower," Ni'kisi said, "That's a pic of flowers."

How did he do overall? Out of 71 trials, N'kisi got 23 hits, as compared with 7.4 hits that would have been expected if the results had been random. Sheldrake points out that this is quite a significant outcome, all the more because N'kisi wasn't aware that he was being tested and often said the right key word after the allotted time was up.

In a small Manhattan apartment this bit of proof was added to mounting evidence that the mind isn't solely human property, and in fact might exist outside the brain. Communication between the animal kingdom and humans may seem odd, but pets can't cheat and they have no ulterior motive for proving they have special abilities. The Vedic rishis long ago asserted that the entire universe is intelligent, because it is permeated by consciousness. Let's see how precisely we can put this in modern terms.

Into the Mind Field

Mind has remained a metaphysical riddle for centuries because it inhabits the physical world like a ghost. But that's a Western perspective based on our bias for solid, tangible things. We insist that the brain must be the source of mind because the brain is a visible object, which is like saying that a radio must be the source of music because it is a visible object from which music emerges. The Vedic rishis adopted the opposite perspective, insisting that visible objects couldn't be the source of mind since the physical plane is the least conscious of worlds. It may seem significant that the brain is active during thought, but a radio is active during a broadcast, and there is no doubt that N'kisi (not to mention human telepaths) picked up a thought that was being broadcast.

Our Western prejudice against the invisible isn't easy to overcome. Mind will only be proved to exist outside the brain if it leaves some kind of footprint, a visible sign that is as convincing as the MRIs that provide concrete evidence of neural activity. One such piece of evidence is information, which we've touched on before. If information permeates the entire quantum field, it can bridge mind and matter in terms more acceptable to a materialist. No scientist has a problem believing that matter and energy cannot be created or destroyed, and the cutting edge of physics is grappling with the notion that information cannot be created or destroyed, either. What we see in the universe is constant transformation. Helium atoms that fuel the sun send heat to Earth that gets transformed by photosynthesis into plants and all other life-forms. It can fairly be said that life consists of the sun's atoms exchanging information with atoms on Earth. (Energy is information in the sense that all chemical or electrical charges can be expressed as plus or minus, positive or negative, zero or one.) It doesn't mater, then, that your body bears no resemblance to a fiery star. Both are part of the same information field, which undergoes endless transformation within itself. Or as Lord Krishna says in the Bhagavad-Gita, "Folding back in on myself, I create again and again."

Amit Goswami, a prominent physicist who writes extensively on the self-aware universe, says that creativity is just another face of transformation. "The universe is always putting new wine into old bottles, or new wine into new bottles." The same energy packets, containing the same information, are being endlessly shuffled in the Zero Point Field. Goswami approaches reincarnation in the same context. Identities are passing through the information field, exchanging data with new identities that feel like a new "me" but are actually transmutations of indestructible zeros and ones strung into long chains of ideas and experiences.

Right now you are a bundle of information in mind and body. You have unique memories; your cells have undergone chemical changes shared by no one else in the world. When you die, none of this information will vanish, because it can't. There is nowhere for plus and minus, positive and negative to go since the field contains nothing *but* information. Therefore their only alternative is to recombine. How do they do that?

The answer lies in the root word of information, which is "form." We inhabit an "in-formed universe" according to Ervin Laszlo, which strings atoms along the double helix of DNA, bits of information in physical form, just as it strings together information in nonphysical form as ideas. This brings us one step closer to the breathtaking notion that the whole universe is God's mind; that is, a dynamic field of infinite information undergoing infinite transformations. But we can't take that step unless we know how small ideas survive, much less cosmic ones.

The rishis taught that ideas survive in the Akashic field as memories. You and I constantly access Akashic memory when we assume that we are accessing our brains. In esoteric circles Akashic memory functions to give us information from departed spirits and past lifetimes. In Jungian psychology the same memory accounts for cultures sharing the same myths and archetypes. Venus and Mars are invisible beings, yet present and alive. The Akasha remembers every god created by humans and every epic battle, romance, and quest. We tap into them all the time as the human story continues from age to age.

The brain has a locatable memory center, but mind isn't confined to the brain. Consider a deeply meaningful experience in your life—a first kiss, or the last time you saw a beloved grandparent. That memory is the remaining trace of an event in time and space. The experience can still be activated in your brain, which means that millions of molecules that could be flying randomly through your neurons *know* that they have to stay together in order for your memory to continue, year after year, without fading. How could they know this, since molecules aren't intelligent? The physical basis for memory remains totally unknown to neurologists, so we can only speculate.

Somehow your first kiss has an afterlife. The afterlife isn't physical, because there's absolutely no difference between the hydrogen, oxygen, nitrogen, and carbon in a neuron and those same elements in a tree, a dead leaf, or decomposed soil. Neurons aren't immortal. They die, just as the rest of the body does, and atoms fly in and out of them every second. How, then, does a memory get transferred to a new atom, or to a new neuron when the time comes for the old one to perish? No physical process for this has been identified, so perhaps memory actually persists on a nonphysical level. Neurologists would defend to the hilt the opposite idea, that mind arises only in the brain, using CAT scans and MRI imaging to prove the point. But those images are only maps. They show the terrain of the brain as an idea or emotion crosses it; they don't prove that the brain *is* the mind, any more than a footprint in the sand is the same as a foot. Imagine that you could map every vibration in the tiny nerve endings that line the inner ear. When graphed on a chart, there would be an extremely complicated pattern for every word and sentence the ear receives, but that pattern is only a map of a word, not the territory itself. A powerful sentence like "I love you" is more than the map of its vibrations, since even the most perfect map cannot contain love's power, meaning, significance, and overall intent.

Memory seems to be a field effect. For you to think the word "rhinoceros" and see a mental image of that animal, millions of brain cells have to act simultaneously. (We will leave aside the more difficult question of why you picked "rhinoceros" out of all the words you could have chosen, since any word choice can be based on reason, emotion, nonsense, or private associations in memory. A computer can be taught to select any given word, but it has no special reason to do so—you do.) The neurons involved in choosing the word "rhinoceros" don't run through the alphabet until they get to "R"; they don't sound out one syllable at a time, nor do they leaf through a zoological photo archive to match the right word to the right image. Instead, the correct brain activity arises simultaneously. The brain is acting like a field, coordinating different events at the same time, except that we know the brain isn't literally a field. It's an object made of seemingly lifeless chemicals.

A compass needle moves because it's responding to the Earth's magnetic field. What if the same thing is true for brain activity? What if the mind field is sending signals, and billions of brain cells arrange patterns in response to what the field is saying? A team of innovative scientists has proposed exactly that. Henry Stapp, a theoretical physicist from Berkeley; Jeffrey Schwartz, a neuropsychiatrist at UCLA; and Mario Beauregard, a psychologist from the University of Montreal, have crossed disciplines to formulate a workable theory of "quantum mind" that may revolutionize how mind and brain relate to each other. Central to their theory is "neuroplasticity," the notion that brain cells are open to change, flexibly responding to will and intention.

They acknowledge, to begin with, the usual scientific explanation that "the mind is what the brain does," but there are many flaws in such an explanation, as we have seen. They propose, therefore, that exactly the opposite is true. Mind is the controller of the brain. In their view, the mind is like an electron cloud surrounding the nucleus of an atom. Until an observer appears, electrons have no physical identity in the world; there is only the amorphous cloud. In the same way, imagine that there is a cloud of possibilities open to the brain at every moment (consisting of words, memories, ideas, and images it could choose from). When the mind gives a signal, one of these possibilities coalesces from the cloud and becomes a thought in the brain, just as an energy wave collapses into an electron. Like the quantum field generating real particles from virtual ones, the mind generates real brain activity from virtual activity.

What makes this reversal important is that it fits the facts. Neurologists have verified that a mere intention or purposeful act of will alters the brain. Stroke victims, for example, can force themselves, with the aid of a therapist, to use only their right hand if paralysis has occurred on that side of the body. Willing themselves day after day to favor the affected part, they can gradually cause the damaged sites in the brain to heal. Similar results have been found with aging. Older people who have begun to show signs of senile dementia such as memory loss can slow down and even reverse their symptoms by exercising their brains (one software manufacturer has even brought out a "brain gym," a program that looks like a video game but in fact consists of exercises that strengthen specific areas of the brain). Children born with cerebral palsy have recently regained use of their paralyzed limbs through similar therapies in which the unaffected arm, for example, was kept in a sling, forcing the child to use the paralyzed arm; in time, the brain healed itself. It showed neuroplasticity.

Putting mind before brain may have many far-reaching consequences in medical therapies. For example, patients suffering from obsessive-compulsive disorder (OCD) are routinely treated with psychotropic drugs like Prozac. Symptoms improve, and physical evidence for that can be found through brain scans; the parts of the brain that malfunction in OCD start to become more normal on the drug.

But obsessive-compulsive patients sometimes seek relief through talk therapy instead. These patients frequently improve, yet only recently did anyone examine their brains with MRIs and PET scans, and what they discovered is startling: the same impaired regions that become more normal with Prozac also become more normal with talk therapy. (Jeffrey Schwartz is an expert in OCD and based the new theory in part on such brain scans.)

In other words, the process of reflection and insight through therapy changed the patients' brain cells. This is exactly what was predicted by the new theory of quantum mind. But the answer was there all along. The mind has always been able to change the brain. If a person suddenly loses a loved one or is fired from his job, sudden severe depression often follows. Depression is rooted in abnormal uptake of the brain chemical serotonin. This physcial imbalance is what antidepressants are typically designed to correct. Yet when someone loses a loved one or gets fired, isn't it obvious that the chemical imbalance came about after the bad news? Reacting to bad news is a mental event. Indeed, the entire world we inhabit of words and thoughts creates infinite brain changes in all of us every moment.

If mind comes before brain, then what if mind belongs to all of us? I can say "my brain," but I can't say "my quantum field." There is growing evidence that in fact we do share the same mind field. This would go far to support the existence of heavens and hells, Bardo and Akashic memory, extending far beyond the brain. To begin with, we need to examine the kinds of ideas that people share as a group. The brain belongs to "me," but if ideas belong to "us," then we are participating together in a field, sometimes quite mysteriously.

The Brain Beyond Boundaries

The human brain processes only a fraction of the information available to it. By some estimates the brain receives 6 billion bits of data per second (such as sound vibrations, photons, X-ray and gamma radiation, electromagnetic static, and various chemical and electrical signals from the immediate environment), a floodtide that gets squeezed into the trickle of experience we actually notice and respond to. But what we notice isn't the same as what we know. For example, some so-called idiot savants with very low IQs can instantaneously compute long strings of numbers, tell the day of the week that any date falls on in the future, remember every detail of their past, or learn difficult languages with incredible fluency. (One savant mastered Finnish, Arabic, and Mandarin at a young age, and only afterward did his caregivers realize he had been learning these languages on his own despite the fact that he'd held the books upside down.) Such savants often lack even the most basic capacity in other areas. One well-documented type of savant is able to perform music or paint pictures with extraordinary facility but cannot calculate change from a purchase, or tie their shoes without help.

When sudden artistic abilities began to appear in a small percentage of normal people who suffer from brain tumors and other neurological disorders, researchers looked at the brains of savants and discovered that they, too, displayed brain abnormalities, particularly in the right temporal lobe. To my knowledge, the current explanation for "savant syndrome" now centers on such physical abnormalities. Thus it seems that when the brain's filtering system is impaired, reality expands in some areas while it contracts in others. All kinds of abilities may inexplicably exceed the norm. Joseph Chilton Pearce, a specialist in child development, writes about the savant syndrome in his book *The Biology of Transcendence*. He makes several striking points. The first is that most children with savant syndrome don't perform on their own but respond when asked. The second is that they are not especially interested in the wider area of their extraordinary ability. If you sit down and ask a savant what day of the week March 12, 2163, falls on, it's like talking to a machine. The child goes inward for a few seconds, then pops up with the answer, but might have little interest in simple math. A calendar savant might not be able to multiply 12 by 12.

The normal brain filters out information for good reason—it takes narrow experience to form a self, a separate person with limited beliefs, goals, memories, likes, and dislikes. We deliberately reject huge portions of information, but a damaged brain is exposed to everything through its inability to select and filter. Pearce is particularly intrigued by how an "automobile savant" could take one look at a parking lot and tell you the make, model, and year of every car in it without being able to read. How does he know this without reading magazines that feature the latest models, including European models that had received no publicity in the United States? It seems as if these savant children are accessing the mind field.

Genius is another way to access the field beyond normal abilities. Musical prodigies like Mozart can see whole symphony scores in their heads. One such prodigy now enrolled in the Juilliard program for composers has been able to switch between four channels of music in his head since early childhood; when asked to write a new sonata for violin, he simply turned to the appropriate channel and took dictation. A direct link to the field of information seems possible, then, and we move closer to the possibility that the brain is the receiver of mind, not its creator.

This is important to the afterlife because upon dying we have no brain but do desire to keep our minds. If the Vedic seers are right, the human brain connects us to infinite consciousness. The fact that we shut out so much of the mind field doesn't mean we have to. Aboriginal peoples don't access higher math, scientific reasoning, or advanced musical harmonies, but if a baby were taken from a New Guinea jungle tribe and placed in the right learning environment, its mind contains the potential for all these skills. Indeed, only in this _____ are certain tribes moving out of the jungles of New Guinea into surrounding cities, and as they do, they make the transition from a culture that never discovered metal-working to one where they can drive a car.

Why don't we access more of the mind field ourselves? In fact, we do. The brain adapts to the field at will. If you intend to learn Chinese ideograms, of which there are thousands, you can apply yourself, and gradually a system of meaningless ink strokes will be transformed into a meaningful area of knowledge. Once mastered, the Chinese language becomes part of you; it becomes second nature, and you can proceed to use it for creative purposes. In essence you have accessed the mind field and willed your own evolution. You have made a leap nearly as significant as when Paleolithic man discovered that meaningless vocal noises could be transformed into spoken language.

Intelligence and meaning aren't only "in here" as a subjective creation of the brain or "out there" as a freestanding object. The give-and-take by which the brain creates meaning is also how it creates the world and creates itself. All these processes actually belong to one process, the self "curving back onto itself to create again and again," as Lord Krishna says. The field is innately creative. It formed the human brain, which is so receptive that it took the next leap and learned to create new thoughts, abilities, and memories on its own. Our brains are still acting out the total activity of the cosmos, but we happen to claim that "I am thinking" when it's just as true to say "the mind field is thinking through me."

Memes and the Behavior of Beliefs

There's another kind of filtering that limits how much of the mind field we can perceive. This has to do with creating beliefs and then accepting them as real. A belief is an idea we hold on to. For example, if you believe that God is good, that women are mysterious, or that life is unfair, you have taken generations of shared experience and reduced it to one conclusion. The conclusion may be right or wrong; that's not important for the moment. Beliefs hold us together as a society. Such shared beliefs give us a clue about how mind might exist outside the body.

We all carry in our minds a large database of information that we consider fundamental. This database holds everything important that we believe about the world. It is our worldview. We depend upon it to survive for even a short time. Beliefs evolve over the centuries, and therefore some researchers look upon beliefs as being like "virtual genes," that become fixed characteristics of the brain. These mental genes were named "memes" by the British evolutionist Richard Dawkins, who founded a new field overnight that has proliferated considerably since then.

A meme is often compared to a virus that spreads from person to person until an entire society gets infected. It wouldn't be beneficial to our species to become infected by everything. If we were actually open to all new ideas, we would not be able to maintain a coherent view of the world. Imagine changing your view of the opposite sex, for example, every time you met a new person. In order to evolve, human beings had to make sure that they accepted only "good" memes—ideas that promoted a coherent, reliable worldview—and rejected "bad" memes, ideas that moved the mind in the opposite direction.

The basic fact that we can track the spread of beliefs the way we track the spread of avian flu provides us with another clue to the nature of the mind field: it is dynamic, shared, evolving, and powerful. It is capable of "infecting" us with good or bad beliefs without the individual actually going through any experience at all. Thus societies fight and die defending a God few have personally experienced. Nietzsche was foreshadowing memes when he said that a mistaken idea "grows from generation unto generation, merely because people believe in it, until it gradually grows to be a part of the thing and turns into its very body. What at first was appearance becomes in the end, almost invariably, the essence, and is effective as such."

Creating a Worldview

The Vedic rishis said that anything we experience in the Akashic field was created by our own consciousness. Memes offer evidence of this, as a means to create the worldview that we then believe in. There may not be much incentive to adapt to new ideas on our own, but when two worldviews clash, as Western culture is clashing with radical Islam, the pressure to cling to one worldview or the other against outside threat is inescapable. Our very survival is said to depend upon it. (I am reminded of a CNN interview with a right-wing Christian operative from Indiana who said, "As long as liberals and atheists despise us, we will never go away.")

Two people with different worldviews can see the same fact and give totally divergent interpretations of it, because no fact or event is perceived by itself. Walking down the street, I may pass a woman with bright red lipstick, a faint whiff of wine on her breath from a lunch at a restaurant, and no hat on her head. In my worldview, none of these facts triggers any particular emotion or judgment, so this is a neutral encounter that barely registers on me. Therefore you might assume that nothing happened in my brain. Yet, as meme theory points out, a great deal happened tacitly. The sight of this woman entered my brain as raw data along the optic nerve, but I couldn't actually "see" her until that data passed through my worldview. Imagine a series of filters marked "memory," "beliefs, "associations," and "judgments." Each filter alters the raw data in some way, invisibly and instantaneously.

Should a person with a different worldview encounter the same woman, he would "see" her through his filters. If he happened to be a traditional Muslim or a Victorian or a medieval monk, all the innocuous features that entered my brain—the lipstick, the smell of alcohol, the absence of a hat—might cause a violent reaction in his brain, and generate considerable stress.

A worldview provides fixed grooves for behavior, which is dangerous, unfortunately, much of the time. Traits like racism and warmaking persist as automatic reflexes. Anatomically the human nervous system is divided into two parts: the somatic and autonomic nervous systems. All information in the body that you are conscious of comes from the somatic nervous system; all information that you are unconscious of comes from the autonomic nervous system. Memes occupy a fascinating middle ground, a shadowland. When you can't get a catchy song out of your head—one classic example of meme behavior—you are totally conscious of the tune but unconscious of why you can't get rid of it.

This is precisely what the Bhagavad-Gita means by the binding effect of karma. You may be completely aware that you have a certain trait, such as being stingy, irritable, easily flattered, or self-important, but you cannot say why that trait sticks to you, however much you dislike it.

Worldviews are built of symbols that fulfill a need. Take any charming thing in the environment—say, the late Princess Diana. For her to stay in your mind and persist there longer than a few moments, she must be significant to you. That is, she is a sign for something you recognize, and I would add something you value and desire. On a global scale Princess Diana symbolized beauty, innocence, vulnerability, motherhood, prestige, sexuality, and more. Like all the best memes, her negative side was also powerfully symbolic. At various stages she represented disability, illness, social liability, addiction, naïveté, wantonness, infidelity, and masochism.

By whatever name we give them, memes are the way we give

meaning to experience. They package meaning into the building block of reality. Insofar as we are creators of reality, we use these symbolic building blocks as our raw material. I find this whole field of meme theory exciting because among those scientists who cannot stomach the notion of inherent consciousness, the parallel notion of memes is gaining considerable credibility. A gap is closing.

The Vedic rishis had their own model for what happens in the mind field. Thought forms that grip us are *samskaras*, impressions made on the nervous system by past experience. A young child frightened when his mother forgetfully left him in a department store might carry that impression, or samskara, for life. Such impressions do not have to be negative—a first kiss can, and usually does, form a lasting samskara. The concept of samskara goes beyond memes because it applies to all mental experience. Whether they are sensations, desires, or ideas, impressions can go as deep into the field as the soul. They constitute the qualities of the self that give each of us an identity we recognize as "me."

Samskaras can be dismantled or changed only by affecting the right level of the mind. A change at the subtlest level is the most powerful. J. Krishnamurti put it beautifully when he said that "the highest form of human intelligence is to observe yourself without judgment." That is, if you can stand aside from how your beliefs are behaving, how various impulses of desire and repulsion are pulling at you, how the "stored consciousness" of memory makes you see the world, you can witness the field itself. This is true enlightenment. In many spiritual traditions, such as Buddhism, the key seems to be stillness, detaching oneself from the internal dialogue whose stream of ideas and impulses comes from the past. Witnessing allows us to see and understand with an intelligence that is holistic, without a win-or-lose orientation. This gives us a chance to experience the mind field, or what we popularly call "having an open mind."

Ultimately, dying will carry each of us into the mind field, which we will experience directly. Yet our beliefs, being stored consciousness, will follow us. The issue of an open mind bears directly upon how much baggage we'll have to carry. I'm reminded of a question posed by Krishnamurti. When someone commented that it was good to have an open mind, he asked, "Is there such a thing as an open mind?" This was a typically ambiguous reply, but if the mind is trapped by either memes or samskaras, it cannot be open, because of secondhand beliefs, opinions, judgments, and other mental "viruses." Or is there some kind of new experience entirely beyond the realm of ingrained beliefs and karmic impressions?

The most profound of contradictions is that to reach enlightenment, which is free from past impressions, you have no choice but to use your brain, and the brain is mired in its habit of filtering, choosing, preferring, rejecting, etc. Krishnamurti stated this elegantly when he asked, "Can a fragmented mind ever experience wholeness?" The answer is that it cannot, but all any of us are equipped with is a fragmented mind. A mind made up of memes and samskaras. Asserting that you have an open mind while someone else's mind is closed, or claiming that you experience reality instead of illusion, seems like a reasonable statement, but in Krishnamurti's terms—which are pure Vedanta—it is impossible to do things like "trying to be more open" or "trying to get more real." You are simply fighting with your own divided self.

So what is the way out of this paradox? There is a way to approach the tricky business of opening your mind.

1. Know that you are going to identify with your worldview at every stage of personal growth.

2. Accept that these identifications are temporary. You will never be truly yourself until you reach unity.

3. Be willing to change your identity every day. Take a flexible attitude. Don't defend an "I" that you know is just temporary.

4. Allow your ability to quietly observe without judgment to replace the ingrained ideas you reach for automatically.

5. When you have the impulse to struggle, use that as an immediate signal to let go. Open a space for a new answer to unfold on its own.

6. When you can't let go, forgive yourself and move on.

7. Use every opportunity to tell yourself that all viewpoints are valid, every experience valuable, every insight a moment of freedom.

These steps cultivate an open mind by exposing you to the mind field itself, witnessing without judgment. They will orient you to the possibility that you can be redefined continuously. In other words, give your allegiance to transformation rather than defending the status quo. Now you are ready to disassemble your worldview. You are ready to stop having a stake in the world limited to the narrow confines of I, me, and mine. The ego-defended worldview you want to dismantle is organized in three layers:

1. Energy
2. Beliefs
3. Structure

These three layers apply both to the whole and to its parts. They are inescapably intertwined because the field itself contains all three. This means that a tree or a cloud is nothing but energy, information, and structure. Your personality is composed of the same three elements, and so is every experience in your worldview.

Energy: When an experience gets stuck in your head, you are holding on to its energy. Every experience has its own energy pattern, which is reflected in the brain as memory, emotion, sensation, etc. When you decide to recall something from your childhood, what comes to mind? Visual images, names and faces, all kinds of emotions, physical details, associations, various sensations. All of these exist at the level of energy. Without the electromagnetic field vibrating in a certain way, specific experiences couldn't exist.

This stuck energy is cleared in many ways: through dreams, insight, imagination, emotional release, deep recollection, confession, prayer, atonement, meditation, love, etc.

Beliefs: Beliefs take us to a subtler level of the mind. Beliefs allow one experience but forbid another to enter. They are like judges deciding whether an experience is positive or negative, right or wrong, desirable or undesirable. The universe is doing a continuous dance with your beliefs. What you believe is reinforced by what you experience, but what you experience also alters what you believe. Anyone who has wrestled with the question "Does he (or she) love me?" knows what it feels like to have tiny things like a glance or a casual word or an unreturned phone call confirm or destroy your belief in being loved.

Beliefs are cleared by being aware of the sticky quality they possess. Beliefs aren't static; they result in behavior. So when you watch your own behavior, you are seeing your beliefs at play. If a poor black homeless person asks you for a handout at night and your response is to say nothing and walk away, consider all the beliefs that could be at work: "Black is dangerous, the night is fearful, strangers can't be trusted, any response will get me entangled, poor people are lazy or crazy or weak, to associate with them means I will be one of them one day." When you stop defending the behavior of your beliefs, they become less sticky. You regain freedom to think and believe in a new way.

Structure: Structure is the foundation of the personality. It includes your vision of life, your purpose for being here, your deepest goals, your view of physical existence, and your attitude toward pleasure and pain. These profound things are overlooked because people are too overwhelmed—and too convinced—by their beliefs and energies. Only after you start clearing energy and beliefs can you look at the "Why?" that is at the bottom of your participation in Maya, or external appearance. Why are you alive? What is your overall purpose? To what higher values have you offered your allegiance? These are structural questions, and when you can see them clearly, they bring their own answers.

Structure isn't cleared the way stuck energy is, and it can't be challenged the way beliefs can be. Structure is your vehicle for this lifetime. It's the boat you use to sail across the ocean of space and time. Without it you would have no identity at all; you would be a cloud of energy without a center. All you can do with your structure is to "witness" it. In that moment of witnessing, you reduce the "I" to its first principles. In other words, you stand at the threshold where the person meets the soul. This is an enormously liberating moment of recognition.

When you build any new structure in your mind—for example, deciding to see your life in spiritual terms or learning parenting skills after a baby is born or replacing the perspective of a victim with the perspective of someone who's in control—you are choosing to evolve. You are taking advantage of certain subtle qualities that pertain to mental structures as revealed by the rishis:

- Structures in the mind organize energy so that it serves the highest purpose.
- They interface this lifetime with universal experience.
- They open you to the higher self and its transmissions.
- They expose you to the force of evolution.

To the extent that you are working on the three levels of energy, beliefs, and structure, you are connecting yourself to the field directly and consciously, which is how an open mind is achieved. How can you tell that your work has paid off and you have gained an open mind? You know yourself as wholeness once and for all.

15

THE MECHANICS OF CREATION

As much as we try to explain it, what happens when we die remains a miracle. We move from one world to another, we shed our old identity to experience "I am," the identity of the soul, and we assemble the ingredients of a completely unique life in our next body. Science supports the claim that the field is capable of creative leaps and endless transformation. An oxygen atom, if it could tell its own story, would feel that a miracle has occurred when it bonds with hydrogen to form water. Its old identity was gaseous, its new one is liquid. Its old world was in the atmosphere, its new one is in oceans, rivers, and clouds. And what if this water molecule happens to become part of the human brain? Would oxygen suddenly experience being conscious?

This question is the final, most mysterious leap we have to explain. Oxygen, like every other atom in the brain, participates in consciousness as it courses through every neuron. Yet to say that oxygen itself is conscious goes too far. So how did consciousness creep in somewhere between oxygen atoms and the cerebral cortex? This is crucial in determining whether or not consciousness survives death. As I've already argued, the answer doesn't lie in the brain. The brain is an inert object formed of organic chemicals. Those chemicals can be broken down into more basic molecules and atoms. Those atoms can be broken down into subatomic particles, which can in turn be broken down into energy waves that have their source in an invisible field.

Taking these steps one at a time, we get *further away* from consciousness rather than closer. The brain is aware, but we cannot say that energy waves are aware, even though the brain is ultimately nothing but energy. To solve this enigma, materialists argue that consciousness has no reality in itself; it is just a trick of the brain. Does this mean that if we could download a person's complete memory into a supercomputer, we would achieve life after death? Would the living self continue to feel intact, experiencing the world just as before but from inside a machine?

This is a perfect example of how we can be victimized by our own explanations. Awareness can't be found in information. The fact that a billion zeros and ones are loaded into a computer won't make it conscious unless each zero and one is conscious already, which leads to the absurd conclusion that the numbers printed in a math textbook are thinking about themselves. You cannot explain consciousness at any level of nature without running into the same contradiction. So do we have to give up on scientific explanations or is science ready for insights that will force it to explain Nature differently?

Creative Leaps

One property we cherish in ourselves is the ability to create something new. We come by this honestly. The appearance of life on Earth depended on the sudden ability of a molecule, DNA, to replicate itself. No molecule before it had ever done that. We can explain the evolution of the universe entirely in terms of such creative leaps, or "emergent properties." Before oxygen and hydrogen could discover how to become water, the cosmos had to create atoms, which weren't present at the Big Bang, and atoms had to turn into gases, solids, metals, organic molecules, and so on. None of these events were simple combinations like pouring sugar into water. The sugar may disappear, but if you evaporate the water you find that the sugar has remained intact. There's no new property in sugar water that wasn't already present in the two components when they were separate.

An emergent property, on the other hand, is a creative leap that produces something out of nothing. In spiritual terms the cycle of birth and rebirth is a workshop for making creative leaps of the soul. The natural and the supernatural are not doing different things but are involved in transformation on separate levels. At the moment of death the ingredients of your old body and old identity disappear. Your DNA and everything it created devolve back to their simple component parts. Your memories dissolve back into raw information. None of this raw material is simply recombined to produce a slightly altered person. To produce a new body capable of making new memories, the person who emerges must be new. You do not acquire a new soul, because the soul doesn't have content. It's not "you" but the center around which "you" coalesces, time after time. It's your zero point.

I was recently reminded of just how uncanny this transformation is. I know a couple from Italy who suffered a terrible family tragedy two years ago when their teenage son, Enrico, killed himself. He had gotten drunk with some friends, one of whom started playing with his father's handgun. It went off and Enrico was killed. His family was devastated, all the more when it was suggested but never proved that their son had shot himself playing Russian roulette.

A week after he died his mother went into his bedroom. She had the impulse to pray for her son, and as she knelt by his bed she heard a noise. A remote-control toy car of Enrico's had fallen off the shelf for no apparent reason. It began to run around the floor, and the mother removed its batteries. Still it continued to run. This strange phenomenon lasted three days, she told me. It was witnessed by the entire family, and Enrico's older sister, the one he was closest to, insisted that her brother was operating the car. She asked it questions, as one would a Ouija board, and the car would go left or right to signal yes or no.

Months later Enrico's father happened to be in India, and he went to a *jyotishi*, or astrologer. Certain jyotishis do not cast your chart but consult already written charts, many dating back centuries, that apply to the person who comes for a reading. (This decision is made according to the time a person appears and by matching certain personal data with charts that the astrologer has on hand.) This was true of my friend, who was told the following story: In his previous lifetime he had lived on the west coast of India. He was desperate to have a son, but unfortunately his wife was barren. The couple adopted a baby boy when suddenly she became pregnant and in time delivered a boy of their own.

After the biological son's birth, the father began to ignore the adopted boy and abuse him. Tormented by this, the boy committed suicide at exactly the same age as Enrico. The astrologer told my friend that there was a connection here. The former son was reborn as Enrico, and he committed suicide again to show his father what it was like to lose a real son. Naturally, my friend was quite shaken to hear this, but when he met me some months later, he said that the final result was a sense of peace. He had come to terms with Enrico's tragic death and understood the karma behind it.

I have no idea how many readers will scoff at this tale and how many will consider it uncanny but possibly true. To me, it says a great deal about how mysteriously life and death are woven together. They are two aspects of the same creative act. Our brains are set up to operate in time and space. We do not witness the mechanics of creation outside that framework. But the life you are experiencing now, the one that preceded it, and the one that will follow didn't appear out of nowhere. They appeared through a continuous, evolving consciousness—the real you. There is a gap between lifetimes that we cannot observe, yet your soul keeps track of you as you enter the gap and reemerge. Consciousness doesn't lose track of itself; the zero point of the soul is just as capable of correlating events across time and space as the Zero Point Field is.

In this story father and son remained joined across the gap between birth and death. They unconsciously recognized each other, they carried out a common purpose, and they worked out karma together—all these things defied death. At the same time their physical bodies, their private memories, and their sense of identity were transient—these didn't survive death. Nature is built from the same intricate relationships. The oxygen atoms locked in a water molecule or in your brain are still themselves, but they have learned to relate in a totally new way, making it seem as if each separate atom has vanished—that is to say, died. I can't emphasize enough that if science cannot explain the emergence of wetness from dryness, it cannot explain the emergence of consciousness in the brain. True creative leaps are always inexplicable and therefore miraculous.

The Source of Everything

What science should do is hold the miracle under a microscope to get closer to where creation occurs. There are faint physical traces to be followed down to a very subtle level. It has long been known that the brain, and the body as a whole, is surrounded by a very weak electromagnetic field. With the proper photographic emulsion, this field can be seen to glow; the minuscule electric charge given off by neurons as they fire is also measurable. If being conscious creates an energy field, can an energy field display consciousness? You would think that since the brain depends on electrical signals, it would be affected by the murky soup of radio, television, microwave, and many other electromagnetic emissions that surround us. Apparently this isn't true. Parapsychology researchers have gone so far as to isolate subjects with psychic abilities in Faraday cages that block all electromagnetic energy without altering their abilities to see at a distance or exhibit other psychic phenomena. The case of "remote viewing" is especially intriguing because so much credible work has been done in this field.

Many experiments have been conducted in remote viewing, commonly called clairvoyance, but one of the most notable took place at Stanford University, where scientists built a machine called a SQUID, or superconducting quantum interference device. It's enough for us to know that this device, which measures the activity of subatomic particles, specifically quarks, is very well shielded from all outside magnetic forces. This shielding begins with layers of copper and aluminum, but to fully ensure that no outside force can affect the mechanism, exotic metals wrap the inner core.

In 1972 a SQUID was installed in the basement of a laboratory at Stanford, apparently doing nothing except tracing out the same hill-and-valley S-curve on a length of graph paper. This curve represented the constant magnetic field of the Earth; if a quark passed through the field the machine would register it with changes in the pattern being drawn. A young laser physicist named Hal Puthoff (later to become a noted quantum theorist) decided that aside from its main use, the SQUID would make a perfect test of psychic powers. Very few people, including the scientists at Sanford, knew the inner workings of the machine.

A letter Puthoff wrote in search of a psychic who would take up the challenge drew a response from Ingo Swann, a New York artist with psychic abilities. Swann was flown to California without being told in advance about either the test or the SQUID. When he first saw it, he seemed a bit put off. But he agreed to "look" inside the machine, and as he did, the S-curve on the graph paper changed pattern—something it almost never did—only to go back to its normal functioning as soon as Swann stopped paying attention to it.

A startled Puthoff asked him to repeat this, so for forty-five seconds Swann concentrated upon seeing the inside of the machine, and for exactly that interval the recording device drew a new pattern, a long plateau on the paper instead of hills and valleys. Swann then drew a sketch of what he saw as the inner workings of the SQUID, and when these were checked with an expert, they perfectly matched the actual construction. Swann was vague about how he had changed the magnetic input that the machine was built to measure. It turned out that if he merely thought about the SQUID, not trying to change it at all, the recording device showed alterations in the surrounding magnetic field.

PEOPLE WHO ARE skeptical of psychic abilities ignore countless studies demonstrating that ordinary thought can actually affect the world. This is particularly important if mind is a field. I once participated in a controlled experiment in which a subject sitting in an isolated room (the sender) would intermittently look at a visual image, while I (the receiver) would press a button every time I sensed that this was happening. My accuracy, like most people's, was far above average. (The British biologist Rupert Sheldrake, who more than anyone has tried to explain how mind extends beyond the body, has done similar experiments. He has tested, for example, whether we can actually sense when someone is staring at us behind our backs. Those experiments have shown a greater than random outcome as well.)

In a long series of experiments in the Sixties, an FBI expert named Cleve Backster hooked plants up to polygraphs, knowing that lie detectors work by measuring changes of moisture on the skin surface. In his own words, here's what happened next.

> Then at thirteen minutes, fifty-five seconds chart time, the imagery entered my mind of burning the leaf I was testing. I didn't verbalize, I didn't touch the plant, I didn't touch the equipment. The only new thing that could have been a stimulus for the plant was the mental image. Yet the plant went wild. The pen jumped right off the top of the chart.

This first startling observation in February 1966 led to a host of follow-ups as Backster measured responses to cigarette smoke, negative thoughts, and strong emotions; it turned out that houseplants register how people feel around them. The most remarkable finding, perhaps, was that if Backster hooked up a pair of plants and injured one plant in a separate room, the other plant registered the same disturbance in electrical activity as if it had been injured itself. The polygraph needle jumped even though the two plants had no physical connection, and it kept jumping even when the plants were separated by a greater distance. One can't help but be reminded of the various studies in which identical twins sense what is happening to each other at a distance, to the point that one particular twin knew the instant his brother was electrocuted climbing a telephone pole and testified to actually feeling the pain himself. Are human twins paired through the same complementarity that bonds electrons in deep space?

To say that consciousness is a field creates only the outline of a proof. Nobody has accounted for the gap, and without that, consciousness remains totally mysterious; in fact, so do fields. The gap is the empty space between events; it contains nothing but itself, and yet it seems that everything comes out of it. When we look at DNA we are told by geneticists that life emerges not from the bits of amino acids strung on the double helix, but from the space between them. These spaces are little understood, but they play a mysterious role in the sequence of genes. In physical terms the DNA of gorillas and humans differs by less than 1%; the gaps between visible matter create the unbridgeable gulf between gorillas and humans. In the gap the source of consciousness must be revealed.

Sat Chit Ananda

The Vedic rishis followed the mind into the gap and declared that three primal qualities were the foundation of existence: *Sat Chit Ananda*. These are usually translated as a single phrase, "eternal bliss consciousness," or individually as Sat (existence, truth, reality) Chit (mind, awareness) Ananda (bliss). But these definitions don't help us much, since they assume an understanding of what we mean in English by reality, truth, bliss, and existence. These are far from settled. If you say, "It was blissful going to Aruba for Christmas. It changed my whole reality," your words have meaning in everyday life, but they haven't described Sat Chit Ananda.

If we unfold what the rishis meant, they were referring to an experience, which can be summarized as follows: Every thought you have, as well as every object you see in the world, is a vibration of the universe—the Sanskrit term is *shubda*. Shubda creates light, sound, touch, taste, and every other quality. In dreams you can also see, hear, touch, taste, and smell, but those vibrations are subtler. They don't have the same feeling as concrete reality. When you go beyond the subtle qualities of the mind, shubda becomes so faint that the mind loses all experience of an outside reality, even shadowy wisps of memory. Eventually it experiences only itself, and there aren't any vibrations at all. You are at the source.

The threshold of the source is silence. But you must step over the threshold into the room where reality is born. There you find that the raw materials are threefold. Creation springs from existence (Sat), consciousness (Chit), and the potential for vibrations to arise (Ananda). These three are the most real things in the universe because everything else that we call real comes from them.

It's this experience of the source, a state beginning beyond silence, that the Vedic rishis considered the field of all fields—what physicists call the ground state or vacuum state. Being pregnant with every possible flicker of energy in the universe, the vacuum state still isn't Sat Chit Ananda. It has no mind, no bliss. It cannot be experienced subjectively. By leaving these factors out, physics leaves out the physicist, who pretends that he isn't part of the field. John Wheeler, an eminent Princeton physicist, decades ago pointed out this flaw: as we make models of the universe, he said, we act like someone with his nose pressed against the window of a bakery, looking at everything on display from the outside. But there is no window separating the observer from the universe; we are not outside what we see.

Wheeler's suggestion that we must find a science that combines subjectivity and objectivity has been meagerly pursued, because science remains stubbornly objective, and it can afford to be when conducting isolated experiments. Ultimately, however, there is a limit that cannot be crossed, and we are quite close to it. We can face the limit of knowledge in a simple problem like prayer.

By now the public is well aware that research on prayer has validated that it works. In a typical experiment volunteers, usually from church groups, are asked to pray for sick people in the hospital. They do not visit the person and often have only a number rather than a name to go by. The prayer isn't specific; they are asked simply to pray for God's help. The results of such experiments have been startlingly positive. In the best-known one, conducted at Duke University in North Carolina, patients who were prayed for recovered faster and with fewer side effects than those not prayed for. Here we have one more demonstration that we are all connected by the same field of consciousness. The properties of the field operate here and now:

The field works as a whole.
It correlates distant events instantly.
It remembers all events.
It exists beyond time and space.
It creates entirely within itself.
Its creation grows and expands in an evolutionary direction.
It is conscious.

The Vedic rishis began with these qualities as their first principles; in that regard they were wiser than we are, with our reluctance to admit consciousness unless we are forced to at the far limits of a difficult scientific issue. The field of consciousness is primary to every phenomenon in Nature because of the gap that exists between every electron, every thought, every instant in time. The gap is the reference point, the stillness at the heart of creation, where the universe correlates all events.

Has science proved that the rishis were right? I think the most we can say—and it is a lot—is that science and the rishis are consistent with each other. They come from different worlds but see with the same vision—almost. Science is still burdened by spiritual materialism, the belief that any explanation of God, the soul, or the afterlife is valid only if matter contains the secret. This is like saying we can't understand jazz until we diagram the atoms in Louis Armstrong's trumpet.

In the end, a book on the afterlife cannot fully reconcile us with the inevitability of death. It can only lead the way to finding personal comfort on your own. You and I are unique people and therefore very different. I may be consoled by a vision of eternity that is foreign or even frightening to you. I may mourn my aging body more than you, or less. We each have our own personal view of God. Yet we are bound together in the field of consciousness, and we do the same work there.

We need to see that we are all entangled in the same reality. Isolation has been outmoded on every front, from ecology to the Internet. We need to remember our common source. The human spirit is degraded when we confine ourselves to the span of a lifetime and the enclosure of a physical body. We are mind and spirit first, and that places our home beyond the stars.

Knowing that I will return to the field one day to find my source provides me with immeasurable confidence in the purpose of life. As fervently as any devout believer, I have faith in this vision. My faith is renewed every time I have a moment of witnessing, in which I can touch the silence of my own being. Then I lose all fear of death—indeed, I touch death right now, and gladly. Tagore said it so movingly:

> *When I was born and saw the light*
> *I was no stranger in this world*
> *Something inscrutable, shapeless, and without words*
> *Appeared in the form of my mother.*

> *So when I die, the same unknown will appear again*
> *As ever known to me,*
> *And because I love this life*
> *I will love death as well.*

Without death there can be no present moment, for the last moment has to die to make the next one possible. There can be no present love, for the last emotion has to die to make a new one possible. There can be no present life, for the old cells in my body have to die to make new tissue possible. This is the miracle of creation, which in every second is one thing: life and death joined in an eternal dance. It would be a catastrophe to exclude death from the dance. That would guarantee a universe with no chance for renewal. Fortunately, creation wasn't set up that way. We live in an endlessly re-created universe. On the other side of our fears and doubts, our deepest prayer should not be for life, which we have in abundance. It should be a prayer to lead the cosmic dance, for then the angels and gods themselves will have someone to follow.

MAHA SAMADHI

THE MONSOON RAINS SWEPT down from the mountain overnight. Ramana could hear it in his sleep like warm dull thunder on the roof, or the knocking of the gods. It was loud enough to make him restless but not to wake him up completely. He had dim thoughts of closing the window by his bed. He remembered the small hole in the roof that needed a bucket underneath to catch the drip. Yet for some reason he couldn't feel rain splashing from the windowsill and heard no dripping sound.

Strange, he thought drowsily.

The dull thunder continued, hour after hour. Too many hours. Ramana opened his eyes, flicking his gaze to the windowsill and the place under the hole in the roof. Both were dry. Where was the water? Why was it still thundering?

Then he knew. It *was* the gods knocking. Death had come like the monsoons, the season of year Ramana loved the best. He wasn't surprised that he could still feel his body or that the room was intact. His old master, who had died sixty years ago, told him how things would be. Sixty years? Could that be right? Suddenly Ramana couldn't remember how old he was himself. Seventy-five, eighty? This confusion triggered a change. His body began to feel lighter, as if age were slipping away. He was rising, the whole room was rising, in fact, and the dull thunder began to fade.

Ramana wondered if he was about to disappear, but the world saved him the trouble by disappearing first. He had never much believed in the world, so this didn't surprise him. For one last moment he was still in bed, looking out the window at a sky that turned from blue to a soft white, and then there was only whiteness and no room. He looked down, and his body was gone too. It had slipped away so easily that he was reminded of something his master had told him: "The body is like a cloak. For the enlightened, dying is like letting the cloak fall to the floor. For the unenlightened, it is like ripping off a cloak that is sewn on."

What would slip away next? Ramana could still pose mental questions, so his mind hadn't left him. He saw himself as a boy of twelve, when he first met his master, who lived in the same forest retreat that became his after the master died. The old man sitting in lotus position on a worn deerskin had said, "Do you want to learn from me?" The boy nodded. "Is it because your parents think it would be a good thing?" The boy nodded again. Then the master waved his hand, sending Ramana's parents out of the room.

When they were alone, the master said, "Come to me when it's your desire, not that of your parents."

"Why?" Ramana asked. "My parents only want what's good for me."

"That's not enough," the master replied. "You can't be with me and remain like ordinary people. Ordinary people need the support of family, or they would die of loneliness. They need the support of society, or they would have no friends or spouse. They need the support of their bodies, or they would starve. And most of all, they need the support of their minds, or they would go crazy."

"I don't see why you're telling me this," said the boy.

"Because if you lose family, friends, your body, and your mind—all of which you must—I don't want you to die. I want you to be free."

The boy didn't come back for ten years, and even then the master laughed and said he had been quick about it. "After what I told you, most people would stay away forever." During his period as a disciple Ramana had found the teaching difficult. He often stumbled but never fell. Everything his master foretold came true. The time came when the disciple no longer needed the support of his family. But this wasn't a loss, because he now saw them with great compassion. He didn't need the support of society, but this wasn't a loss, because he saw himself as part of all humanity. He didn't need the support of his physical body, but this wasn't a loss, because his body took care of itself better when he stopped worrying about it.

The one thing Ramana never quite gave up was the support of his mind. "Ah, you fear that without a mind you will die," his master said patiently. Ramana adopted the same patience. He learned to go inward in *samadhi* to experience silence, and over the years this became home to him, a place free of the constant activity of the mind.

On the day his master died, Ramana knelt by his bed and wept. "So you imagine that I am leaving you," his master whispered. "Your mind still has you in its spell." He said this affectionately, not in reproof, and that consoled Ramana. An hour later his master went into the deepest of all silences, *maha samadhi.*

Ramana could remember all these things now that he too had died. He looked around. There was no one to greet him, no family, not even his master. For a second a shiver of fear gripped him, then it faded, and with it the power to think. Ramana didn't even get to think, *There goes my mind.* He slipped effortlessly to where mind was no longer needed. There was no whiteness around him anymore, but even this perception lasted for only an instant, because there was no darkness, either. When his mind slipped away, it took light and dark with it.

Now he was enveloped in silence, which came as an indescribable relief. Like thieves in the night, whole worlds wanted to enter him and take his silence away. But all they could do was glance off him ever so lightly, like feathers off a rock. He was impenetrable now. There was no universe and no God, no divine presence, no love.

He lingered like that, in the womb of the timeless, for a while. Then Ramana felt a soft breath, and it beckoned him back. He was stirring to life again. Not because he wanted to live on earth, for that would have been a thought. The breath was its own reason. There was a split second when he could choose not to return. Eternal peace was just as possible as another lifetime.

Only then did he realize that he was free at last. Human life could be his again, only now he also would have eternal peace, the two together. Ramana smiled to himself, if one can say that the cosmos smiles. The breathing grew louder. He relaxed and let it carry him downward back to earth. One breath, then another, always louder, until it became like the monsoons drifting down the mountain, or the knocking of the gods. He couldn't see what family he would be born into, but Ramana knew his new purpose: to show these dreaming humans, whom he loved so much, how to wake up.

READING NOTES

There will never be a definitive book on the afterlife, which I think is good, because no single book will ever convince skeptics or console everyone who has wondered what happens after death. What might change society's fear and doubt is a rising tide of evidence. Below I have listed every book and Web site that helped me write this book. They constitute a mountain of evidence that life continues after death; more important, each one is a symptom of rising consciousness. Too long has death been a mysterious subject. The best I can hope for is to shed a little light into that darkness, but I couldn't have done it without the countless other people trying to shed the same light.

Chapter 1: Death at the Door

We have entered a new era in research where the Internet has become as valuable as standard book references. Besides Googling any general topic (e.g., ghosts, near-death experiences, heaven) at www.google.com, one can turn to the ever-expanding online encyclopedia at www.wikipedia.com. The only flaw with Web references is that they tend to be overwhelming in number but sometimes shallow in coverage.

The great virtue of online referencing is that the reader can go deeper than the author on any particular topic with the push of a button.

I touched only briefly on the physical changes caused by death. Sherwin B. Nuland won a National Book Award on the subject with *How We Die: Reflections on Life's Final Chapter* (Knopf, 1994). Nuland, a senior Yale physician, goes into clinical detail about the biology of the dying process, covering heart disease, cancer, Alzheimer's, and AIDS, among other topics, in his exploration of how every person's death is as unique as his life.

Spiritual experiences also cause physical changes, making them just as real, if you are a materialist, as the changes caused by death. An early popular book on the subject is Nona Coxhead, *Mindpower* (Penguin, 1976), which emphasizes research into ESP and other areas of parapsychology. For a contemporary study of how current break-throughs in brain science are changing our view of consciousness, I turned to Joseph Chilton Pearce, *The Biology of Transcendence: A Blueprint for the Human Spirit* (Park Street Press, 2002), which is refreshingly humane and far-ranging. Pearce writes for the general reader and intersperses neurology with intriguing anecdotes.

I have tried to be as nontechnical as possible when discussing the vast philosophical system known as Vedanta. Readers who want to go back to the source should begin with *The Concise Yoga Vasistha* (State University of New York Press, 1984), in a clear and readable translation by Swami Venkatesananda. This great work describes the education of Lord Rama, an incarnation of God in human form, at the feet of an immortal rishi, Vasistha, who tells his young pupil all the Vedantic knowledge about death, reincarnation, and the projection of all worlds from the Self. I've kept this book at my side for many years.

TEXT NOTE:

p. 25   Modern attempts to weigh the soul at the moment of death are discussed online at http://www.snopes.com/religion/soulweight.asp.

Chapter 2: The Cure for Dying

The story of the Tibetan delog Dawa Drolma is recounted by her son Chagdud Tulku in his introduction to her book, *Delog: Journey into Realms Beyond Death* (Padma Publishing, 1995). This is the best entry into personal experiences of the Bardo that I've found. The classic work on death and dying in the Tibetan tradition is the now-famous Tibetan Book of the Dead. It may strike many Westerners as too exotic and detailed in its Buddhist ritualism, which is the product of many centuries of religious practice. More accessible is Sogyal Rinpoche, *The Tibetan Book of Living and Dying* (HarperSanFrancisco, 1993), which covers the same ground.

Near-death experiences were introduced to the public in the 1970s through several bestsellers, one of them being the immensely popular *Life After Life* by Raymond Moody (Mockingbird Books, 1975), a quick read that still retains the excitement of a physician who has just discovered a remarkable phenomenon. Since then the literature on NDEs has grown enormously. A great deal of it is summarized and updated on a Web site, www.near-death.com. This site gives details of some of the most prominent and widely publicized experiences, but it branches much further into almost every aspect of death and the afterlife.

The near-death experiences of children are particularly fascinating because they are considered to be innocent, unbiased witnesses. Of the several books on the subject, I turned to another physician's book, Melvin Morse, *Closer to the Light: Learning from the Near-Death Experiences of Children* (Ivy Books, 1990). Dr. Morse has several other titles in the near-death field. Another notable writer is P. M. H. Atwater;

the book of hers I read was *Beyond the Light: The Mysteries and Revelations of Near-Death Experiences* (Avon Books, 1994). The mainstay of such books, of which there are dozens, are real-life stories told first-hand by those who have come back from clinically dying.

The best clinical study on NDEs was conducted in Holland by Dr. Pim van Lommel. It is well described in Mary Roach, *Spook: Science Tackles the Afterlife* (W. W. Norton, 2005), a book told from the perspective of a bemused journalist. An even more detailed account, told without the bemusement, can be found online at www .odemagazine.com/article.php?aID=4207&l=en.

TEXT NOTES:

p. 37   The percentage of Americans who tell pollsters they've had a near-death experience is cited in the online article "Religious Interpretations of Near-Death Experiences" by David San Filippo: http://www.lutz-sanfilippo.com/library/counseling/ lsfnde.html. The doctoral essay contains many other academic references to the NDE phenomenon as well.

p. 38   The story of the historical delog Lingza Chokyi is told at http:// www.inference.phy.cam.ac.uk/mackay/info-theory/course.html.

p. 42   "Science isn't about knowing the mind of God . . ." is quoted from "What Was God Thinking? Science Can't Tell" by Eric Cornell (*Time*, Nov. 14, 2005, p. 100).

p. 43   "At that moment these people are not only conscious . . ." is quoted from an online interview with van Lommel at http://www.odemagazine.com/article.php?aID=4207&l=en.

Chapter 3: Death Grants Three Wishes

Religious belief is a vast topic, but for a thumbnail sketch of where religion is headed in modern America, I consulted a leading poll, *The Next American Spirituality: Finding God in the Twenty-First Century,* by George

Gallup Jr. (Cook Communications, 2000). The Gallup organization is dedicated to documenting the actual beliefs of every faith around the globe, which is especially needed in the Islamic world, where reliable data has been scarce, even in recent years. You can do your own browsing of opinions across the board on Google, entering topic phrases like "church attendance" or "believe they will go to heaven."

TEXT NOTE:

p. 49   Figures about church attendance in the United States come from an online article: http://www.religioustolerance.org/ rel_rate.htm.

Chapter 4: Escaping the Noose

I didn't rely on any specific book for the Christian conception of heaven, but for official theological answers I consulted *The Catholic Encyclopedia,* which "proposes to give its readers full and authoritative information on the entire cycle of Catholic interests, action and doctrine." The home page for the encyclopedia is http://www.newadvent .org/cathen/. I did not explore the thicket of contrasting beliefs stemming from Protestant theology, although as always there were many helpful articles at Wikipedia.

For anyone who wants to browse the religious landscape, the easiest way to begin is to take a question like "Where is heaven?" or "What is heaven like?" and enter it at Google—innumerable results crop up. One can browse the beliefs of various denominations online at http://www.religioustolerance.org/heav_hel.htm.

The vagaries of the Old Testament God, with his many faces and changes of mood, are thoroughly covered in Jack Miles, *God: A Biography* (Vintage, 1996). The book is nonreligious, treating the Old Testament as source material in the life of a fascinating, captious, mercurial person who happens to be God.

When I contend that Jesus often sounds like a Vedic rishi, I have in mind the Book of Thomas and other Gnostic gospels. The fascinating history of how these seminal Christian writings came to be unearthed accidentally by a wandering Egyptian shepherd in 1945, and their subsequent suppression by the Church, is told best by Elaine Pagels in *The Gnostic Gospels* (Vintage, 1989). Hers is one of those exceptional books on religion that hugely influence public opinion; it came as a revelation that the Christian tradition had an early, authentic mystical tradition that allowed women full status and told an alternate Christ story that doesn't end with suffering and dying on the cross.

For anyone who wishes to read every single word attributed to Christ in any gospel, official or unofficial, an invaluable source is Ricky Alan Mayotte, *The Complete Jesus* (Steerforth Press, 1997). It is usefully arranged by topics, such as Commandments, Parables, Jesus Speaking About Himself, etc.

Chapter 5: The Path to Hell

One of the major points I emphasize throughout this book is that the afterlife is still evolving, as it must since life as a whole is always evolving. This is true of hell, too, as described in Alice K. Turner, *The History of Hell* (Harvest, 1995), a readable survey compiled by a freelance journalist. Similar surveys on both heaven and hell have appeared regularly, but a more in-depth reference is Elaine Pagels, *The Origin of Satan* (Vintage, 1996). Her approach is to trace Satan, not as a real personage but as a concept whose basis can be found in anthropology, psychology, and literary analysis. Such a humane approach appeals to me because it shows so clearly and in detail how the devil can be considered our own creation.

A similar approach can be taken to Christ, who is boldly explained in mythic terms by Timothy Freke and Peter Gandy, *Jesus and the Lost Goddess: The Secret Teachings of the Original Christians* (Harmony Books,

2001), which puts Jesus in the context of the ancient world and its belief in the Goddess. Here the attempt is to fill in how early Christians used Jesus for the archetypal purpose of fulfilling the myth of God-as-man that exists in every ancient culture.

Chapter 6: Ghosts

Akasha is the subtlest of the five Mahabhutas, the five elements from which creation is constructed (the others being earth, air, fire, and water). Readers who want to study the system of Mahabhutas might begin online at http://ignca.nic.in/ps_04012.htm. For traditional Indian beliefs in Akasha and how they affected Western spirituality, see the online discussion at http://www.saragrahi.org/.

There are, of course, many popular books on ghosts and communicating with the dead. Mary Roach's *Spook* gives a readable survey of these topics, told from a skeptical and amused point of view that will either immediately appeal or irritate. Popular books by psychics that have reached millions of readers include James Van Praagh, *Talking to Heaven: A Medium's Message of Life After Death* (Signet, 1999) and Allison DuBois, *Don't Kiss Them Good-Bye* (Fireside, 2005).

The phenomenon of psychic communication has been researched at the university level by psychiatrist Gary Schwartz, whose experiments have engaged me personally. The same research brought Allison DuBois to light and resulted in a television series on NBC, as recounted in Gary E. Schwartz and William L. Simon, *The Truth About Medium* (Hampton Roads Publishing, 2005). Schwartz gives a thorough account of his academic research, the leading findings in the field, in *The Afterlife Experiments: Breakthrough Scientific Evidence of Life After Death* (Atria, 2003), for which I wrote the introduction.

Chapter 7: The Invisible Thread

Readers who are interested in the historical perspective of the afterlife may want a survey like Harold Coward, editor, *Life After Death in World Religions* (Orbis, 1997), which collects essays on each faith by various experts. I came up with my own synthesis, relying heavily on a classic work, Huston Smith, *The World's Religions: Our Great Wisdom Traditions* (HarperSanFrancisco, 1991), which is still a model of fairness and ecumenical tolerance, not to mention graceful writing and valuable insights. If there is one book that every person interested in religion should begin with, this is it.

TEXT NOTE:

p. 105 "There is no salvation for those outside the Church . . ." is quoted from a press interview with Mel Gibson, cited online at http://www.msnbc.msn.com/id/4224452/.

Chapter 8: Seeing the Soul

The subject of spiritual materialism is incredibly important because so many people, especially in the West, are driven by ego needs even when it comes to spirituality. We turn spiritual to gain things from the world that we otherwise couldn't through work and struggle, and thus we transform work and struggle into spiritual processes. The book that started me thinking along these lines was Chogyam Trungpa, *Cutting Through Spiritual Materialism* (Shambhala, 2002), which is told from a Buddhist perspective but with a Western audience in mind.

Chapter 9: Two Magical Words

It goes without saying that eternity is indescribable, but the Vedic rishis were comfortable living in unbounded awareness. Therefore their descriptions are the most reliable that we possess in the world's wisdom traditions. It helps to have someone who continues to have similar experiences. I would point to Nisargadatta Maharaj, a humble Indian farmer who became a renowned guru in Bombay after enlightenment. His book, *I Am That* (Acorn Press, 1990), is one of the purest spiritual testimonies we have in modern times. Not only is it completely unspoiled by any trace of the guru game, which has been played in India for centuries, but Sri Nisargadatta seems to be witness to a very expanded state of awareness, fully comparable to the ancient rishis. This is another of the few books I've kept by my side for years.

TEXT NOTES:

pp. 122–26 My account of Mellen-Thomas Benedict's journey into the afterlife comes from online: http://www.near-death.com/experiences/reincarnation04.html.

pp. 135–36 The story of Dawn J., the woman who healed with miraculous oil, is told in Cheri Lomonte, *The Healing Touch of Mary* (Divine Impressions, 2005), which contains dozens of similar firsthand accounts.

Chapter 10: Surviving the Storm

Readers who are interested in theories of consciousness face a bewildering number of choices, and in the context of science almost all those choices are materialistic. That is, they assume that mind arises from matter. Since I disagree with the assumption, I am halfhearted about recommending even a good survey like Susan Blackmore, *Con-*

sciousness: An Introduction (Oxford University Press, 2004), which does a thorough job covering the many philosophical questions raised by current theories. The most praised authors in the field seem to be skeptics who believe that mind is actually an illusion created by neural activity and outmoded thinking about the brain. See Daniel Dennett, *Consciousness Explained* (Back Bay Books, 1992), which argues aggressively for the proposition that consciousness is a materialistic phenomenon and nothing more. Therefore, human consciousness could (and one day will) be duplicated by a computer.

For a more pluralistic, open-minded discussion, see Susan Blackmore, editor, *Conversations on Consciousness: What the Best Minds Think About the Brain, Free Will, and What It Means to Be Human* (Oxford University Press, 2006), in which twenty-one thinkers talk in conversational interviews about the whole problem of relating mind and brain. Finally, for a perspective that is more neurological, I read the fascinating speculations of Humberto R. Maturana and Francisco J. Varela, *The Tree of Knowledge: The Biological Roots of Human Understanding* (Shambhala, 1998), which attempts an all-inclusive theory that follows the evolution of mind from a basis in organic chemicals. It is up to each reader to decide if Vedanta, whose own all-inclusive theory begins with consciousness instead of chemicals, stands up to modern skepticism as I have claimed.

The discussion of the five Koshas is my own synthesis of traditional Vedic ideas. Those ideas are easy to explore online at Web sites such as http://swamij.com/koshas.htm.

Chapter 11: Guides and Messengers

The literature on angels is vast, but I found that what I wanted to say did not involve the many historical surveys describing how angels appear in various world religions. However, there are many fascinating accounts from people who have learned to cooperate with the devas, creative agents that are the Indian parallel of angels. These are all New Age books that center on Findhorn, a famous Scottish community that claimed to use devas to grow crops on barren soil, among other remarkable things. See Dorothy MacLean, *To Hear the Angels Sing: An Odyssey of Co-Creation with the Devic Kingdom* (Lindisfarne Books, 1994) and Machaelle Small Wright, *Behaving As if the God in All Life Mattered* (Perelandra, 1997) for two sympathetic stories of women who suddenly found that they could talk to devas and use them to manifest desires. Both are at polar opposites to skepticism and materialism.

Chapter 12: The Dream Continues

The literature on reincarnation is quite unwieldy since it spans every religion and spiritual movement. The main source of popular belief in reincarnation is probably Theosophy, a movement that grew out of nineteenth-century spiritualism but also incorporated a broad range of ideas from India. See James S. Perkins, *Experiencing Reincarnation* (Theosophical Publishing House, 1977), for a readable introduction. For me personally, it was fascinating to discover how many spiritual notions I absorbed as a child at home have been adopted by the Theosophists, and the New Age in general.

For the scientific proof of reincarnation, I am indebted to an excellent survey article, "Death, Rebirth, and Everything in Between: A Scientific and Philosophical Exploration," by Carter Phipps, in the journal *What Is Enlightenment?* (Issue 32, March–May 2006, pp. 60–90). The Web address is http://www.wie.org/, where subscribers can read the entire article.

This led me to the important research by the University of Virginia psychiatrist Ian Stevenson on children who claim to remember past lives. His Web site is http://www.healthsystem.virginia.edu/internet/personalitystudies/. On the same topic an invaluable book is Carol Bowman, *Children's Past Lives: How Past Life Memories Affect Your Child*

(Bantam, 1998), in which a mother finds that her children's irrational fears of loud noises and house fires is cured by past-life regression, leading her to explore the field in depth. A Web site devoted to regressing children to their past lives is http://www.childpastlives.org/.

TEXT NOTES:

pp. 173–74 I first became aware of the boy who remembered dying in a World War II air battle from an ABC News report: http://www.reversespins.com/proofofreincarnation.html.

pp. 174–76 et passim The anecdotes of children who remember their past lives, mostly derived from Ian Stevenson's database, are recounted in Phipps, pp. 63–70 (see above).

p. 175 The quotes from children reported by their parents is from Ian Stevenson's Web site, http://www.healthsystem.virginia.edu/internet/personalitystudies/.

p. 176 The source of out-of-body research at the Monroe Institute can be browsed at http://www.monroeinstitute.org/. Another good article, linking out-of-body experiences and NDEs, can be found online at http://www.paradigm-sys.com/cttart/sci-docs/ctt97-ssooo.html.

Chapter 13: Is Akasha Real?

I had already started writing about Akasha before discovering Ervin Laszlo's *Science and the Akashic Field: An Integral Theory of Everything* (Inner Traditions, 2004), the most wide-ranging argument for incorporating consciousness and science. Since my topic was the afterlife, I wasn't able to include the dozen or more mysteries, ranging from advanced quantum theory, cosmology, biology, and neuroscience, that according to Laszlo will never be solved until consciousness is taken into account. Readers who want to investigate these prevailing enigmas should start here.

Laszlo discusses the Zero Point Field, but there is a complete and very readable book devoted to it—see Lynne McTaggart, *The Field: The Quest for the Secret Force of the Universe* (Harper Perennial, 2002), which describes many experiments and gives detailed anecdotes of various discoveries, in contrast to Laszlo's method, which is to outline and survey prevailing theories with a minimum of narrative.

TEXT NOTES:

pp. 202–204 Helmut Schmidt's experiments, followed by the Jahn team at Princeton, are recounted in McTaggart, *The Field,* pp. 101–16.

p. 204 "On the most profound level . . ." quoted from McTaggart, *The Field,* p. 122.

p. 209 An easily accessible presentation of the paradox known as Schrödinger's cat can be found online—see http://whatis.techtarget.com/definition/0,,sid9_gci341236,00.html

Chapter 14: Thinking Outside the Brain

Current speculations about "extended mind"—the possibility of intelligence outside the brain—cover a wide range of science. A good overview is provided in Part 2 of McTaggart's *The Field,* pp. 99–179, told largely from the perspective of field theory in physics. For first-hand research and in-depth thinking, the best source is Rupert Sheldrake, who made a first impression with his impressive book on evolution, *The Presence of the Past: Morphic Resonance and the Habits of Nature* (Park Street Press, 1995), in which he brilliantly speculates on how life could have evolved, and continues to evolve, through its own self-interacting intelligence.

Undaunted by the outrage his nonmaterialistic theory causes among Darwinians, Sheldrake has challenged them to replicate his own experiments. His research into the telepathic parrot and other psychic pets is contained in *The Sense of Being Stared At: And Other Unexplained Powers of the Human Mind* (Three Rivers Press, 2004) and *Seven Experiments That Could Change the World: A Do-It-Yourself Guide to Revolutionary Science* (Park Street Press, 2002). His entire output has been immensely influential on me, and I cannot imagine an open-minded person who would not be deeply intrigued.

I have only sketched in the burgeoning field of information theory, which is fascinating but not yet expanded to cover a topic as specific as the afterlife. My introduction to the subject came from Hans Christian von Baeyer, *Information: The New Language of Science* (Weidenfeld and Nicolson, 2003), which is readable and free of higher mathematics.

Savant syndrome has become a widely publicized phenomenon. My first acquaintance with it came from Oliver Sacks, *The Man Who Mistook His Wife for a Hat: And Other Clinical Tales* (Touchstone, 1998), which gives a neurologist's firsthand account of meeting autistic children with extraordinary abilities. Sacks's interest in "other brained" people ventures into no spiritual speculations. Joseph Chilton Pearce does, in *Evolution's End: Claiming the Full Potential of Our Intelligence* (HarperCollins, 1992). His lengthy first chapter on savant syndrome links it to a nonmaterial field of intelligence that we all tap into. A nice online article on savant syndrome and its link to genius, "The Key to Genius," can be found at http://www.wired.com/wired/archive/11.12/genius_pr.html.

I became intrigued by memes from online reading. The Internet is rife with discussions of these "mental genes." For the definition of memes, see http://www.intelegen.com/meme/meme.htm. For examples of memes, see http://memetics.chielens.net/examples.html. The evolutionist Richard Dawkins, who invented the term, discusses it in *The Selfish Gene* (Oxford University Press, 1990). My fascination with memetic theory falls short of agreeing with it, however.

TEXT NOTES:

pp. 216–18 A full account of N'kisi, the telepathic parrot, is in Sheldrake, *The Sense of Being Stared At,* pp. 24–27; the statistical
analysis of the research results is on pp. 300–305.

p. 220 Amit Goswami's statement "The universe is always putting
new wine into old bottles . . ." is quoted from a personal conversation.

pp. 225–26 The remarkable story of a musical savant named Rex can
be found online at http://www.cbsnews.com/stories/2005/10/
20/60minutes/main957718.shtml.

p. 226 The story of the "automobile savant" is told in Pearce, *The
Biology of Transcendence,* p. 82 (see above).

p. 226 The story of the child prodigy who is enrolled at Juilliard was
told on CBS News and can be found online at http://www
.cbsnews.com/stories/2004/11/24/60minutes/main657713.
shtml.

Chapter Fifteen: The Mechanics of Creation

The topic of emergence—the appearance of a new phenomenon in
Nature—is discussed lucidly for the general reader online at Wikipedia
(see http://en.wikipedia.org/wiki/Emergence). I have also benefited
enormously from the physicist Amit Goswami, who has written
extensively on creative leaps made in nature—see *The Self-Aware Universe* (Tarcher, 1995). One of the boldest attempts to combine the
physical and spirituality can be found in Ervin Laszlo, *Science and the
Reenchantment of the Cosmos: The Rise of the Integral Vision of Reality* (Inner
Traditions, 2006). Both authors are scientists who refuse to accept the
schism between the scientific and spiritual views of the world.

Remote viewing, the preferred term now for what used to be
lumped under the rubric of clairvoyance, is emerging from the fringes.
Readers can browse a dedicated Web site, http://www.farsight.org/

that contains copious information on the subject. There is also a recent, extensively researched book, *Remote Viewing: The Science and Theory of Nonphysical Perception* (Farsight Press, 2005). A veteran of the military's secret remote viewing program, Project Stargate, has written about his experiences and outlines how anyone can learn the skill with enough self-discipline and dedication—see Joseph McMoneagle, *Remote Viewing Secrets: A Handbook* (Hampton Roads, 2000).

TEXT NOTES:

pp. 242–43 The story of the psychic who could see inside the SQUID comes from McTaggart, *The Field*, pp. 142–46.

p. 243 The experiment in remote viewing that I participated in was run by Marilyn Schlitz, director of research for the Institute of Noetic Sciences. See their home page at http://www.noetic .org/. This site leads to a wealth of material on every aspect of science, spirituality, and the paranormal. To my knowledge, this is the most extensive and wide-ranging institute of its kind, and I have been inspired by their work for twenty years.

p. 244 "Then at thirteen minutes . . ." quoted from an online interview with Cleve Backster in which he also discusses his astonishing research on telepathy in plants—http://www. derrickjensen.org/backster.html.

p. 248 All the Tagore poems are from Deepak Chopra, *On the Shores of Eternity: Poems from Tagore on Immortality and Beyond* (Harmony, 1999).

INDEX

Aboriginal peoples, 96, 226
Acceptance, 114, 115
Addiction, 13
Adversaries, 99
African gray parrot, 216–18, 268
Afterlife:
  and bad deeds, 74
  belief in, 194
  choice in, 173
  Christian view, 26, 61
  and consciousness, 42, 58, 194
  control of, 182
  creation of own, 42, 47, 53–54
  creative possibilities in, 83, 91
  dawning of, 40–42
  desire to join loved ones in, 10
  and disconnection, 185
  expanded awareness of, 97–103
  Indian view, 2, 97
  and Judaism, 61
  meaningful, 32
  nature of, 26
  positions on, 51–53
  powers needed for, 113–17
  punishment in, 72
  questions about, 100

  and religion, 41
  responsibility for, 75
  self-exploration as preparation for,
    102
  Tibetan Buddhist, 38
  as transformation chamber, 177
  Western view, 2
  See also Heaven
Aging, 223
Agnostics, 51–53
Air element, 3
Akasha:
  and awareness, 102
  and choice, 88, 103–4
  dreams, 84
  explanation of universe, 205–13
  as field of consciousness, 87–89,
    106, 167, 203, 211
  interpretation by various cultures,
    94-95
  memory, 220
  questions about afterlife, 100
  reality of, 195, 197–213
  as source of creativity, 95
  and states of consciousness, 128,
    129–30, 135

Death (*continued*)
as fulfillment of purpose on earth,
26
Indian parable of, 1, 21–23,
35–36, 45–47, 55–57, 69–70,
81–83, 93–94, 107–9, 119–21,
139–41, 155–57, 169–70,
251–54
materialistic view of, 30
miracle of, 24–33, 37
mystery of, 24–25
sudden, 8, 9, 109–10
survival of consciousness after,
237–38
See also Afterlife; Dying; Near-
death experiences
Delhi (India), 3
Delogs, 38–39, 41, 122
Dementia, 223
Departed spirits, 110–13, 143, 220,
261
Depression, 224
Desire, 8, 11, 88–89, 114, 115, 142,
160
Destination, 99
Deva, 156, 164, 265
Devaloka, 161
Devata, 162, 164
Devata effect, 163–68
Devil. *See* Satan
Directedness, 10
Disconnection, 185
Discrimination, 114, 115
Dissolution, 96
Distinctions, 114
DNA, 24, 49, 172, 178, 200, 201,
220, 238, 239, 245
Dogs, 215, 216
Don Juan, 132
Doubt, 58, 115, 131, 255
Dreams, 6, 84, 128, 131, 132, 142,
143, 144, 157

Dream time, 97
Drolma, Dawa, 37–38, 39, 41, 257
Drowning, 8
Drugs, 42
Duke University, 247
Dying, 7, 256
and arrival at eternity, 121
conscious, 183
cure for, 35–43
departure of soul, 4, 25
and mind field, 232
over weeks and months, 9
personal nature of, 29
qualities one can bring to, 32
and reality, 98, 121, 210
seeing life flash before one's eyes,
8–9, 184–85
See also Death; Near-death
experiences

Earth, 212
Earthbound souls, 73
Earth element, 3
Ecosystem, 146, 152, 200–201
Ecstasy, 65, 124, 149
Ego, 102, 144, 148, 149, 150, 153,
164, 233, 262
Einstein, Albert, 143, 197
Electromagnetic field, 241–42
Electron, 163, 181, 201, 205, 209,
223, 244
Elijah (Elias), 104
Eliot, T.S., 66
Emergent properties, 238–39, 270
Emerson, Ralph Waldo, 104
Emotions, 176, 221
Energy, 198–200, 205–6, 212, 213,
219, 233–36, 238, 242
Enjoyment, 10
Enlightenment, 231, 232
Epiphanies, 142

DEEPAK CHOPRA'S many books have become classic texts of health and spirituality as well as national bestsellers. He is the founder of the Chopra Center for Well Being (www.chopra.com) and the president of the Alliance for a New Humanity (www.anhglobal.com).

Deepak Chopra and The Chopra Center for Well Being at La Costa Resort and Spa, Carlsbad, California, offer a wide range of seminars, products and educational programmes, worldwide. The Chopra Center offers revitalizing mind/body programmes, as well as day spa services. Guests can come to rejuvenate, expand knowledge or obtain a medical consultation.

For information on meditation classes, health and well-being courses, instructor certification programmes, or local classes in your area, contact The Chopra Center for Well Being at La Costa Resort and Spa, 2013 Costa Del Mar Road, Carlsbad, CA 92009, USA. By telephone: 001-888-424-6772, or 001-760-931-7566. For a virtual tour of the Center, visit the Internet website at www.chopra.com.

If you live in Europe and would like more information on workshops, lectures or other programmes about Dr. Deepak Chopra or to order any of his books, tapes or products, please contact: Contours, 44 Fordbridge Road, Ashford, Middlesex, TW15 2SJ. Tel: +44 (0) 208 564 7033; fax +44 (0) 208 897 3807; email: info@spiritualityworks.com; website: www.spiritualityworks.com

If you live in Australia and would like more information on work-shops, lectures, or programmes presented by Dr. Deepak Chopra, please contact What's On The Planet Pty Ltd, PO Box 161, Brighton Le Sands, NSW 2216, Australia, or email deepak@theplanet.com.au